MY HAPPY HUNTING GROUNDS

WITH NOTES ON SPORT AND NATURAL HISTORY

BY

ALFRED ERSKINE GATHORNE-HARDY

AUTHOR OF "AUTUMNS IN ARGYLLSHIRE," "THE SALMON," ETC.

WITH ILLUSTRATIONS BY

G. E. LODGE, SIR FRANK LOCKWOOD
W. A. TOPLIS

AND FROM PHOTOGRAPHS

LONGMANS, GREEN AND CO.
39 PATERNOSTER ROW, LONDON
NEW YORK, BOMBAY, AND CALCUTTA
1914

All rights reserved

TO

MY DEAR FRIENDS

ETHELBERT AND LOUISA LORT PHILLIPS

IN GRATEFUL REMEMBRANCE

OF MANY HAPPY DAYS IN NORWAY

PREFACE

PORTIONS of this volume have appeared in the form of Articles in the *Cornhill* and *Badminton Magazines*, *Country Life*, and *Land and Water*. I desire to express my acknowledgments and thanks to the Editors and Proprietors of those periodicals for permission to reproduce them, and also beg to thank Mr. Watts-Dunton, the proprietor of the copyright, for permission to quote extracts from Mr. Swinburne's poems.

A. E. GATHORNE-HARDY.

CONTENTS

CHAPTER I
PLEASANT PLACES 1

CHAPTER II
THE ISLAND OF COLONSAY 24

CHAPTER III
BIRD LIFE IN COLONSAY 43

CHAPTER IV
SEALS GREAT AND SMALL 63

CHAPTER V
GOLF AT COLONSAY 85

CHAPTER VI
SARK: THE GARDEN OF CYMODOCE 100

CHAPTER VII
NORWAY IN 1865. MY FIRST SALMON 113

CHAPTER VIII
HVILESTED, 1901 128

CHAPTER IX
HVILESTED. THE UPPER WATER 145

CHAPTER X
TODAL AND LILLEDAL, 1903 166

CHAPTER XI
A HOME ON THE HIGH FJELD—ALFHEIM, 1902 . . . 180

CHAPTER XII
ALFHEIM, 1913 193

CHAPTER XIII
LILLEDAL, 1913 211

CHAPTER XIV
CHRISTMAS SPORT AT POLTALLOCH 225

CHAPTER XV
HOME AT LAST. DONNINGTON PRIORY 246

INDEX 269

ILLUSTRATIONS

LANDING A SEA TROUT IN FLADVAD (*Photogravure*) . *Frontispiece*
   (From a Drawing by G. E. LODGE)

"FANCY AND FACT" . . . . . *between pp.* 110 *and* 111
   (Coloured Drawing by Sir FRANK LOCKWOOD)

                                        FACING PAGE

PORTRAITS OF THE ARTIST AND SIR WILLIAM HARCOURT . . 1
   (From the Braemore Visitors' Book, 1875. By Sir JOHN MILLAIS)

"IN A BAD PLACE FOR A SHOT" 14
   (From the Braemore Visitors' Book, 1868. Pencil Sketch by Sir EDWIN LANDSEER)

"HERO AND LEANDER" 16
   (From the Braemore Visitors' Book, 1871. By General HOPE CREALOCK)

"A DISCONSOLATE BACHELOR" 18
   (From the Braemore Visitors' Book, 1873. By General HOPE CREALOCK)

ARTHUR'S SEAT 22
   (From the Braemore Visitors' Book, 1870. By Sir JOHN MILLAIS)

PORT LOTHA, COLONSAY 24

PEREGRINE FALCON AND RAVEN 55
   (From a Drawing by G. E. LODGE)

STALKING A SEAL 80
   (From a Drawing by G. E. LODGE)

THE HANGMAN'S ROCK, COLONSAY } 85
A QUIET PIPE ON THE LINKS }

LES AUTELETS, SARK 102
   (From Pen-and-ink Sketch by W. A. TOPLIS)

LIGHTNING SKETCHES BY SIR FRANK LOCKWOOD . . . 112

A NIGHT'S CATCH } 160
THE SUNDAL IN FLOOD }

	FACING PAGE
Low Water above Stor Pool: Salmon Traps	164
Todal	166
A Large Todal Foxglove } Part of a Large Todal Family }	168
Head of the Valley above Todal } Todal }	174
The Bull Valley above Kaarvand	176
Shooting the Rapids } Ole at the Ferry }	182
Svart Snuta: The Summit } Svart Snuta from the Lake }	189
A Lake on the High Fjeld } The Bridge at Vangen }	195
Ladies Fishing at Vangen } Vangen }	200
Old Pine on the High Fjeld } Root of Same }	205
Lilledal and Kalken from the Fjord } Rapids on Lilledal River }	211
Lilledal } The Record Sea Trout }	216
A Rival Fisherman: The Osprey	218
(From a Drawing by G. E. Lodge)	
Red Deer in Ballimore Wood	243
(From a Drawing by G. E. Lodge)	
Feeding the Trout } The Big Gunnera }	247
Donnington Priory } Returning from Church, Donnington }	266

PORTRAITS OF THE ARTIST AND SIR WILLIAM HARCOURT
(From the Braemore Visitors' Book, 1875. By Sir JOHN MILLAIS)

HAPPY HUNTING-GROUNDS

CHAPTER I

PLEASANT PLACES

HAPPY hunting-grounds! How many delightful visions swim into the focus of my memory as I strive to recall the early scenes of my rambles with rod, gun, and rifle!

> "Thro' many an hour of summer suns,
> By many pleasant ways,
> Against its fountain upwards runs
> The current of my days."

The lines have indeed fallen to me "in pleasant places." From the earliest time when I was permitted to toddle after my father as he strolled round the garden with a gun, or to watch him as he filled a bucket with eels from some flooded backwater of the Lune near Kirkby-Lonsdale with bunches of worms threaded on worsted, I have loved sport and nature—and have had ample opportunities of enjoying the delights of both.

I have found happy hunting-grounds everywhere, but I do not invite the reader to accompany me in pursuit of the "rats and mice and such small deer" on which my early prowess was exercised. Perhaps the first sparrow I bagged with my own gun, or the gudgeon which took my exceedingly early worm at Henley-on-Thames in the fifties may have produced in my breast a "fine careless rapture" that I could not quite "recapture" when in later days I landed a twenty-pound salmon or grassed a ten pointer, but such memories are for myself alone. Nor shall I go back to my schoolboy days in Sussex, although then the heathery sides of Blackdown were still untouched by the speculative builder, and the combe where we lived was sixteen miles from Godalming, the nearest railway station. Black-game were still to be found there, and I remember my eldest brother returning in triumph from a solitary ramble, with a fat grey hen which he had succeeded in bagging with the little sixteen bore by Egg, which passed shortly afterwards into my hands, and acquired a capacity for missing it had not displayed in the hands of its former owner.

My father entrusted us all with a gun very early, but made and enforced very definite rules as to its use. In the first place, the muzzle must never be pointed at anyone. "Loaded or unloaded it may go off." Then no bird or beast was to be shot at unless it was either destructive, or good for food; and all game birds were strictly tabooed until we became the proud possessors of game licences. He always inculcated what would now be considered a quixotic reverence for law and order. He considered smuggling a breach of the eighth commandment, and would never even import a Tauchnitz novel when returning from one of his rare visits to the Continent, as he held that by so doing he was defrauding the authors. For a gentleman to shoot game without a licence he considered doubly culpable, because it was not only a fraud upon the revenue, but a breach of the law made for the protection and preservation of game, and rigidly enforced against poachers of humbler origin. This particular injunction we always obeyed, and I think we at least observed the spirit of his other instructions, to which I ascribe some measure of my good fortune in never having been present at a serious shooting accident. I still remember the horror I felt when I went to pick up what I supposed to be a rabbit and found that I had massacred a hen pheasant. I trembled lest I should be haled before the magistrate and fined, and was quite delighted when my father instead of playing Brutus merely drew the mild and salutary lesson that it would be well in future for me to make quite certain what I was aiming at before I pulled the trigger.

Happy hunting-grounds! Let me name a few of the earliest, with heart-felt gratitude to the generous hosts who made me welcome to their Northern homes. What days and nights I spent at Murthly Castle, where the best and kindest of friends, Mrs. Graham, found sport by day, and inexhaustible merriment by night, for an enchanted circle of privileged guests. It seemed as if the conjuror's magic bottle from which each could taste the drink which pleased him best, found its counterpart here, where every sportsman could choose and enjoy at will his favourite pursuit. Below the picturesque old castle and the gaunt unfinished modern shell which stood beside it, the winding Tay flowed through beautiful hills fringed with silvery birch and dark pine; and just above Dunkeld, Birnam protested that all its wood had not marched to Dunsinane.

Here hourly through each day Miller, the skilful boatman, rowed two, or sometimes three of the party across and across the long stretch of water between Dunkeld and the ferry below Delvine, the fortunate "sitters" taking their turns to seize the rods which hung over the stern when the scream of the reel announced that a "fish" had taken the fly or minnow. Perhaps a second salmon would be hooked before the spare lines could be reeled in, and then some moments of breathless excitement would ensue before the rival anglers could be landed to play their fish; or sometimes a foul would free one or both of the hooked salmon. Still many a big fish succumbed, and the fortunate captor would return radiant to boast of his twenty-five pounder, oblivious of the fact that the honour really rested with the boatman, whose skilled and practised movements had hung the lure in every nook and corner where a fish might be expected to rise. If the party was large, and the number of would-be fishermen excessive, one or more would be seen dotting the banks, and exploring with the fly the few pools which were fishable from the shore, consoling themselves for their inferior prospect of sport by the proud consciousness that the whole merit of any capture would be their own. Or an overflow party would visit the stretch by Burn Bend, and, commandeering a boat, try their prentice hands at harling for themselves, or try their luck from the bank where a cast could be reached in that way. My brother-in-law Henry, now Sir Henry Graham, K.C.B., never harled when alone, and even when fishing from the boat had it let down by a rope a yard at a time, and explored the casts in that more scientific manner; but it was only by means of harling that two rods could fish the same water at one and the same time, and it was for that reason that this method was so often adopted at hospitable Murthly.

Other guests would splash through Murthly Moss, immortalised by the pencil of Millais, himself a later tenant of the shootings, or where the bog was impassable would walk just outside the thick reed-grown swamps, picking off the snipe or water-fowl which the keepers put out by means of a rope held between them and dragged through the rushes. Never was there such a place for getting a mixed bag; eight varieties was thought nothing of, ten or twelve were quite likely to have been obtained when the lucky sportsmen returned happy in the evening. Duck and teal, snipe, whole and jack, grouse and black-game, rabbits and hares, were certainties, while woodcock, golden plover, capercailzie, roe, and wood-pigeons were often got. Another amusement was still-hunting in the coverts, where an expert rifle shot might find opportunities of adding the pretty head of a roe to his sporting trophies. I more than once killed roe there myself, and I remember an occasion when one of the visitors killed two fine roebuck right and left, which he came upon fighting near the water garden.

The evenings were not less delightful than the days. Music and song, much of the latter improvised, kept the party merry till a late hour; and all in turn enjoyed the good-natured chaffing verses in which Henry used to chronicle the adventures of the day. As I write I find snatches of these ephemeral lyrics running in my head, although it is nearly half a century since I listened to them. Then there were other amusements, such as thought-reading, improvised charades and dramatic duologues, but I cannot profess to give an exhaustive list. I remember particularly a can-can danced by the nimble forefingers of Archie Stewart Wortley, his two hands personating the male and female performers. Scotsmen are wrongly supposed to be devoid of a sense of humour, but I can still see in my mind's eye the tears of merriment running down the cheeks of one of the spectators of this remarkable *tour de force*.

Another pleasant place where I was frequently a guest during the same decade, was Fasque in Kincardineshire, then the home of that fine old Tory, Sir Thomas Gladstone. Unlike his more famous brother in tastes as in political views, he was a keen sportsman, and an excellent shot. There was no grouse ground in the immediate neighbourhood of the house, but there were plenty of roe deer and black-game in the coverts, and wild duck frequented the home lake in the park where I enjoyed some good days' fishing, getting capital baskets of trout of an average weight of about half a pound. There was also excellent partridge shooting, and I had many a long day's walking in company with my host himself, although he had already passed his seventieth year. There was no driving; that easier and more luxurious way of getting partridges was never during his reign introduced at Fasque.

Sir Thomas protected his long nether limbs on these occasions with a pair of many-buttoned leather gaiters reaching far above the knee; and after each field of roots had been thoroughly worked, he used to call a halt, and solemnly remove these leggings, resuming them when the stubble or pasture had been crossed, and roots or potatoes again reached. Perhaps some of his younger guests occasionally felt, if they did not show, some impatience at this leisurely method of procedure, but it is surely right that he who pays the piper should call the tune, and probably we were all really the better for the enforced delays which so frequently interrupted the arduous tramp through the heavy root crops and matted potato haulms of Kincardineshire. Perhaps the shooting lunches would be looked upon as somewhat Spartan in these degenerate days, but there was always abundance of sandwiches, biscuits, and bread and cheese, with whisky and water in moderation. There was also a very prolific snipe bog in the neighbourhood of the house, where I once enjoyed an excellent day's sport in company with one of Sir Thomas's nephews, a midshipman who afterwards, if my memory serves me rightly, became an Admiral. Glendye, the famous grouse moor, was within a ride, or drive, and occasionally the guests at Fasque had the good fortune to take part in a grouse drive there, although the regular shooting was then usually compressed into a fortnight or three weeks in August, when Sir Thomas and his friends used to migrate to the little lodge and enjoy excellent sport over dogs on the well-stocked slopes that surround Mount Battock. Here also he used to walk with the best of them; and, to complete the catalogue of the sports which he permitted me to share, I must not omit to add that there was a cricket ground in the park at Fasque where he and I have taken part in a game with his servants and retainers. I can boast— or perhaps "record" would be a more appropriate word—that I have been bowled out by the elder brother of the "Grand old man"!

How happy too were the weeks spent on Speyside as the guest of Dr. Deane, afterwards Sir James Parker Deane, the Queen's Advocate, where my dear friend and college companion, Bargrave Deane, who now presides in the Court where his father was then so distinguished a leader, invited me to share the sport. The grouse shooting was of the best, and there was also capital rough shooting in woods where Bargrave's rifle used to account for many a fine roebuck. The fishing in the Spey was indifferent, but there was a stretch of the Avon which fished well after a spate; and I remember a picnic expedition with Bargrave, when with our knapsacks we walked across the hill, and after sleeping out in a shake-down, brought back in triumph two or three somewhat red kippers.

As a grouse moor Millden stands supreme, and I should be indeed ungrateful if I did not recall with special thankfulness the many seasons that I spent there as guest of the first Lord Cairns, and the magnificent sport and genial welcome I ever enjoyed at the hands of that kind host. I can never hope to see again such a perfectly trained kennel of pointers as he then possessed, or to be one of a party of four guns who bagged over fifteen hundred brace of grouse over dogs in ten days' sport. The family were then all quite young children, and Arthur, the eldest boy, was only occasionally allowed to walk with the shooters for part of a day. The beautiful North Esk ran through the middle of the ground, and salmon might often be seen moving in the pools, but I only once succeeded in catching a fish there. I used, however, to catch plenty of small trout on off days, and I remember one occasion upon which I met the children out with their nurses, and carried two of them on my back over the river. The little rogues instantly started up the brae, and the next thing I saw was the nurse and maid with kilted petticoats wading across the stream in pursuit, doubtless cursing my officious good-nature. Grouse driving was not then recognised in Forfarshire, although I enjoyed one or two days with our neighbour, the old Lord Dalhousie, at Invermark. He made fine practice with a little twenty-four bore gun; his swollen fingers, crippled with gout, could not stand the recoil of a larger weapon. After about three weeks' shooting, the grouse at Millden used to pack and become almost unapproachable. I am afraid to suggest a probable figure for the bag that might have been secured in the great year 1872 had we adopted the modern method of driving with suitably arranged butts and a party of practised guns. I feel sure that the total would have amounted to at least 5000 brace.

Better broken dogs were never seen on a moor. Mickie, the keeper, was a genius, and possessed all the patience, skill, and good temper which are necessary to constitute the perfect dog trainer. He never shouted or whistled; a signal with his uplifted hand was enough to make either or both of the ranging pointers drop and remain still as stones until his signal of release set them free. Lord Cairns was a Sabbatarian, but he did not take such a rigid view of the obligations of the day as those extremists satirised in Hood's "Ode to Rae Wilson"—

> "That bid you baulk
> A Sunday walk
> And shun God's work as you should shun your own."

It was one of the pleasures of a Sunday at Millden to stroll to the kennels, and see the whole pack released to race over the adjoining heather, when each and all of them would drop at their trainer's sign, however fast they might be galloping in the enjoyment of their liberty.

Here let me digress for a moment to pay my tribute of regard and esteem to my lost friend. Biographers have not done justice to the rare and sympathetic kindness, transparent sincerity, and strong sense of humour he veiled under a somewhat stiff and reserved manner. Religion was a part of his life, but he feared no person but his God. Shy by nature, he revealed his true self best in his home, surrounded by his family circle and friends. There was no trace of condescension or patronage in the delightful freedom with which the great statesman, judge, and advocate, chatted to such fledgling barristers as Edward Ross and myself, and I always felt natural and at my ease in conversation with him. He had a most retentive memory, and illustrations and quotations from his favourite Scott were often on his lips. Now, after the lapse of half a century, I seem to hear him now prophesying a sturdy and spirited resistance in some political or legal battle which he happened to be discussing, in the spirited words the poet puts into the mouth of Marmion—

> "Many a banner will be torn
> And many a knight to earth be borne,
> And many a sheaf of arrows spent,
> Ere Scotland's king shall cross the Trent."

His household servants, keepers, and gillies all worshipped him, for he seemed to enter into their feelings, and made their troubles and difficulties his own. A mistake of his boy Arthur illustrates this. The morning chapter of the Bible read by him at family prayers contained the passage "He that exalteth himself shall be abased." Arthur was heard afterwards explaining to his brother: "So nice of father! *If he had said 'a beast' none of the Scotch servants would have understood him!*"

I first visited Millden in 1869, when my father was joint-tenant with Lord Cairns of the Lodge and moor. Lady Cairns undertook the housekeeping, and the two large families had a delightful time together, in spite of the fact that it was not a great grouse season. It was the year of Mr. Gladstone's Irish Church Bill, and the two friends had passed a strenuous Session in the Houses of Lords and Commons as protagonists among the opponents of the measure. They had certainly earned their holiday, which they enjoyed like released schoolboys. Among my father's papers I find a letter of Lord Cairns, written to him in September of that year, describing the sport in the adjoining forest of Invermark, from which it appears that he had been given a day's stalking there, and had been so unfortunate as to wound a stag! The letter gives a graphic account of the sport, and concludes with a prophetic political allusion.

"MILLDEN, 29 *Sept.* 1869.

"MY DEAR HARDY,—You will like to hear of the doings in Invermark Forest since you left. Sir Thomas Moncrieff came up the day after you went South, and on the Monday killed two, and on the Tuesday four stags. On the Monday one of his stags was the one wounded about a week before by Captain Young, and on the same day they saw, but did not get, your cripple. The Buccleuchs and ourselves went to Invermark on Tuesday, and on Wednesday the Duke stalked in the South Forest, and Sir T. M. and myself in the North. The Duke had a good chance, but missed. We also came upon a herd of stags about eleven o'clock. I got the first shot and killed a good stag, fourteen or fifteen stone, shooting him through the heart, and breaking both fore-legs. Sir T. M. had two shots at the same time, and two afterwards, and as we thought without success. Since then old Ross and Mr. Forbes (Newe) have been there and have killed two or three more stags.

"I heard of your splendid sport at Murthly, the best I think I ever knew anyone have there.[1] It was a great achievement, and you must be very proud of it. We have had little shooting since you left: a few brace of grouse; and we have brought our slain partridges up to one hundred brace. The weather has been wet and stormy, but with intervening days very fine. We feel the break-up of our large and pleasant party very much.

"I infer from Hartington's speech that there are decided breakers ahead about the Irish Land Bill.— Ever yours, very sincerely, CAIRNS."

Another very happy hunting-ground where I was a frequent visitor at a later period was Braemore, the beautiful Ross-shire home of Sir John Fowler, the great engineer. The natural surroundings were of match-

[1] Diary of Gathorne Hardy, Sept. 24, 1869. "My last day at Murthly was spent 'harling' alone, and my success was extraordinary and almost unparalleled there, as I killed 2 salmon and 8 grilse. The largest 19, the second 12, and the grilse varying from 10 to 6. I did not lose one."

less beauty, and all the resources of great wealth and marvellous technical skill had been employed to make the place perfect. After Sir John (then Mr. Fowler) purchased the estate he set to work to select a site for a residence. "I must have," he told his architect, "a view of the valley, the river, and the sea, and the house must stand so high that there will be no danger of feeling enervated by the relaxing West coast climate."

Careful and exhaustive inspection failed to show any site possessing all the advantages required. No matter; a plateau was scooped out of the side of the mountain, just where a brawling torrent leaped in a succession of cascades down a steep birch-clad ravine into the narrow valley through which that delightful salmon river the Broom finds its way to the sea. A dam above the house turned the little torrent into the "Home Loch," which when I knew it was well stocked with excellent trout, sporting risers, although not very large. The overflow, directed and controlled, supplied electric light and power for the establishment, as well as an inexhaustible supply of excellent water for drinking and other purposes. As every inch of space had to be hardly won from rock and moss, the stables and gardens were put in the valley just below the house, three miles distant by a beautifully constructed winding road, although a stone could almost be thrown upon the roof of the coach-house from the terrace above. Two paths, one very steep, the other, afterwards known as Lady Fowler's, gently winding across and beside the stream among fern-clad rocks which were a vision of loveliness, provided a shorter access for pedestrians or deer ponies.

Every kind of rare and lovely British fern flourished in these congenial surroundings, from the tall *Osmunda Regalis* to the tiny film fern, of which both varieties, Wilson's and the Tunbridge, abounded. I fancy that Sir John was almost a pioneer in the use of the telephone and the electric light in a private residence. The higher part of the river, above a fall no salmon could negotiate, cuts its way through a deep inaccessible gorge, crossed and recrossed by threadlike iron bridges, which carry the path through the most magnificent scenery commanding lovely views of mountain, torrent, and rapid. The eagle floated on noiseless wing round the mountain peaks, and the osprey, which nested on the shores of Loch Luichart, in the adjoining forest of Lady Ashburton, might frequently be seen in the neighbourhood of the house.

The road from Garve, the nearest station, ran through deer forest for nearly twenty miles; rather a long drive when I first traversed it, but nothing in these days of motors. The journey was enlivened by frequent visions of stag and hind upon the sky-line, earnest of the sport that awaited the traveller at his journey's end. It was at Braemore that I had the never to be forgotten thrill of bagging my first stag, and many much more important persons—artists, statesmen, and even bishops and archbishops—were beguiled there into undertaking their maiden stalk. I suppose the big-game book is still at Inverbroom, in which it was more than once my fate to read my name, coupled with the melancholy entry: "Missed a stag."

I paid my first visit to this terrestrial paradise somewhere towards the end of the seventies, but not

(From the Braemore Visitors' Book, 1868. Pencil Sketch by Sir EDWIN LANDSEER)

by road. Braemore's steam yacht, *The Southern Cross*, came to Poltalloch, where I was then spending one of my many very happy "Autumns in Argyllshire." We had a lovely cruise up the beautiful coast, calling on our way at Oban, Loch Hourn, and other places, and taking toll of the sea fish with trawl and hand-line. Arthur Fowler, the eldest son, then a lad—now alas! no more—was our host and companion; his father was not on board.

The first morning the ponies were brought to the door after an early breakfast, and I started with Monty Fowler along the Garve road, which divides the Braemore Forest conveniently into two beats, Ben Dearig and Strome. The stalker, McHardy, was somewhat of an autocrat, and as I afterwards thought a little too much inclined to treat the sportsman accompanying him as an automaton, and to direct his movements arbitrarily without taking him into his confidence as to the why and wherefore—

"Theirs not to make reply,
Theirs not to reason why,"

but he was a magnificent stalker, and knew every stone in the forest, and every trick of the currents of air which drew through the corries. He was also a keen observer of Nature, and used to bring back many rare plants and ferns from distant heights, to be planted in his mistress's cherished rock garden and fernery by the side of her path below the house.

Every little incident of that day forty years ago comes back to me as I write,

"As tho' 'twere yesterday; as tho' it were
The hour just flown."

Once more I seem fretting to start with a boy's impatience while my host reads his letters before issuing the orders of the day. Then, when we are fairly mounted and away, comes another delay. About a mile from the gate the two stalkers dismount, and deliberately search with their glasses the portion of the hillside on their left between us and the sanctuary. "Braemore" had greeted us on his return from the forest the evening before, full of regrets for the loss of a magnificent stag which he had hit and followed to about this point, when the mists of evening veiled it from sight. I am afraid that my inward prayer was that it might not be discovered, as I knew that if it was, it meant further delay, and I grudged every moment. Alas! the sharp eye of McHardy marked a reddish-brown object near a cairn on the hillside, and leading a pony behind them the two stalkers left us in the road, and made their way up the hill to the spot where the big stag (he turned the scale at 18 stone, clean) lay motionless and dead. More than an hour passed before they returned, having performed the last rites. However, we made up for lost time when they returned, pressing our ponies to their utmost speed, which, as they were grass-fed and thick-coated, did not exceed the "speed limit."

We parted by the forester's house opposite to Loch Druim (the summit loch), and McHardy proceeded to seat himself on a flat stone on the road and "spy" the hillside on the right beyond the lake. In a very few minutes he rose and signalled to me to follow. He had found a small herd of stags, and in response to my eager inquiries condescended to tell me that the wind was all right, that it would be quite easy to get up to

"HERO AND LEANDER"

them, and that there was one "worth a shot." We walked rapidly to the boat-house, where a light skiff hung suspended by pulleys, so that a child's hand could move it up and down, crossed the lake, and our stalk began at once. There was a certain amount of crawling, but the approach was neither long nor difficult, and soon, after peering over a heather-clad brae, McHardy took the rifle from its cover, slipped back the safety bolt, and pointed below him, whispering as he handed me the rifle, "The second to the right is your beast." The stag—how enormous he looked to my unpractised eyes!—was lying down broadside about 120 yards off. McHardy advised me to wait till he rose, but when I urged that I was sure I could not miss him, he left me to take my own wilful way. I took a low sight behind the shoulder, pulled the trigger of the rifle, a 450 express with black powder (it was before these happy days of cordite and 303), and with a bound my stag disappeared behind the mound.

There was a moment of agony when I believed that I had missed and disgraced myself for ever, but McHardy reassured me, shouting, as he started in pursuit, "He is hit hard, and cannot go far." In a very few minutes he had administered the *coup de grâce*, and I was standing breathless by my first stag, a nice fifteen-stone beast carrying a pretty head of nine points. I got a second in the afternoon, but will not go into details. It was more of a drive than a stalk, as the deer were in an unapproachable position, and had to be moved by showing them a glimpse of something, while I ran to waylay them in the pass they would be pretty sure to take. Six stags passed me at a hand gallop within a hundred yards; I was told to take the third, and this time hit him right through the heart, and marvelled that he ran on more than fifty yards before he fell dead and lay motionless as a stone.

It was well that my first day on the hill proved successful, as I was not destined on that occasion to pay a prolonged visit to Braemore. A telegram greeted me on my return; my son, a baby in arms, had developed a rash at Poltalloch where we had left him in charge of an aunt, and nothing would induce his mother to remain away. Our thoughtful friends once more placed the yacht at our disposal, and early next morning we started for home. It was a flat calm; a day's steaming brought us to Loch Aline before nightfall, and the skipper suggested that we should go in there and anchor for the night, "as he could easily land us at Duntroon in time for breakfast at Poltalloch on the following morning." The plan sounded most satisfactory, so after despatching a telegram ordering the carriage to meet us at the little pier at eight, we turned in, rejoicing that we should so soon be home. Next morning according to orders the skipper weighed anchor at the first dawn of day, but a little later a dismal succession of blasts from the hooter notified that all was not well. I hastily dressed and ran on deck, to find myself enveloped in a dense fog of the colour, I had almost said of the texture, of cotton wool. We were somewhere in the Sound of Mull, but even in that narrow strait no vestige of land was visible, and after a consultation with the captain we decided to anchor and wait till it cleared. But our waiting, like that of the clown in Horace, was in vain. Breakfast came, then lunch, but

"A DISCONSOLATE BACHELOR"

[From the Braemore Visitors' book, 1873. By General Hope Crealock.]

still the fog continued. All day we had seen nothing but one fishing-boat which anchored a few fathoms from us. Hour after hour this unlucky craft, and one or two floating bottles, swung round us with the tide, always keeping the same distance from the yacht. As the long hours passed all hope of reaching home that day vanished, and the skipper became anxious. It was all very well to remain where we were in a flat calm and a slack tide during daylight, but we might be, and probably were, close to the cliffs of Mull; there was no holding ground, and if it should come on to blow in the night we might quite easily be wrecked. We determined therefore to proceed dead slow, blowing the whistle at intervals of two or three minutes, and listening for the echo from the cliffs, which shortly afterwards gave back the sound on the port-side. Working the lead, and consulting the chart, we forged cautiously ahead, keeping just within sight of the low cliff, and at last distinguished moving figures on the sky-line, and, shouting inquiries, obtained the information that, as we expected from the soundings and coastal indications, we were close to Loch Spelve, a loch with a bottle-necked entrance near the south point of Mull opposite to the Firth of Lorne. Our chart disclosed that there was capital anchorage and shelter within, but it was rather risky to enter in a fog without a pilot or someone with local knowledge. However, it was a choice of evils, and we cautiously felt our way in, and were soon comfortably at anchor. The mist never showed any signs of clearing, so we turned in, after giving orders to the skipper to weigh anchor as soon after dawn as possible, if the fog had then lifted.

Next morning I woke with the comfortable sensation that the yacht was once more steadily progressing through the water, but shortly after I had completed a hasty toilet and come on deck the atmosphere thickened, and we were soon once more enveloped in dim and almost impenetrable mist. It was quite unsafe to anchor; we were in the strong tide near the point of Craignish, and there was nothing for it but to try to make our way through the "Door," the narrow strait which forms the entrance to Loch Crinan through which the flood and ebb rush boiling and eddying at the rate of eight or nine knots an hour at spring tides. We were in familiar waters, where many a time both my wife and myself had fished round the rocky islands for saith and lythe, but the shapes of the rocks as they loomed gigantic through the fog all looked the same. We manœuvred about, with my wife as the one most familiar with the locality looking out on the prow, and at last, when she reported that she certainly recognised the point of Craignish, we faced the channel and were soon safely through the strait, quickly passed Rabbit Island, anchored under the old castle of Duntroon at about nine in the morning, and were home in time for a late breakfast.

All is well that ends well! but I had undergone an experience somewhat trying in a friend's yacht. The risk to passengers and crew was infinitesimal in the calm weather and always close to land, but we might easily have done serious damage to the yacht so generously placed at our disposal. I am only a moderate sailor, but I infinitely prefer a blow to a fog. As it turned out we need not have cut short our visit,

PLEASANT PLACES

as the interesting invalid was already quite convalescent, and some twenty years later enjoyed the hospitality of Braemore and, like his father, killed his first stag there.

The visitors' book was a most interesting and valuable possession, as the most distinguished artists and literary and scientific celebrities had enriched it with their contributions. Sir Edwin Landseer, Millais, and General Crealoch had sketched various incidents of the sport in the forest, and Sir William Harcourt had celebrated the delights of a holiday in verse. The pen-and-ink sketches of Millais were especially interesting. One exaggerated the drawbacks of a wet season. An ark of the well-known Lowther Arcade type floated over a dreary expanse of water, a black-cock perched upon its chimney. The legend inscribed below recorded that it contained " Braemore and his family," but it would have needed a deluge greater even than the historical spate on the Findhorn to submerge the eagle's nest from which the Laird looked down upon the valley. In another sketch Sir John's partner was depicted landing his first salmon, and a Cupid fluttering above an admirable likeness of Harcourt crowned him with a laurel wreath on the occasion of his shooting his first stag. Another sketch by the same hand portrayed an angler casting from the narrow platform beside the boiling foss at the top of the river Broom, his gillie supporting him by a gaff firmly fixed through his nether garments. This bore the legend, " A necessary precaution when fishing the Lynn pool."

Some of these sketches were reproduced as illustrations to an article on " The Game Book of a Famous

Estate," written by the Reverend Montague Fowler, and published in the *Badminton Magazine* for November 1898, but the reduced and faint reproductions of amateur photographs necessarily did scant justice to the delicate lines. The first Sir John Fowler made this precious book an heirloom by will, and I am deeply indebted to his grandson, the present baronet, and his mother, Lady Fowler, for trusting me with the precious volume, and permitting me to reproduce some of its unique contents. The sketch of a group of deer, "In a Good Place for a Shot," was drawn by Sir Edwin Landseer in 1868, and the two excellent studies of stags by General Crealoch, "Hero and Leander" and "A Disconsolate Bachelor," in the following decade. I give also two out of several sketches by Sir John Millais. The first, "Triumphs of the Year," gives excellent portraits of the artist himself and of Sir William Harcourt in 1875. The second illustrates a feat of Sir Arthur Fowler, the second baronet, when a lad of seventeen. On September 10, 1870, he killed three stags with three consecutive shots, while Millais on the same day missed three. Arthur is portrayed seated on a pyramid of slain, with the punning legend "Arthur's Seat" subscribed, while in the corner a duck with three eggs represents the artist's less successful "innings."

The whole volume is full of interest with its mementoes and autographs of the numerous soldiers, statesmen, churchmen, and leaders of science who enjoyed the hospitality of the great engineer. The names of Lord Strathnairn and Earl Roberts, Archbishops Benson, Maclagan, Thomson, and Magee,

ARTHUR'S SEAT
(From the Braemore Visitors' Book, 1870. By Sir JOHN MILLAIS)

Professor Owen, Sir Roderick Murchison, and many other great men of the Victorian age are to be found in its pages.

Those friends who did not care for the strenuous joys of the forest could angle in the river for salmon or sea trout, or visit the numerous lochs among the mountains and make good baskets. The yacht conveyed many a merry party among the lovely summer islands in Loch Broom, or on more distant excursions to Loch Maree, or some of the other beauty spots on the West Coast. It carried a beam trawl, which used to bring up not only magnificent turbot and other sea fish, but many rare objects among the "rubbish" to delight the heart of a naturalist—quaint long-legged spider crabs with their clothing of sea-weed, strange pennatulidæ, the long sea rope (*Funiculina quadrangularis*), the rosy sea pen, and sea rush; countless starfish of all colours and shapes, and other samples of the scaly and shelly marvels which strew the bottom of the sea. A sportsman's paradise indeed!

> "Braemore! what brush can paint? what tongue express
> The fullness of its perfect loveliness?
> O, 'would I were a bird' to linger there,
> A willing victim of the Fowler's snare."

CHAPTER II

THE ISLAND OF COLONSAY

I ALWAYS had a hankering after Colonsay long before I ever visited its shores. It was visible as a dim cloud on the horizon as one looked over the whirlpool of Coirevreachan between Jura and Scarba from many of the high points round Poltalloch. But, although the distance was not very great as the crow flies, it required a daring pilot and a favourable tide, to face the dangers of the gulf with its galloping rush and roaring whirlpool even in a steam yacht, and the voyage round, either southward through the Sounds of Jura and Islay, or northward round the end of Scarba and the Garvelloch leaving Mull on the port helm, was rather an undertaking. The anchorage was notoriously difficult and risky; in fact in anything like an easterly gale even the mail-boats were, it was said, often unable to land their cargo and passengers. More than once when my brother-in-law, John Wingfield Malcolm, afterwards the first and only Lord Malcolm of Poltalloch, but then member for Argyllshire, sailed in the *Guillemot* to visit that Ultima Thule of his constituency, he came back disappointed, having found the weather too uncertain to risk landing and leaving the yacht outside in the open roadstead. So it befell that it was not until 1898 that my desire was gratified. That year I was looking out for a small moor in

Scotland where to spend my autumn holiday, and heard that my western Utopia was to be let for August and September. I visited Sir John M'Neill at home in his apartments at St. James' Palace, and found him more than willing to accept me as a tenant at very moderate rent. In his downright way he ridiculed the idea that his island home was at all out of the way or difficult of access, and indeed all my own later experience went to prove that the danger of being cut off from communication with the mainland was greatly exaggerated. During the six or seven visits I afterwards paid there, many of them prolonged for two or three months, I do not recall more than two or three occasions when the steamer was unable to call and disembark mails and passengers.

At his suggestion we paid a picnic visit to his house at Killoran to spy out the land. The weather was lovely, and one of his nephews was there to do the honours. It seemed enchanted ground. The gulls and cormorants were building on the cliffs, where also were then to be found a few nests of the chough, a bird now rare in the British Isles. Plovers and oyster-catchers were busy on the links, from which the eye searched the broad Atlantic to catch a sight of the distant lighthouse of Dubheartach, the only inhabited land between us and America. It was early for loch fishing, but we sampled the trout in West Loch Fada, and visited that mountain gem, Loch Sgoltaire, which is situated so exactly upon the watershed that the overflow sometimes discharges itself from both ends, one stream flowing into Killoran bay and the Sound of Mull, the other finding its way into Loch Fada and thence into the Atlantic. We could not of course exhaust a quarter of the charms of the island in the short time at our disposal, but we looked across from the beetling precipice of the Cailleach towards Iona and the Ross of Mull, and visited the golf course and some of the caves.

The Cailleach, so called from its fancied resemblance to an old woman's mutch, actually overhangs the rolling breakers, and we admired, but did not emulate, the feat of a former Laird, the celebrated Scotch judge, Lord Colonsay, who took his title from the island he loved so well, who used to display his intrepidity and soundness of head by standing here just on the verge of the precipice on one leg—

> "With his arms serenely glued
> On his breast,"

like Sir Lancelot Bogle in Aytoun's parody of Mrs. Browning's "Rhyme of the Duchess May."

His head was as clear when listening to an argument on the Bench as it was unmoved on the precipice, in spite of the bitter tongue of his forensic colleague and contemporary, Lord Westbury. The story runs that this latter once met the ex-Chief Justice Erle strolling in the neighbourhood of his former haunts. "Chief Justice," he said, "how is it that you never give us the benefit of your assistance in the Privy Council?" "Well, the fact is, my dear Bethell, that I am so old, and so deaf, and so stupid that I do not think I could be of any use." "Tut! tut!" replied Westbury, in his most acid and satirical manner, "I am old, Vaughan Williams is as deaf as a post, and Colonsay's stupidity surpasses belief, yet I assure you that we three make a most reliable tribunal."

THE ISLAND OF COLONSAY

When we got back to London we at once clenched the bargain, and began to count the days which separated us from our holiday. A joyful party started from Euston on the night of the 1st of August. We had prevailed upon MacBrayne's firm to take our party on to Colonsay in the regular Islay steamer, so our voyage on the following morning was once more in the familiar *Columba* as far as Tarbert, where we left her, and drove over the narrow strip of land across which Bruce dragged his bark on the famous occasion described in the "Lord of the Isles"—

> "Ever the breeze blows merrily,
> But the galley ploughs no more the sea,
> Lest, rounding wild Cantire, they meet
> The southern foeman's watchful fleet,
>   They held unwonted way:
> Up Tarbat's western lake they bore,
> Then dragg'd their bark the isthmus o'er,
> As far as Kilmaconnel's shore,
>   Upon the eastern bay.
> It was a wondrous sight to see
> Topmast and pennon glitter free,
> High raised above the greenwood tree,
> As on dry land the galley moves,
> By cliff and copse and alder groves."

Our course was in the reverse direction, as we joined our steamer at the end of west Loch Tarbert, and left Ardpatrick on our right, while on the left we spied a flock of lazy seals on the rock, so accustomed to the passage of the steamboat that they hardly condescended to look up. Soon we emerged into the Sound of Islay, and after landing passengers and goods at Port Askaig, an hour and a half brought us to our destination—the little harbour of Scalasaig.

Here we were met by the whale-boat, which, with its sturdy and obliging boatmen, we had hired from Sir John for the term of our tenancy, as well as the stable establishment, consisting of a pair of good horses, a strong waggonette, and an old buck-board imported from Canada, where it had seen service at the time of the Red River expedition. The little harbour is too shallow for anything bigger than a fishing-boat, so our steamer left its anchorage in the open roadstead, and steamed back to Islay as soon as our party and the luggage had got into the boat. Happily the wind was favourable, and in some ten minutes we landed on the pier where the waggonette was waiting to take us to our destination. There are two roads by which Killoran House can be reached from the harbour. One, across the island to Machrins and round between the north end of the coast and the chain of three lochs, is nearly four miles in length, while the other is under two; but the shorter road traverses a desperately steep brae, and with a heavy load little time is lost, and some strain upon the horses saved, by adopting the longer route. Some of our party drove round with the luggage, and some strolled up the brae past a circle of prehistoric stones, which is only one of the many interesting primeval remains with which the island abounds. There are cromlechs and circles, relics of the stone age and of remote antiquity; there are ancient middens where bones of red deer and of the extinct great auk reveal the former existence of a now vanished fauna. Two buried boats with the skeletons of horse and Viking, with the broken axe and sword of the latter, were exhumed to bear their testimony to the raids of the old Norwegian sea

THE ISLAND OF COLONSAY

kings; and cloisters, chapel, cross, and shrine carry on the story to a later date, and tell how dear the sacred soil was to the Fathers of the early Christian Church. It was only an unfortunate accident that prevented Saint Columba, from whom the island derives its name, from settling on its shores. He fully intended to remain, but unfortunately he had made a vow that he would never see Ireland more. On a clear day soon after he landed his eyes caught sight of three misty humps in the south-west, which could be nothing but the mountains of the island he had abandoned and forsworn. He was sorry, for, like all sensible people, he had taken a fancy to Colonsay, but like Agamemnon, Jephthah, Herod, and others, he was a man of his word even when his vow was a foolish one, and he ordered out his coracle and paddled across to Iona, where he passed the remainder of his life.

Happily I was under no such rash vow as the Saint, and I learnt to love Colonsay and to regard it almost as a second home. The old house at Killoran close to the grand bay with its magnificent sands made an ideal residence for a naturalist and sportsman. The lochs, full of excellent trout running up to a pound and a half in weight, afforded capital sport for the fisherman, and the sea provided plaice, haddock, and whiting, as well as the common saithe and lythe, although the resident fishermen already complained sadly of the manner in which stream trawlers coming from a distance had depleted their once teeming waters. There was first-rate black-game shooting, a fair proportion of grouse, a good many partridges to vary the bag, and abundance of ducks, teal, snipe and plovers. As for rabbits, they might be counted by thousands, and we generally reserved them for the pea rifle, unless some were specially wanted for the pot. The caves which honeycombed the rocks abounded in rock-pigeons, but it was only very rarely that the Atlantic rollers which dashed their foam up to the very summit of the cliffs were sufficiently smooth to enable the sportsman to shoot these birds from a boat. The rock scenery was magnificent. It was hard to believe as one strained one's eyes over the beetling precipices on the north end of the island that no portion of the island exceeded in height 800 feet. Lobsters and crabs formed the principal commodities for export, and there were always plenty of magnificent fellows which the fishermen were glad to dispose of at a moderate price at home to save the middleman's profit. My game book lies before me as I write, and I jot down our bags for 1898 and 1899.

	1898.	1899.
Partridges	50	105
Pheasants	10	2 [1]
Grouse	222	100
Hares	32	13
Rabbits	422	392
Woodcock	3	5
Black-game	64	68
Snipe	88	137
Wild duck	104	111
Various	55	112
Total	1045	1050

It must be remembered that this bag did not by any means represent what might have been got by a party who wanted to make a record. There was, of course,

[1] We left on the 10th of October, and did go after these birds.

THE ISLAND OF COLONSAY

a limit as to grouse, which we took care not even to approach, as we were not fortunate in hitting upon good breeding seasons. We were the despair of the keeper, as we rarely took a set day with dogs and men. What my sons, and perhaps their father also, loved best was to wander out alone with a ruk-sack, glass, and pea rifle, and bring back as much as a solitary sportsman cared to carry. It can readily be imagined that under such circumstances hares were severely let alone, and rabbits only shot at in the evening when we had got very near home.

What happy days we spent there during those two autumns! The old house was large enough to accommodate a numerous party, and I never knew anyone who visited the island who did not succumb to its charm. There was amusement to suit all tastes; the old whale-boat was out most days, unless the wind was unfavourable, bearing a merry party to picnic either northward or southward as tide and wind happened to serve; others would visit the golf links at Machrins, taking with them gun, rifle, or fishing-rod; for West Loch Fada was close to the links, and the evening hours were best for a rise, while duck, pigeon, and snipe abounded in the bays and rushy marshes on the edges of the green turf, and along the sides of the three lakes which stretched below the road between Killoran and the bay. These lakes must at no very distant date, geologically speaking, have formed part of the sea itself. They discharge their overflow into Port Mor and the Atlantic through a low marshy field, and the whole conformation of the valley in which they are situated nearly resembles such sea lochs as Loch Swen and West Loch Tarbert in the Mull of Cantyre.

Numerous raised beaches along the shore indicate considerable alteration of the level of the land, and explain how salt water lochs have become fresh. It cannot be expected that the climate of a western island should be particularly dry, but that of Colonsay compares very favourably in this respect with that of the adjacent islands of Mull and Jura. Often and often have I stood dry and comfortable looking out with a feeling of pharisaical superiority at the dense clouds discharging their contents upon those less favoured shores, diverted to our north and west by the mountainous peaks of Ben Mor and the Paps of Jura.

I soon became reconciled to the comparative inaccessibility of my island home. If it were not for its difficult anchorage and its dangerous and reef-strewn coast, Colonsay, close as it is to Oban, the Charing Cross of the Highlands, would be constantly visited by the thousand and one yachts which flit like so many butterflies over the blue waters which encircle the inner and outer Hebrides. The flora and fauna of Colonsay would not, it is to be feared, remain so distinctive and characteristic as they are if it became a regular calling place for the steam palaces which convey Midas and his guests for their cruise among the Western islands.

Here reigned supreme, beloved by all the inhabitants of his little kingdom, most of whom were his clansmen and bore his name, the late Sir John M'Neill. He did not inherit his property, but had to buy it back from the heirs of the famous judge. Unfortunately for him, land at the time of his purchase stood at a high figure, and the interest of the price, which he had to raise on mortgage, crippled his finances all through

THE ISLAND OF COLONSAY

his career. At his death it passed into the hands of Lord Strathcona, fortunately a lifelong friend and one sure worthily to carry on his traditions; but it is sad to think that Colonsay knows the M'Neills no more. I seem to see the old chief still: his upright gait, his abrupt and alert manner, his kindly face, and to hear his brusque but ever genial welcome. A gallant soldier, his prowess had been shown in many lands, and the Victoria Cross "for valour," and a host of other less-prized orders decorated his breast. He was a beloved and honoured servant of Queen Victoria, who visited him in his remote kingdom. He rode by her side as equerry at her two Jubilees, and again by the gun-carriage which bore her remains to her burial. He did not long survive his Royal Mistress, but passed away, full of years and honours, on 25th May 1904.

He loved all kinds of natural objects—bird, beast, and fern; but perhaps the seals have the best reason of all for cherishing his memory and lamenting his loss. It was said of another king, William the Conqueror, "that so he loved the high deer as if they had been his own children," but he preserved them only as beasts of chase, whereas Sir John protected seals because he loved to watch them; and it was only on rare occasions and for some adequate reason that he or his tenants ever molested them. Great was his indignation when a predatory yacht trespassed along his shores, and wantonly fired on his pets. Several seals were killed, and many others wounded. The letter which he wrote to the headquarters of the Northern Yacht Club at Oban is still remembered. It described in cutting and sarcastic terms the conduct of "the crew" of the yacht, of which he gave the name, adding that "of course they must have trespassed in the absence and without knowledge of their master, as no gentleman could possibly ever have acted in such a manner." The owner had the grace to admit his offence, and to offer a handsome apology, attributing his fault to ignorance of Sir John's wishes, and promising not only never to repeat it, but also as far as possible to prevent others from following his bad example. Probably the castigation inflicted by the letter, which was duly posted over the mantelpiece of the smoking-room of the club, was sufficient to deter any but the most brazen culprits from a repetition of the outrage. But the seals of Colonsay are a sufficiently distinctive feature of the island to demand a chapter to themselves.

The situation of Killoran House, like that of most residences of the period, was selected rather for shelter than for view. The original structure was like a large Scotch farm-house—a square two-storied building, to which two wings were added, one on each side; one containing a suite of bedrooms and servants' offices, and a comfortable smoking- and gun-room; the other a billiard-room and library, a corridor, a dining-room, and a drawing-room opening into a conservatory. The dining-room contained some excellent busts and portraits of the M'Neill family: the judge, the diplomatist of Persian celebrity, and last—not least—a portrait of Sir John himself by the hand of her Royal Highness Princess Louise, Duchess of Argyll.

The old-fashioned garden, which is of an earlier date than the house, which occupies the site of a Priory, is indeed a delightful spot. In front of the windows sweet-scented verbenas grow to a height of ten to twelve feet, and a hedge of hydrangeas blossoms profusely between the conservatory and a walled kitchen garden producing excellent fruit and vegetables in abundance. Peaches and nectarines ripen in the open air. In those gardens on the adjacent mainland which I know best, they only come to maturity under glass. At the foot of the garden below the lawn runs a fine burn through which doubtless sea trout would find their way into the lochs beyond, but for the fact that the outlet into Killoran bay expands over a wide tract of sand, and is therefore too shallow for migratory fish to ascend. I have sometimes thought that it might be possible to cut, or blast, an artificial channel through the rocks at the southern extremity of the bay deep enough to enable migratory fish to enter, and thus add another charm to the many which the place already presents. Where the stream runs through the garden its banks are almost concealed by the growth of *Osmunda Regalis* and the Lastreas of various kinds. Many rare and beautiful ferns flourish all over the island; both varieties of the hymenophyllum, the Tonbridge fern, and Wilson's, carpet the damp boulders with their moss-like growth; and in every cave and cleft along the shore the long shining fronds of the *Asplenium Marinum* depend in luxuriant profusion.

At the back of the house, between the garden and the end of east Loch Fada, are beautiful woods now containing some fine trees. A M'Neill could now have his death sentences executed near home without having to go as far afield as the "Hangman's Rock," an ominous-looking pointed projection overlooking the Strand opposite to Oronsay, where, according to tradition, the justice of former Lords of the island was carried out. The entire absence of trees suitable for the purpose compelled the use of this projecting rock, and the hole through which the rope was passed still bears witness to the truth of the story. The whole of the little kingdom, comprising the two islands of Colonsay and Oronsay, contains only 12,000 acres, and numbers about 460 inhabitants. The two islands are separated by a narrow strait which bears the familiar name of the Strand. To a Londoner's mind this carries with it the suggestion of a crowded thoroughfare, with hurrying passengers thronging its pavements, and divided by a stream of motor buses, taxicabs, and a few specimens of the rapidly vanishing hansom; and yet I suppose that even our familiar London Strand was once the border of a tidal river whose sandbanks at low water were the haunt of avocet, dunlin, ring plover, and a host of waders and shore birds. The Colonsay Strand is dry at low water, when carts and foot-passengers can pass between the two islands; but caution and a knowledge of the tides is desirable, as the flood rises rapidly, and the expanse of sand is soon turned into an arm of the sea through which sailing-boats and yachts can pass. There is a story that one yacht came in and anchored half-way in what her captain imagined to be a permanently navigable strait, to find itself shortly afterwards lying over on its side in absolutely dry ground. There is an anchorage here where a good-sized yacht can lie in safety and shelter, but it can only move out under suitable conditions of wind and tide. I think the most useful sort of boat for a wealthy proprietor of the property to acquire would be a stout steam-trawler with powerful engines, small enough and strong enough to lie stranded at low

THE ISLAND OF COLONSAY

water in the little fishing-boat harbour at Scalasaig, with which it would almost always be possible to maintain a connection either with Oban to the north, the "Small Isles" of Jura, or some point in Islay where regular steamers call daily. Such a boat would always be useful also for fishing and trawling, and for getting about to different points on the island without being dependent on wind and tide. A large yacht drawing much water would be a comparatively useless toy. I was twice tenant of Killoran House and the shootings, and also visited the island on several other occasions, usually at Easter, but once for a much longer period commencing in September. On these occasions we stayed at the little inn at Scalasaig whose friendly proprietors, then the Misses M'Neill, did everything possible for our comfort, and provided excellent homely fare and clean and comfortable quarters. Our experience in 1900 was not altogether a pleasant one, as we came for rest and change, bringing with us my son who had been wounded at Lindley in the South African war, and invalided home. Shortly after our arrival he developed enteric fever, which he had caught on the troopship on his way home. This was not an agreeable experience either for ourselves or for the inhabitants, who had once before suffered from a serious outbreak of typhoid causing many deaths, and were naturally anxious that the disorder should not again be introduced. Happily on this occasion there was no second case of fever, but my son's attack proved a severe one with numerous relapses, and the long detention and the distance from consulting physicians was certainly trying. I managed to amuse myself with golf and with a pea rifle which Sir John allowed me to use. Old blackcocks used to feed all round the inn, and even in the garden; and the patient had a looking-glass so arranged that he could see their reflection as he lay in bed. His convalescence dated from the day when he was tempted to creep out of bed, and put a bullet through the glossy ebony neck of one which tempted him beyond endurance. Our stay was prolonged into December, and I was able to see something of bird life in winter when the great flocks of Brent, Barnacle, and Lag geese used to pass over my head in wedge-shaped cohorts. What pleasure may be derived from watching the life of bird and beast under natural conditions, and yet how unobservant some are! We had a maid-servant who said to my wife one evening when brushing her hair, "I saw a gull to-day." This was about the third week of our second autumn at Killoran, and it is hardly an exaggeration to say that the eye could never sweep the horizon without encountering the sight of many gulls. Another of her quaint remarks ran as follows: "The young gentlemen brought in a funny bird to-day. I think they called it a handrail!" But to those that have eyes to see, the pages of the book of Nature are everywhere open, and full of ever fresh interests and delights.

Gaelic was the prevailing language, and those linguists who could understand and speak the Sassenach tongue were obviously translating as they went on. Witch, spectre, and fairy had not been altogether driven away by the advance of civilisation, and the votive offerings of devotees on the stone at the side of the well of St. Columba testify that passers-by still

THE ISLAND OF COLONSAY 39

pay for wishes as they drink, and hope for their fulfilment. Many of the fairy tales still current in the island may be found in a delightful little book, *Summer in the Hebrides*, printed in 1887, in which the authoress, Mrs. Murray, describes her experiences of six seasons spent on Oronsay. I take this opportunity to acknowledge my debt to this volume, which the authoress kindly presented to me, of which I have made use to refresh my memory of names and scenes. The stories, taken down from the mouths of *cailleach* and boatmen, are variants of the folk-lore of many lands, and offer an interesting study to the archæologist.

For instance there is a familiar ring about the tale of the humpbacked man who lived at Balnahard, and left his home on Hogmanay to buy stores for the new year at Scalasaig. Passing a green knowe overlooking Killoran bay he suddenly came upon the fairies dancing on the hillside to a measure, the tune of which went to the words, "Monday, Tuesday, Wednesday, Thursday, Friday, Saturday." There was something wrong with the dance, and the little revellers were evidently disconcerted; they were out of time and tune. The mistake flashed upon him suddenly; he called out "Wednesday" at the proper moment and set them right. The fairies took up the correction, sang the song right and trod the measure correctly. The hillock then opened and the fairies disappeared, taking the man down with them to their subterranean home where, to reward his kindness, they removed his hump, and sent him back to earth loosed from his infirmity. Another humpback on the island heard of the good fortune of his fellow-sufferer, and went out in search of the fairies on the next anniversary of Hogmanay, and found them again at their revels. Unfortunately his correction, "Thursday," was wrong and misleading, and put them all out of time, although they had been right before. They punished his interference by giving him the hump they had taken off his friend's back the year before, so that he had to pass through the remainder of his life with two humps like a Bactrian camel. Many parallels will suggest themselves to any student of folk-lore, or even to the child who has loved and studied the well-known fairy tales collected by the brothers Grimm.

I had not the same opportunities as Mrs. Murray enjoyed for inviting the confidences of the old inhabitants of cottage and clachan, but I have no doubt that old world beliefs are still prevalent in Colonsay, although it would require tact and sympathy to prevail upon the shy witnesses to impart their experiences of ghost and fairy. One curious instance occurs to me as a proof that superstition still had a strong grip upon my boatmen and their neighbours. I was very fond of occasionally spending an hour or two at low water catching prawns in the rock pools with a long-handled spoon-shaped net. My *modus operandi* was to dig the end of the iron rim into the sand at the near side of the pool, and push it along the bottom, stirring up the sand and searching the seaweed. I had many pleasant days at Port Ornsa, on the Strand opposite Garvard, and in many other bays; and there was no one to say me nay, until one day I announced my intention of trying a very likely-looking spot near the golf links at Machrins, which takes its name, "Traigh na Tobar Fuar," from the beautiful spring of crystal water which bubbles

THE ISLAND OF COLONSAY 41

out of a deep pool in the grass at the edge of the bay, and discharges a strong stream across the sand into the Atlantic. I detected hesitation and disapproval on the part of the keeper who accompanied me with my nets and gun, but could not get to the bottom of his objection, which accordingly I disregarded. I had a most successful morning, filling two or three pickle bottles with large prawns, mostly of the Æsop variety, which next day made a satisfactory appearance on the breakfast table. There is a great charm about the rock pools; in addition to the prawn the net brings to bag many strange fishes and crabs; and bright-coloured anemones, corallines, and algae present a feast to the eye in the natural aquaria and water gardens. But never again did I go prawning there. Next day,

"Or ever the evening ended a great gale blew."

The Atlantic billows rolled in from the west, the white horses dashed over the rocks scattering the spindrift far and wide, the lobster fisher's heavily-weighted pots were washed ashore in all directions, the borders of the links were covered thick with slimy jellyfish, and I, as I found out, was responsible! "There will be no good weather again as long as Mr. Hardy goes on digging up Traigh na Tobar Fuar," said my scowling boatman. There was no more apparent connection of cause and effect than between Tenterden Steeple and the Goodwin Sands, but the storm, one of exceptional violence, had certainly come opportunely to confirm the prejudices of the natives. I never quite got to the bottom of the nature or origin of the "taboo," but it was certainly strong and widely prevalent. I believe there was some legend of a battle on or near the spot—perhaps a Viking raid—and there was a risk of violating the resting-places of the dead if the sand was turned over or disturbed. I acknowledged my error, and never offended in like manner again, and in due time once more

> "The sun smiled out far over the summer sea,"

and when the next tempest raged some other reason had to be found for the misfortune. Superstitions may be foolish and irrational, but it seemed to me to be an act of ill-natured and needless pedantry to run counter to them unnecessarily.

CHAPTER III

BIRD LIFE IN COLONSAY

THE whole coast of Colonsay is indented with little bays; and all along the west and south are miles of reefs and wicked-looking rocks of all shapes and sizes, many of them large enough to be dignified with the name of islands. Eider-ducks swarm there at all times of the year; they are indeed so much a characteristic feature of the bird life of the island, that they are locally known as "Colonsay ducks." They are far more numerous than all the other species of duck put together, and it was hardly possible to turn the glass upon any bay or inlet without seeing specimens of three kinds—the drake, with his handsome plumage of white shading into a delicate pink; the immature males, less handsome and attractive, presenting a general effect of black and white; and the sober-plumaged ducks, resembling in colour but not in shape the ordinary mate of the mallard. They seek their food in the surf, and seem to love to battle with foam-capped breakers and rushing tideways. Other diving-ducks prefer comparatively calm and sheltered nooks, but no wave, back-wash, or eddy seems too strong for these powerful swimmers. They breed in large numbers in the heather, but I was generally either too early or too late for the nesting season, which comes in May. Once only was I privileged to find a nest with the duck already sitting upon it, and as yet it contained only one egg instead of the usual number of from five to eight. The bird was already there upon the soft heap of down, and allowed us to approach quite close to her. When the tale of eggs is complete, and the process of incubation has begun, you may touch and even stroke the attentive mother without causing her to leave her nest.

The young birds usually do not take to the water until nearly half-grown. It was no uncommon thing to come upon nearly full-grown birds left on shore at high spring tides, which waddled away in front of us and made no effort to fly. They seemed quite helpless out of the water; and in early days we knocked one on the head from quite benevolent motives, under the supposition that it was a wounded bird. The post-mortem failed to reveal any traces of injury, and I am happy to say that it was the only member of its tribe killed by us during our many visits. During the nesting season the drakes have a queer note, which my son describes in his note-book as "a kind of ōōōh, with a shocked intonation." He adds that "the drake throws his head up and down, and then puts it back, resting on the body with the bill pointed upwards. The ducks when put off their nests quack like an ordinary duck when alarmed."

I believe the eider-down industry, so common and lucrative in Norway, might easily be introduced into Colonsay; and I have no hesitation in suggesting it, as it involves no cruelty to the birds, and indeed makes for their protection. In Norway the only bird which it is absolutely illegal to kill is the eider, and I doubt whether much of the sentiment expressed by early Victorian poets and moralists on the cruelty of robbing birds' nests is not thrown away. Courthope, in his *Paradise of Birds*, gives in his charming verse a description of the manner of taking eider-down, derived from Hartwig's *Polar World:*

> " For where the brown duck stripped her breast
> For her dear eggs and windy nest,
> Three times her bitter spoil was won
> For woman ; and when all was done,
> She called her snow-white piteous drake,
> Who plucked his bosom for our sake."

But I have my doubts whether birds whose nests have been robbed, for down or eggs, think any more of it in half an hour's time than the domestic hen does of the new-laid egg which steams upon the breakfast-table. Bird memories are short, and the bereaved matron whose nest has been taken soon sets calmly to work to make another, happily oblivious of her wasted labours. Gallantly as bird and beast defend their young by force and stratagem as long as protection is needed, family affection does not survive the passing of the period of immaturity, or interfere with the struggle for life or the survival of the fittest. As the Communists would have it here, the State soon claims and adopts all children alike, and no gratitude for the toils of incubation prevents the young drake from fighting his father when he thinks he is strong enough to supplant him. Where man pays for the tribute he exacts by protection and encouragement, I think the bird or beast, if it appreciated and was able to weigh the circumstances, would not grudge the price.

The ordinary duck, teal, widgeon, pochard, golden-eye, and so forth, are too familiar to need much notice. They all, however, afforded abundance of sport, and we had many delightful evenings flighting by the corn and potatoes at Killoran and Machrins. How well I remember one beautiful autumn evening at the latter place, when we went a party of four and made a very good bag. I can still remember the sunset over the Atlantic, and seem to hear the weird sounds and sights as the light gradually faded into dusk, and dusk deepened into darkness so impenetrable that the whistle of wings overhead told in vain of invisible flocks. There is always some enthusiast among a flight-shooting party, who insists upon staying long after accurate aim has become an impossibility; and it is not to be wondered at, for just as one is deciding to make tracks, one hears another shot to the right or left, or sees a distant wedge clear against the horizon where a faint light still lingers.

That September night ended in an adventure, for the united weights of our party of four, and their impedimenta, proved too much for the long-suffering old buckboard, which split asunder with an unearthly groan, scattering ducks, guns, and cartridge bags over the road, and pinning my nephew Dougal between the two seats as they collapsed together. How we laughed at his unhappy plight; and yet he might have been hurt had the old pony thought proper to take fright and start, struggle, or run away. Happily the beast was of a philosophical disposition, and only too glad to be relieved of his heavy load, and free to crop the rank grass under the dyke. We had a long tramp before us, and it

BIRD LIFE IN COLONSAY

was late before we sat down to our dinner, but we enjoyed it with appetites sharpened by our sport and adventure.

As to teal, I think that I established a record by killing three with a throw of a walking-stick on the rocks at the end of Oronsay. Truth compels me to confess that the little family of nine, three parts grown, scrambled across in front of me within a few yards, and that it was hardly possible to miss the lot. It is the first and only time that I have ever partaken of the "petit poussins" of teal, but they were very good, although there was extremely little on them. I do not profess to make an exhaustive catalogue, but in addition to the ducks already mentioned I noted pintail, sheldrakes, and of course mergansers in abundance.

I pass on from the ducks to their nearest relatives, the beautiful little red-breasted phalarope, whose small feet with web-like membrane attached to each toe indicate a sort of link between the duck tribe and the waders. One remarkable characteristic of these beautiful little creatures is their extraordinary tameness. Those I have watched seemed to have lost all dread of human creatures, and my first interview with a member of the family, which took place in another part of Scotland at an earlier date, afforded an example of this tameness. I was fishing my favourite stream, the Add, near Dunadd Bridge, one day in late August, when I espied a small grey-backed bird swimming about close to me in a large shallow pool which the heavy rain of the night before had formed in the ill-drained rushy field on my right. His appearance seemed unfamiliar to me, and he was so close that I could almost reach him with my landing-net. I stretched it out toward him and almost touched his tail, but he just managed to evade capture. I had on long waders, so I splashed after him in the water, and he half swam, half fluttered on in front of me, always managing to keep just, but only just, out of reach. Of course I had made up my mind that he was wounded or injured in some way, and that his capture was in the interest of true humanity, and could only be a matter of time. My surprise may be imagined when, after a chase which had lasted at least a quarter of an hour, the supposed cripple suddenly developed renewed energy, spread his wings, and flying high over the top of Dun Add in the direction of Crinan Bay, was soon lost to sight. At Colonsay I saw specimens pretty often, but having realised that the reason they kept so close was that they had no fear, or desire to avoid mankind, I contented myself with watching them with ever fresh delight. It is not only in their semi-webbed feet that they form a link with the duck tribe. Their manner of swimming about in the tidal pools closely resembles that of a miniature duck. Their position in the water is exactly like that of a mallard, with head, neck, back, and half the breast out of water.

The sands at low tide were covered with vast quantities of wading-birds of every description, varying in size from the heron to the tiny ringed plover. I do not profess to give the names of all the smaller varieties. I found it impossible, even with a powerful glass, to identify their species with accuracy; and I did not feel the collector's instinct sufficiently strongly to induce me to destroy the harmless little lives on

BIRD LIFE IN COLONSAY

the mere chance of adding to the list of "Birds of the Hebrides." I could see enough to determine that there were many varieties, including all the smaller species of sandpiper, dotterel, and ringed plover. Curlew and whimbrel dug their long curved beaks into the soft sand for worms and molluscs, or flitted overhead repeating their weird musical cry; black and bar-tailed godwit found their way into the bag, and justified the testimony of our ancestors to their excellent flavour at table. Redshanks and greenshanks, golden plover and lapwing were ubiquitous; but the wader which was on the whole the most in evidence at all times and in all places, was the oystercatcher, locally known as the sea-pie. They were to be found everywhere—on the rocks and on the links, as well as feeding on the shore—and their scarlet beaks and legs, and neat black and white marking, would have rendered them always conspicuous even had they been less tame and confiding, but they hardly took the trouble to get out of the way.

One curious thing which I noticed about these birds was that very often one or more in a flock was lame, and sometimes had one leg completely gone. I asked the keeper, who was a fairly accurate observer, whether he could account for this mutilation, and his suggestion was that it was done by the dog-fish. This puzzled me, for although these predatory and rapacious miniature sharks are quite capable of attacking waterfowl as well as fish, and sometimes follow the shoals of saithe, lythe, or herring in incredible numbers, I could hardly credit their coming so near inshore as to attack and mutilate a wading-bird which confines itself entirely to shallow water not exceeding an inch or two in depth. Further cross-examination proved that my informant had misunderstood me. Gaelic was his native language, although like most West Highlanders the English which he spoke was remarkably pure and accurately pronounced. When I made it clear to him that the object of my inquiries was the sea-pie, he at once agreed that their mutilation could not be laid to the account of the dog-fish, but he stuck to his guns about these latter being often known to attack waterfowl. The whole episode taught me a lesson as to the necessity of carefully sifting second-hand information, even when it comes from trustworthy sources. I was certainly in this instance within an ace of believing and recording a misleading and inaccurate anecdote.

I heard a curious instance of a fish attacking a bird from my old boatman and companion on many a dredging expedition on Loch Craignish, Duncan Macallum. He told me that he had found a full-grown teal in the stomach of a dead angler fish, and I never knew him to exaggerate or invent. Many a strange object, from the sea-pen (*Pennatula phosphorea*) to the rare and curious-looking angular crab (*Gonoplax angulata*), which Bell in his *British Stalk-eyed Crustacea* had not heard of having been taken in Scotland, was brought by him for my inspection. This latter is a strange-looking creature, with its unrounded carapace, its long claws, and eyes mounted on long movable peduncles, shifting back when not in use into a sort of groove at the side of the carapace. If trawlers and lobster fishers were in closer touch with the naturalist, and could be prevailed upon to bring them back the "rubbish" they daily throw away as

BIRD LIFE IN COLONSAY

useless, I suspect that many crustacea and molluscs now considered rare would turn out to be fairly common, and new species and varieties would be added to the list of British fauna.

Gulls and terns abounded, but I was not able to identify any but the usual varieties—herring gull, greater and lesser black-back, kittiwake, and laughing gull. Richardson's skua was common enough, and could be often seen harassing its unfortunate cousins and robbing them of the fruits of their labours. Its dark feathers and hawk-like flight appropriately designate the corsair of the air. It is a pretty, if not an edifying sight to watch this bird pursuing some unfortunate kittiwake or tern, and compelling it to drop the glittering prey which it is bearing away in its beak. The larger gulls are terrible poachers and egg stealers, and attack young lambs and even sickly sheep. They are as true carrion-feeders as the raven or crow, and a flock of them on the hillside, rising and settling again in the same place after a short flight, is a sure indication of the presence of some carcase, usually that of a sheep. They are formidable customers with their sharp, powerful beaks. I have always been thankful that my dear old spaniel Ben did not lose his eye when I incautiously sent him for a black-backed gull which I brought down with a pea-rifle bullet as I was sitting eating my sandwich on the brae overlooking the Strand.

It was no great feat of marksmanship, as the big bird close overhead, and almost poised in the wind, presented something very like a sitting shot. Both master and servant were, however, rather surprised and pleased to see him come down, and the latter rushed off to retrieve him as fast as his four legs could carry him, but was rewarded for his impatience and excess of zeal by a vicious dig which made him speedily drop the flapping quarry. The bullet could not have penetrated any vital part, for before I could come to the rescue the bird had recovered sufficiently to fly away, and I never saw it again. I cannot myself from my own personal observation convict the smaller gulls of poaching, but I have heard keepers lately give them a bad character as egg robbers; and even after giving them all credit for the undoubted good which they do in the destruction of wireworms and grubs, I question whether their protection and preservation is not now a trifle overdone.

They destroy fish and fry in enormous quantities, and the angler owes them another grudge for the persistent way in which they hawk and kill May flies, March browns, and other ephemera as they emerge from the water before they have had time to deposit their ova. It is quite a sight to see gulls hovering in flocks over the Tweed at Coldstream when there is a strong rise of fly, and taking the nymphs as fast as they come to the surface. No wonder that these persecuted insects are becoming less common than of yore, preyed upon as they are in all stages of their career; first in their embryo state by the larvæ of the dragon-fly and water-beetle, next by the fish both before and after their first flight, and lastly during their brief sojourn in the upper element, by innumerable feathered enemies, among which the gull and the chaffinch are not the least persistent and destructive. Beautiful and graceful as are the plumage and flight of these engaging birds, now so familiar a spectacle to Londoners, I am afraid that their numbers have increased unduly. But I could not persuade myself to lend a hand in their destruction; I love too well to watch them under all conditions, whether following the plough and swooping down upon the prey disclosed in the upturned furrow, or accompanying the *Columba* in its swift voyage from Gourock to Ardrishaig, poised in the air above the tiller, and keeping up with the vessel with just an occasional turn of their strong pinions. I love also to throw them crumbs, as they circle round the children and nursemaids feeding the waterfowl by the Serpentine and the ornamental water in St. James' Park, but I cannot agree with those who think that these pauperised pensioners are in any danger of starvation. To my eyes they seem plump and well-fed enough, and it is only occasionally that they will take the trouble to pay for their entertainment by displaying their marvellous feats of catching. The experience of the hard winter which first brought them to town has taught them that in addition to the voluntary benevolence upon which they can confidently rely, abundance of waste and refuse food floats down the Thames; and it is not for nothing that they return again and again to the discovered treasure-house, bringing in their train "their sisters, their cousins, and their aunts."

Black-headed laughing gulls do not breed in Colonsay, but depart for that purpose to one of the large inland lakes on the mainland, where they congregate in great gulleries during the nesting season. Numbers of their eggs are sent to London and elsewhere for food, although I have not often seen them exposed for sale under their own name in the poulterers' shops.

Their egg is more oval and less pointed than that of the green plover; the yoke is redder and the white less transparent and the flavour somewhat stronger, but they are excellent food, as I can testify from experience. Other rock-building gulls whiten the cliffs with their numbers, building there with cormorants, guillemots, razor-bills, and land birds; but the society is not mixed, each species keeps to its own ledge, and forms a separate community. The solan geese nest elsewhere, perhaps on the Bass Rock or Ailsa Craig. A journey of a hundred miles or so after the herring-shoals is a mere nothing for these strong-winged birds, and they can often be seen fishing off the shore, dropping like plummets with unerring aim upon their prey; not pursuing the fish under water as do the divers and cormorants, but spying them from on high, and only going so far below the surface as the impetus of their flight carries them.

Puffins were not common, but an occasional one could be seen among the guillemots, conspicuous for its brilliant parrot-shaped beak. Guillemots, both of the common and black varieties, abounded; razor-bills were also to be found, and great numbers of the two common sorts of cormorants. The water-hen, dabchick and coot, as well as the common merganser, were to be found on the burns and inland lakes; and the retiring water-rail was occasionally flushed from the reed beds. The Arctic and common tern pursued the fry in myriads, and nested on the low rocks and the shingle. I have no doubt that other varieties of terns might also have been identified, but as in the case of the small waders my eyes are no longer good enough to distinguish minor differences with

PEREGRINE FALCON AND RAVEN
(From a Drawing by G. E. Lodge.)

certainty. I often saw the Great Northern diver, which is pretty common everywhere on the west coast of Scotland.

The crow tribe were well represented, ravens were numerous, and there were nearly always a pair of these birds on the shore of one or other of the bays by the golf links at Machrins, feeding on some of the refuse washed up by the tide. I do not know whether they care for jelly-fish, but there were occasions when these were washed up in such abundance as to create a nuisance. In a strong westerly gale I have seen the shore covered with them to the depth of some inches, and decomposing into a slippery and evil-smelling slime. I confess to an affection for the bird of ill omen, and if ravens had brought me ill-luck every time I have seen them or heard their unmistakable bark, I hardly think that I should be alive now to tell the tale. I would far rather wage war with the ubiquitous and mischievous jackdaws than with these grand and picturesque birds. Often I came quite close upon them as I rounded some knoll or rock, and could distinguish their broad wings and strong spadelike beak as they flapped lazily away. They seemed to be particularly obnoxious to the pair of peregrine falcons which haunted the cairn on the summit of the hill at the back. I have frequently seen the falcon pursuing one or other of the ravens for quite a long distance, not swooping down upon him from on high with deadly intentions, but flying behind or beside him at a distance of some ten yards, and from time to time making short and ineffectual "dabs" towards him. Each time the raven would turn his beak towards him like the bayonet of a foot soldier prepared to receive cavalry, and the pursuer apparently considered discretion was the better part of valour, for I never saw him actually strike his quarry. I should imagine that food could be easily obtained on easier terms than by an encounter with so powerful and awkward a customer, and the whole proceeding looked more like some sort of game than the thrilling and exciting chase after duck, curlew, and grouse which it has more than once been my privilege to witness.

One bird of the crow tribe, once common enough, but now nearly extinct in England, was an everyday sight in all the northern part of the island. I allude to the chough, whose shrill metallic cry, glossy plumage, and dark orange beak and legs, made it easy to distinguish from the jackdaw. Why have these birds become so uncommon in all their old haunts? I have seen a few on Jura, and on portions of the mainland of Argyllshire, but never come across one during my occasional visits to Devonshire and their native Cornwall, although I have heard that they have not altogether disappeared from those coasts. Not only song and ballad, but Statute and picture, testify to their former abundance. A Statute of Henry the Eighth, passed in 1532, proves that even the attractions of Anne Boleyn, whom he married that year, could not divert his attention from "the innumerable number of Rooks, Crows, and Choughs which do daily breed and increase throughout the realm, which Rooks, Crows, and Choughs do yearly destroy, devour and consume a wonderful and marvellous quantity of Corn and Grain of all kinds; that is to wit as well in the sowing of the said Corn and Grain, as also at the ripening and kernelling of the same, and over that a marvellous Destruction and Decay of the Covertures of Thatched Houses, Barns, Reeks, and Stacks, and other such like." The Act (24 Henry VIII, c. 10), of the preamble of which the above quotation forms a part, goes on to enact that "everyone shall do his best to kill and utterly destroy all Rooks, Crows, and Choughs on Pain of a grievous Amerciament, and that every Town and Hamlet shall provide and maintain Crow Nets during ten years. The Taker of Crows, Rooks and Choughs shall have after the Rate of Two Pence the Dozen." His "manminded offspring" revived the Statute (8 Eliz. c. 15) and provided that "in every Parish Sums should be raised for the destruction of noyful fowl or vermin; and for the heads of three old Crows, Choughs, Pies or Rooks, or of six young ones, or for six eggs, was to be given a penny."[1]

Two choughs, apparently pets, are prominent objects in the beautiful portrait of three children by Van Dyck, which by the kindness of Lord Lucas adorned for some time the south wall of the right-hand vestibule of the National Gallery. I can hardly attribute the scarcity of these birds in our day to the success of the efforts of our ancestors, spurred on by the Statutes I have quoted. Certainly the rooks are still with us in more than sufficient abundance in spite of their proscription.

I was able in Colonsay to trace another reason for a diminution in their numbers there. One of the farmers told me that when he was a boy they were so numerous that they were commonly eaten

[1] My attention was called to this Statute by a correspondent of the *Spectator*, but I rather fancy the choughs alluded to were really jackdaws.

for food, being, as he assured me, very palatable. At that time there were no jackdaws on the island, and he could remember when the first pair of these "grey-headed crows" found their way over from Iona. Jackdaws now swarm all over the island, and have usurped in many cliffs and cairns the nesting-places of their comparatively harmless cousins. In spite of the Tudor sovereigns, I do not believe that choughs do much damage to corn and grain. I often saw them feeding on rushy pastures, seldom if ever upon the arable land. I should think that about a hundred couple breed upon the cliffs, but I was assured that their numbers have neither increased or diminished to any perceptible extent in recent years. The note somewhat resembles that of the jackdaw, but is more shrill and metallic. They are seldom seen alone, usually in small flocks of three or four. They fly about a good deal with no apparent object, and in strong winds often rise and drop about ten feet. I quote again from Alfred's note-book:

"On 22nd August 1899, I saw some choughs quite close on the ground, and was much amused at their actions. They were not actually playing together, but all their movements reminded me of a clown in a circus company out for a holiday. They were busily engaged in feeding—picking the beetles and insects out of some dry cow-dung, and using their curved beaks in the most scientific way, nearly always putting them under the far side of the object which they wanted to turn over and 'howking' towards themselves. They appeared to be in a hurry, running at a great pace from spot to spot, although they evidently felt the heat very much and seemed to be panting through their open beaks. One of them appeared to have a game leg, as he kept hopping instead of running, and was very top-heavy in consequence. However, I saw one or two of his companions hop once or twice heavily, as if they wanted to frighten the worms, beetles, &c. on which they were feeding to the surface. I noticed that they were very fond of stretching out their wings at right angles to their bodies. As a rule they are quite as hard to stalk as jackdaws, although they often fly quite close past one's head. One day, however, as Geoffrey was out with his rifle, a party of four or five choughs came so close over him that he could have touched them with the barrel. He was crawling at the time, and the birds evidently did not like his appearance, for they settled about three yards off, craned their necks and simply cursed, even following him as he crawled."

I did not often see carrion crows, but hoodies were very common. I never saw an eagle or osprey, although the golden eagle was fairly common in Jura, protected by that keen naturalist and sportsman, Henry Evans, at that time the tenant of the forest at the south end, and resident at his fine house just above the "Small Isles," the harbour where his yacht lay at anchor. Kindred tastes attached him to Sir John M'Neill, and he used often to visit Colonsay to study, but not to molest the seals, and take the Chief back with him to enjoy a day with his red deer round the Paps. Besides the peregrine falcon already alluded to, the falcon tribe were represented by large numbers of kestrels, and a good many merlins. The common buzzard and the hen harrier were also to be found, the former a regular, the latter an occasional, visitor, and the weird banshee note of the wood owl was audible every night. The pigeon tribe were represented by the wood-pigeon, the stock-dove and the blue rock, the latter of which abounded in the numerous caves to which they resorted to roost and nest. More fell to the gun and rifle when on or upon their way to the fields to feed, than darting out of the caves. The north-west coast was so unsheltered, and possible landing-places below the beetling cliffs were so few in number, that the usual and most sporting method of getting these birds was seldom practicable, much to our regret, as there is certainly no more difficult or attractive mark than a wild rock-pigeon startled out of a cliff cave. The flight of the bird is so swift, and the angle he takes so uncertain, that even if the sportsman is on terra firma his skill is tested in a high degree, and the difficulty is doubled when he is tossing in a little boat on the rollers of the Atlantic. Such difficulties are the salt of sport, and make the swift-flying little bird a prize coveted out of all proportion to his merits as an addition to the pot.

In May the note of the cuckoo mixes everywhere with the shrill cry of the wildfowl, and their hawk-like flight is a familiar object. A cuckoo of the American yellow-billed species was picked up in 1904, freshly dead from exhaustion, by Captain Adeane, and its skin is now in the Natural History Museum at South Kensington. It seems hard that, driven before the westerly gales right across the broad Atlantic, it should have made the shore alive only to perish after its record voyage. Its fate recalls that of the two human aeronauts, pioneers of their craft, who perished just

BIRD LIFE IN COLONSAY

after accomplishing the transit of the Channel and the Alps. After a heavy gale I often picked up birds of more familiar species dead, and have wondered what mischance proved fatal to such strong-winged birds as the solan goose, and the black-backed and herring gull. I have also picked up the body of a rarer visitor, the fork-tailed petrel, both here and on the mainland, a proof that even the bird of storm, most daring of mariners, may tempt the gale too often. Among smaller birds I can recall nothing sufficiently special to demand individual mention except the tree sparrow and the snow-bunting. I often put up this latter beautiful little bird in its bright summer plumage out of the bent grass on the sandhills that fringed the links and bays. The indigenous game birds were black game, partridge, woodcock, full and jack, snipe; there were also plenty of pheasants and grouse, but these latter had been brought over from the mainland, although I see no reason to doubt that the red grouse could easily traverse the narrow straits if they thought fit, and cannot definitely deny its claim to be considered a native. For black game a flight of twenty miles or so is all in the day's work, and flocks can occasionally be seen crossing even wider straits than the Sounds of Jura and Islay, from shore to shore.

A day in September after the stout hill partridges which feed on the stubbles, but take refuge when flushed among the heather, gorse or bracken, is particularly delightful. They run like greyhounds, and test the skill and endurance of men and dogs to the utmost in the broken ground and thick cover. The multitudes of rabbits that abound on the same ground spoil the scent, and add to the difficulties of the pointer or setter. But by September the grouse we flushed were all strong fliers, very different from the young coveys on the 12th of August; and young black game were really worth a shot. The infinite possibilities of variety added to the excitement; one never knew whether duck or teal might not rise from some reedy ditch or sheltered bay; snipe were sure to be found in any soft boggy place, and plovers, rock-pigeons, and even at that early period an occasional woodcock, probably bred in the island, had to be reckoned with as possible items of the day's bag.

CHAPTER IV

SEALS GREAT AND SMALL

I HAVE often thought what an ideal place Colonsay would be for a sanctuary in which to permit all the fauna of the Hebrides to grow up in a state of nature unmolested. The absence of such carnivora as the fox, the marten, the polecat, the stoat, and weasel, make the little island especially suitable for such a purpose. I was told, but had no opportunity of verifying the statement, that in consequence of this absence of stoats and weasels, all attempts at ferreting had proved failures, as rabbits declined to bolt at the sight of a ferret, being ignorant of the dangerous character of their strange visitor. No deer of any kind now exist within the boundaries of the island, but the antlers of the red stag are frequently found in the caves and old middens, which looks as if they were at one time indigenous. Both the black and the Norway rat are fairly common, the latter being unpleasantly and mischievously numerous. But the characteristic native mammal is the seal. As I have mentioned in a previous chapter, these amphibians were the special favourites of the Laird. Each of the leases under which I rented the privilege of shooting over the island, contained an express stipulation that not more than six of the common seal (*Phoca vitulina*) were to be shot, and any interference with the rarer grey seal (*Gryphus*) was rigorously prohibited. I myself never fired a shot at either species during the whole time I was there, and it was only very rarely and for special reasons that any member of my family or guest availed himself of the opportunity of stalking seals. We never came up to our limit or even approached it, and the few specimens that were sacrificed in the interests of science or sport were fairly stalked on the rocks, and seldom heard the shot that killed them. In the water, owing to the immunity they enjoyed, they were extraordinarily tame, and would approach a boat with a curiosity and fearlessness which contrasted forcibly with the behaviour of the more persecuted denizens of the lochs which intersect the mainland in the neighbourhood of Crinan. Where every boat may have a rifle on board in the hands of some enthusiastic tripper to whom a seal in the water is an irresistible temptation, the dog-like head that disappears as you round a corner reappears at such a distance as to be only visible when the waves are still and unruffled. Off Colonsay curiosity kept them close, any unaccustomed sight seeming to attract them when in the water. Old Pennant relates in his Arctic Zoology that "if a Greenlander sees a seal lying near its hole upon the ice, he slides along upon his belly towards it, wags his head, and grunts like a seal; and the poor seal thinking 'tis one of its innocent companions, lets him come near enough to pierce it with his long dart." I do not think this primitive method of seal-hunting would be much good in Colonsay. There I always found that seals when out of the water were suspicious and vigilant, mounted their sentinels, and made off at once on the approach of any strange object.

The discovery of cheap and plentiful mineral oil has, no doubt, been the principal cause of their present immunity from molestation. In the old days when their oil was the only illuminant easily procurable, the natives of the island used to net them in large numbers in the "rivers" formed among the reefs by the outgoing tide. Now there is no great inducement to molest them. Colonsay contains no fresh-water streams up which salmon and sea-trout can run from the sea, and therefore there is no necessity to protect those valuable fish from their natural enemies. Permitted to multiply unchecked, the interesting mammals abound, and afford abundant opportunities for the study and observation of their uncouth gambols on land, and their graceful and ever-varying manœuvres in the clear water.

I had heard of the abundance of seals in Colonsay, and on my first visit of inspection I told Malcolm M'Neill, the "manager," that I should like to see some. We drove together in the old buckboard across the links at Machrins to the point of Ardskenish where it overlooks the Western mouth of the Strand. The sea was calm, and the sun bright, and in the middle distance a whole archipelago of long and apparently flat rocks just showed above the tide. Without a glass I could detect no seals, although I am pretty sharp-sighted, but Malcolm knew well enough the nature of the tiny specks that gave a serrated appearance to the broken lines of the islets. "Just turn your glass there, and I am thinking you will see some." I obeyed his injunctions, and the low rock upon which I focussed the lens resolved itself into a wriggling mass of slug-like amphibians, those nearest to the water curved into a semicircle like the lower half of a broken hoop; some scratching themselves with their strong fore flippers, others shifting uneasily from side to side, and one big fellow apparently doing sentry upon the highest point. They were of different sizes and colours, some only half grown, some patriarchs nearly six feet long, and their skin showed at that distance every variety of shade from nearly black to an almost wool-like whiteness; but this latter appearance, I fancy, characterised those among them that had been basking longest and whose fur was driest. Later on, when I frequently saw large flocks quite close, I did not note any very great variety of colour. The typical Colonsay seal was profusely covered with round or oval spots on a lightish ground. There were about fourteen on the first rock that came into focus, and as I swept the glass round I found that hardly one of the many reefs was untenanted, and that they afforded resting-places for great numbers. Altogether there must have been many hundreds taking their siesta, and I returned home satisfied that there would be no lack of opportunity of studying their habits. As we jolted back over the short green turf of the links the air was musical with the cry of sea-birds, from the liquid rippling note of the redshank to the familiar "peewit" of the nesting plovers that tumbled awkwardly above our heads in their time-hallowed endeavour to distract attention from their nests.

Come with me on a bright August afternoon to Traigh na Tobar Fuar when the high tide covers the whole of the sandy bay. I have had a round of golf, I have eaten my sandwich, and I may as well have a look at the seals as I smoke my midday pipe. As I raise my head cautiously above the rocky boundary which separates the smooth close turf of the links from the water, I can see more than twenty coasting about within a range of a hundred yards; the nearest, a big grey fellow, has just risen after a dive and is standing head and shoulders out of the water, his head thrown aback and his mouth wide open as if he was submitting his glistening fangs to a dentist's inspection. I suspect that he has been after the prawns and shrimps which abound here, the former in the rock pools at low water, the latter all over the smooth shell sand. Others swim quietly round, turning their bright intelligent dog's eyes to right and left, sometimes plunging forward, raising the body out of the water above the head as they turn their somersault, sometimes gradually sinking backwards with a slow almost imperceptible motion till the extreme tip of the muzzle at last disappears below the surface. Sometimes they pass within ten yards of the place where I am sitting, but take no notice of my presence. I can even see them when swimming under water, grey ghostlike forms shooting along, followed by their shadows on the sand; sometimes they swim on their backs, sometimes with a breast-stroke, for it is all one to them which way they move, as they twist and turn hither and thither with a scarcely perceptible motion of the flippers. But all their movements are leisurely, very different from the mad exulting gambols with which they pass through the narrows when the flood tide is making strongly in the Strand. Then they shoot along like arrows, or leap like salmon out of the rushing stream, darting along in a succession of bounds and splashes like a shoal of travelling porpoises or dolphins.

I also found opportunity of observing the great grey seal (*Halechoerus gryphus*). His long pointer-like face, and short fleshy lips contrast forcibly with the round bullet-head of the common seal; he makes his haunts on the most distant and inaccessible reefs, and the female is more cunning in concealing its young at the time of birth than other seals. The babies are born about the last week in September, and are pure white, with very fine and silky fur. I heard from my boatmen that on one occasion they found a young gryphus jet black, but all the specimens I have ever seen were white; such instances of melanism must be very uncommon. I believe the parents to be monogamous: father and mother certainly share the care of their offspring, and, conquering their natural fear of man, cruise round almost within an oar's length of intruders who approach their breeding-places.

My second son, Alfred, has made a special study of the habits of both species of these interesting mammals, and I insert his notes as they stand. They are so clearly expressed and suggestive that I prefer to let them speak for themselves; my own observations confirm them in every particular. With regard to the incident which he reports on the authority of a West Highland gamekeeper, of a seal taking a wounded teal, I believe that the fact that the common seal occasionally varies its fish diet by making a meal of ducks is clearly established. Their fresh-water cousin, the otter, often feeds on birds and rabbits as a change from its usual Lenten fare, and I see no reason why a seal should not when hungry take anything he can get, although he would generally find fish and crustaceans not only more palatable, but more easy to obtain than any other kind of food.

NOTES ON SEALS

BY ALFRED CECIL GATHORNE-HARDY

Away on the outskirts of the Hebrides there lies a certain island. On one side it raises a frontage of black irregular cliff to meet the full power of the Atlantic; southward it reaches long fingers of rock, reef beyond reef, into the water, the furthest showing in mere points of surf away to sea. Throughout the whole of its length and breadth the island is a paradise of rare and curious birds and beasts and plants, but to my mind perhaps its chief attraction lies in the innumerable seals that find their home along its coasts. There, on the remoter rocks, the great square-snouted grey seal is still to be found. There any day you care to look, if you know where to go, and the tide is not too high, you may see the common seal in hundreds. For among these reefs, whatever the conditions of wind or water, there must always be found low-lying sheltered places where nothing but the sound of the breaking seas can penetrate. In such places do our western seals love to lie, not basking on the sand, as I am told their east coast relatives generally do, but low down on a reef where two kicks and a wriggle will send them into the water should danger arise.

No beast that I know is better worth watching, and perhaps no British beast, before the publication of Mr. J. G. Millais's monumental work on *British Mammals*, had been so inadequately described. Even to-day few people image a seal as anything else than either a round black head in the water, or at most as lying head up, tail down, in the attitude depicted on the old-fashioned Newfoundland postage stamps.

Watch them on Ardskenish reefs, lying like great grey slugs, fifty together on a rock: the first thing that strikes you is the number of different attitudes they take up. Low down by the water two or three big black fellows have cocked up both ends high in the air, till they are bent stiff, with a curve like the rockers of a chair. Above them the rock is literally yellow with seals, some lying prone, some on their backs, others on their sides. Most of the yellow-looking seals, the dry ones, are more than half asleep, and lie very stiff, but now and again one or other of them, with a grunt of disgust, will hitch round his rudimentary-looking fore-flipper, and start scratching himself where the salt drying into his skin has made it irritable. I believe it is this, and not, as some people say, the attacks of amphibious parasites, that makes these proceedings necessary, inasmuch as I cannot ever remember to have seen a wet seal so engaged.

And it is perhaps worth while to turn your attention for a moment to that same fore-flipper. Short and rudimentary as it looks, it will reach to almost any place on a seal's body, and it is so double jointed that its owner can scratch the tip of his nose and the small of his back with almost equal ease. It is said that seals use the sharp cutting edge when fighting, which would account for the number of short straight scars with which some skins are literally seamed.

But far more interesting to unaccustomed eyes are three or four black-looking seals that are lying head and tail in air balanced upon the very smallest available part of their diaphragms. One wonders why a seal should delight to lie in this apparently unrestful attitude. The question is rather a puzzling one, but a little observation will make one thing at least clear. The seals in this position are as a rule those freshest out of the water. You will see a seal cruise with head held low two or three times past a suitable rock, and then select the easiest landing-place and gallop awkwardly up. After that he will rest for a while and meditate. Then suddenly up go his hind flippers, and he begins washing them against one another with "invisible soap," spreading out first one and then the other to its full extent, clenching the remaining flipper like a fist, and rubbing them both quickly together. Probably he does this to dry them. His flippers, especially the great expansive hind ones, are at once the most important and the least protected parts of his body. They are not covered like the rest of him with a thick coating of blubber, and here if anywhere the cold of the water evaporating from him might do him harm. Therefore he begins by wringing them out. This done he lies head and tail up with as little of him as possible against the rock. In this position he has three advantages, the water drains freely off him, the air reaches him as much as possible, and he avoids lying in a pool of his own making. It is the waving of these hind-flippers that as often as not betrays the presence of a wet seal. A dry one is at all times a showy object and, in his yellow summer coat particularly, is as easy for the eye to pick up as a sheep in a field of grass, but the black body of a seal just out of the water is by no means so easy to find.

When once dry he hardly ever resumes this curved position, except for a momentary stretch, until the rising tide once more begins to submerge them. Then, if he be too lazy to move away, you may see his head gradually rising higher and higher, and with it the other end rising by way of balance, till his back is covered and only his head and hind flippers are visible; finally there comes a wavelet which washes in his face. This is too much for him, and with a wriggle of disgust he slips off into deep water.

Once there what a change comes over him! Seals on a rock are but ill-conditioned brutes at the best. They come up to get dry and to bask, and if any other seals threaten a disturbance even by clambering past them, they are not slow to show their resentment, swearing and spitting like angry cats. I have seen a little yearling seal snap repeatedly at the face (always the face) of another old enough to be his grandfather, that happened to roll too near his resting-place. But in the water all that is forgotten. The ungainly surly brutes become all at once the most graceful sportive creatures imaginable, racing, diving, romping; sometimes, especially when they feel the tide, leaping like great salmon out of the water and falling back with a splash and a glitter of spray. With what an air of luxury too will an old bull boom out his call across the water, raise his nose into the air, and slowly, slowly draw himself under!

In the water moreover his attitude towards man changes altogether. No one whose object is anything but mere destruction should ever shoot a seal except on land. There he is a really sporting animal, with finely-developed senses of hearing and smell; and eyesight, according to my experience, far better than is possessed by most of the larger mammalia. In the water his sense of danger (I am speaking of course only of our island seals) is entirely subordinated to his curiosity. If he does see a suspicious object his instinct is to lift himself out breast high to obtain a better look. I have known seals to approach within twenty yards of me when I was within full view of them, and it was only when I began tossing stones at them that they splashed under water and disappeared.

It is difficult to estimate with accuracy the diving power of a seal. One difficulty is that where there is one seal in the water there are often several, and they have a distressing habit of being under water together, which confuses the reckoning. My father once timed a seal to stay under water for four and a half minutes, but this is obviously nothing to what they can do if put to it. A seal, both on land and water, seems only to breathe when he happens to think of it. It is easy to distinguish when he is taking in breath and when he is exhaling. In the former case the nostrils, situated on the exact point of his nose, dilate into two little round o's, each about the size of a sixpenny piece. When he exhales, the strong muscles on the outside of each nostril automatically contract, leaving two tiny crescent-shaped openings for the air to pass out through, an arrangement which must be very convenient for keeping the water out of his nostrils when diving deep. I have often observed the expansion and contraction of these muscles with a strong glass, and have been struck with the strange irregularity of breathing. Generally, as far as I was able to ascertain, a seal took about five times as long to exhale as to draw in breath; but sometimes, especially just before diving, he would draw breath three or four times very slowly, and take practically no time to exhale.

Seals feed of course mostly upon shrimps, prawns, and fish, always bolting the latter head first. A relative of mine who, when a child, kept a tame seal, told me that she used often purposely to give him a fish tail first, and that he invariably turned it round before swallowing it.

Does the common seal ever take birds? I have never seen an instance of this recorded, but incline to believe that he occasionally does. It must be remembered that the harp seal (*Phoca Greenlandica*) undoubtedly does so, and there is therefore nothing inherently improbable in the idea. My evidence, for what it is worth, was given me by a keeper in Argyllshire whom I know well, and know too to be a particularly keen and careful observer. He told me that one day, when he was out with the rabbit-catcher to shoot what he could for the house, he managed to get within range of a flock of widgeon, and disdaining the niceties of sport, fired at them on the water and hit five. Four were dead or disabled, but the fifth had only a wing broken. He ran down to the shore to send his dog to retrieve them, while James the rabbit-catcher sat down upon a high rock to watch. Four were gathered without difficulty, and the dog was swimming out for the fifth, when the keeper, who had turned away for a moment, heard James sing out, " Did you ever see the like of that? The seal has taken the duck!" He turned round, and sure enough the widgeon had disappeared, and although the water was like glass, was never again seen. James from his vantage ground above had seen the seal come up and swallow the bird. This evidence may not be conclusive; but for my own part I am inclined to accept it as accurate. James was positive as to what he had seen, and my informant dwelt strongly upon the absolute calmness of the sea which rendered it almost impossible for even so elusive a bird as a wounded widgeon to escape unseen.

Alfred above describes the gryphus or grey seal as " square snouted." This is an apt enough description of the short fleshy lips, but the head, as contrasted with the bullet-shaped cranium of *Phoca vitulina*, seems to me long and pointer shaped. I have watched them pretty often, but only in one place. I believe that I once saw a specimen near the mouth of Loch Craignish, but I should not like to speak positively to the fact, but it was certainly much larger than any other seal I had ever seen off the mainland. As a rule they frequent only the most remote and inaccessible rocks in the Hebrides.

I well remember one beautiful late autumn day when I visited their haunts with Sir John M'Neill and his friend Colonel Pearson, who was anxious if possible to obtain photographs of them, and had brought his camera for that purpose. After a long progress in the whale-boat we had reached the distant reef which they were known to frequent at that time of year. We landed and scrambled over the sharp and slippery rocks, but for some time saw none of the animals we were looking for, although we disturbed plenty of specimens of the common seal. At last our host pointed to a long low object lying on a rock not more than thirty yards from us, well in view. It was motionless, and its fur looked ruffled and staring; and when Sir John said to his companion, "There is something for you to photograph," Colonel Pearson replied with a laugh, "Yes, I dare say! any one can see that that beast has been dead at least three weeks." Sir John smiled and gave a shrill whistle, and the supposed corpse, galvanised into life at the sound, floundered into the water, leaving behind a little newly-born cub, not too young to show temper by snarling and spitting when approached. The young do not take to the water for about three weeks after birth, and one that either by accident or intentionally slipped in when we came close up to it, did not seem at all comfortable in its movements, so we left it to the care of its parents, the old bull and cow which were swimming close at hand in evident anxiety. The bull is larger than the cow; one very fine specimen, the head and skin of which was preserved at Killoran House, was said to have weighed forty-four stone. It is difficult to judge the exact weight of any animal when in the water, but some of those I saw quite close at hand when they were anxious about their babies looked enormous. Ordinary seals, which measure some five feet or more from nose to flipper, and weigh up to fourteen stone, looked mere pigmies when near them.

During my two seasons in Colonsay I never myself drew trigger at a seal, but there was one occasion upon which I must plead guilty to having instigated, aided and abetted, the killing of a specimen. I had noticed that the stuffed examples in the National

Collection at Cromwell Road were but poor specimens, as was only to be expected when allowance is made for the difficulties of the taxidermist who probably had nothing better than a dried skin to relax and stuff long after death. In a good cause I considered it perfectly legitimate to sacrifice a seal, and I made the offer, which was gratefully accepted, that I would send up a first-rate specimen in the best condition, and undertake that it should arrive at Rowland Ward's within forty-eight hours of the time when it had been basking on its native rocks. Had I been bound for any other part of the British Isles it would perhaps have been rash to have made more than a conditional promise, but as I had watched these interesting mammals in their hundreds only a year before, I felt no doubt that I should be able to carry out my undertaking.

I waited for some time before I took steps to carry out my project. I knew that September would be the best month to be sure of securing a mottled skin in the best condition, and I had also to choose a day warm and still, with a favourable tide and a bright sun. Besides all this, it was necessary that the day should immediately precede one upon which the bi-weekly steamer called at the little harbour on its way to Glasgow, railways and civilisation. At last the hour arrived. The man was already chosen in the person of my eldest son Geoffrey, whom I could rely upon as a steady and accurate shot, and a skilled and careful stalker.

The best time for stalking seals on the rocks off shore is at about half tide; at dead low water they no doubt are there, but the reef is such a confused mass of boulders and tangle that it is not easy either to make out or to approach them, while at high water they shift their ground, and are swimming about and fishing in the strong currents. On this occasion first of ebb was due at about ten in the morning, so we arranged to have a round of golf at Machrins before proceeding to Ardskenish, where we made certain of being able to find seals in an accessible position. We drove down to the links in the old buckboard, which was just the thing for the job, as the road to Ardskenish was only a rough farm track over grass, rock and swamp; and the carcase of a seal, if we proved successful, could be stowed in the back of the machine without making any mess which could not be obliterated with a little hot water and a mop.

On we jogged over the road, which runs nearly due west till it bends towards the links, passing through a long narrow strip of arable land bordered by moor, moss, and loch. A large flock of black game, most of them old cocks, were feeding on the stubble on our right, and would have invited a drive or a stalk if we had brought guns with us, and many blue rock pigeons passed over our heads within shot before we descended and outspanned by the first tee. Campbell, our keeper, was commandeered to carry our clubs. He was keen enough at all kinds of sport, and what he did not know about woodcocks and their haunts was not worth knowing, but golf was a game he only tolerated. Once, piqued by his indifference, I asked him whether he thought he could drive a ball, and received the complacent answer that as he was the local champion at shinty he had no doubt he could do so very well. I handed him my driver and invited him to try. He balanced the ball on the summit of a huge molehill of sand, grasped the club with both hands with an air of grim determination, and after flourishing it round his head, made a mighty but ineffectual swipe. The ball still maintained its position on the tee. After one or two more failures he gave in and admitted that he could not drive, but his opinion of the poor merits of golf as a game was only confirmed by the incident.

Our game was as enjoyable as ever; we lost the usual number of balls in rabbit holes, and Ben, my black spaniel, caught three or four of the little pests which honeycomb the sandy turf with their bottomless residences. Without crying "fore," we drove straight into the middle of big flocks of gulls, plovers, and oyster-catchers. We watched a pair of sheldrakes feeding at the mouth of the little burn just below the spring. Eider-duck, teal, and widgeon dotted the clear surface of the two little bays where numerous seals also swam round, unterrified and confiding, turning their big lustrous eyes with a curious stare at their odd-looking visitors. It would have been easy enough to accomplish the object of our expedition without going any further, to select the best out of more than a dozen, and shoot him with the certainty of recovering his body as soon as the tide had ebbed a short distance; but it never even occurred to us thus to betray their confidence. As there would be no difficulty in shooting them, so also there would be no sport. The veriest cockney who had even practised at floating bottles in a pond could not have missed such a mark as the round heads presented, as the poor brutes circled round within twenty yards of the shore; whereas to stalk them when basking on the rocks, their watchful sentinels on the lookout for the slightest indication of danger, with all their advantage of acute vision and power of hearing, and even more useful sense of scent, demands so much skill and care that I rather wonder at my temerity in having already directed the label which a failure will render useless or premature.

At about half-past one, having finished our round and our sandwich, we started on our walk over the narrow neck of ground which divides the links from the long promontory of Ardskenish. We had already spied a number of seals from the hill just above the twelfth green, which is crowned by an ancient Celtic fort, and commands a view of the reefs beyond the peninsula. A survey with the glass had satisfied us that the nearest rocks were not untenanted, but it would require a much closer inspection to enable us to select our specimen and plan the stalk.

At length we three—father, son, and spaniel—emerged upon a sand dune thickly covered with the wiry bent grass so obnoxious to golfers who slice their ball off the line at Westward Ho or Sandwich. Here we all halted, and after I had put a leader on Ben, we began to explore the rocks with our glasses. We had not far to look. Just below us a mass of tangle-covered reef stood out above sand and water, and stretched away towards the south and west, and less than half a mile away sixteen seals, all good specimens, basked upon a flat rock divided from the beach and the mainland by a narrow channel of water. There was very little wind, but what there was fortunately came from a favourable quarter, and a small boulder projecting from the sand about a hundred yards from the herd looked as if it should provide some sort of cover. The stalk seemed practicable but by no means easy, as very flat crawling over wet sand would certainly be necessary. The channel which appeared so narrow from our post of observation was really at least fifty yards wide, and too deep for wading, but we were prepared for this contingency, as Geoffrey had nothing on which would spoil, and would be so wet and dirty by the time his crawl was over that a swim would be rather an advantage than a detriment. He had girded himself with a coil of rope which he could attach to his quarry for the purpose of towing it ashore. Without some such precaution it is no easy task to bring a dead seal to land through a deep strait, as these mammals are both heavy and slippery to handle.

My part of the business was over for the present. I found a comfortable seat, lighted my pipe, adjusted the focus of my glass, and awaited developments. Ben nestled beside me, conscious that sport of some kind was going on, but uncertain what we were after. I know nothing more interesting than to watch a good stalk with a telescope from beginning to end. In some ways it is even more amusing for the spectator than for the actor, as the latter is precluded from having a view of his quarry during a large portion of the stalk, while the former watching from an eminence can keep both hunter and hunted in view, although both objects may not be within the circle of his telescope at one and the same time. There ought to be some prearranged method of signalling by which the watcher can let the stalker know any alteration in the position of the herd. I know nothing more maddening than to watch a friend advancing to certain failure, which might have been avoided had I had the means of conveying my knowledge to him in time to be of use. There is not so much risk of this calamity in the case of seals as in that of deer; the former seldom leave their position on a rock except to take to the water if alarmed, and this must necessarily bring about failure, whereas a herd of deer, even if lying down when spied, may at any time rise and move slowly on, when a well-informed spy can furnish information of the utmost use and importance.

This time, however, there was no contretemps. First I saw the figure disappear behind the sand dune on my left, and after a short interval a recumbent shape emerged on the beach at the angle which interposed the favouring boulder between the stalker and the herd. Now came the opportunity for the exercise of all his hunter's craft; an absolutely serpentine method of progress was essential, as the rock, the only available cover, was neither wide nor high. As he wriggled slowly forward my attention was next riveted upon the group of seals. Whenever any one of them lifted its head I feared that ear, eye, or nose had perceived some indication of danger; but all went well, and when I shifted the direction of my glass I ascertained that the moving form had nearly reached the rock, and that a few minutes more would bring him within sight and shot of his quarry. He reached his destination, and I saw him raise his head very cautiously and slowly, to choose the best beast before putting himself into position to shoot

STALKING A SEAL.

I was not conscious of showing any visible tokens of excitement, but Ben certainly knew that the psychological moment was at hand, for his whole body was trembling, and his stump agitated at the rate of 150 strokes a minute. I pressed my left hand on his head as a gentle hint to keep quiet, and then once more focussed the glass upon the group of seals. I had just settled in my own mind that the third one from the left was the finest, and therefore the one most likely to be selected, when I noticed a slight, hardly perceptible, sinking of its head, and its fifteen companions splash into the water with every sign of haste and terror. Before I heard the shot which almost immediately awakened the echoes, I knew that the stalk had been successful, and that the slight drooping of the head of the seal, which still rested upon the rock, was its last movement.

The interesting martyr in the cause of science had certainly had a swift and merciful end, as he certainly never could have heard the shot that killed him. The next moment all was hurry and excitement! The stalker deposited his rifle on the sand behind him, took off his coat and prepared for a plunge. Ben, released from his lead, was already bounding along the shore towards him, and another figure became visible for the first time, that of Campbell the keeper, who had been told to bring the buckboard to the nearest point on the farm road and then advance to the sand dunes and await events, with strict injunctions to keep carefully out of sight until he heard the shot. No doubt like myself he had watched the stalk from beginning to end; he was the second on the scene of action; the dog was first, I a bad third. By the time

I was beside Campbell he had picked up the rifle, wiped it, and placed it in its canvas cover, and the swimmer had crossed the channel with a few vigorous strokes, and climbed on to the rock beside his motionless seal. Not very far off dog-like heads emerged from the water, looking back for the companion that would never follow them again; but they soon disappeared, and the next time they emerged to take breath they showed as mere specks upon the unruffled surface of the channel, far on their way towards the open sea.

Inspection proved all to be satisfactory. The wound just below the eye had neither injured the skin nor shattered the bone of the skull. The beast was a big one, and the pelt in perfect condition and handsomely marked. This was the hunter's report; and we were soon to be able to judge of its accuracy for ourselves, as the rope had been fastened to the hind flipper, and the swimmer soon stood up in the shallow water on our side of the strait, hauling steadily at the line, at the end of which the heavy shape progressed slowly towards us, sometimes just above and sometimes just below the surface. Its specific gravity was only slightly denser than that of the water, but it would certainly have sunk if the hitch had failed to hold. Soon the end of the rope was handed to us to do the rest of the hauling, while the successful sportsman shook himself like a great Newfoundland dog—all the drying he could get until he reached home, a fire and a change of clothes.

The most arduous part of the whole performance had yet to come. Only those who have tried it can realise how difficult it is to convey a beast weighing in full thirteen stone, very slippery, and singularly inconveniently constructed for purposes of transport, more than three-quarters of a mile; first over wet sand and rock covered with tangle and bladder-weed, then up and down hill over loose sand in which the foot sinks deep at every step; lastly up the brae face to the spot where the buckboard waited for us where the track crossed the moor. First Campbell and I each grasped one of the fore-flappers at the thinnest point, and half lifted, half dragged, the seal along between us, but the handhold proved very unsatisfactory, and we soon had to press the third party into the service, and take it by turns to lift and carry the hind flippers. As far as mere weight was concerned the keeper, a stout West Highlander, could have managed the whole job by himself, but we could not contrive any satisfactory method of adjusting the beast on his back, as there were no hind and fore legs of convenient shape to tie together round the neck so that the weight of the body might rest just below the shoulders. At last we found a good large piece of drift-wood, which had once formed part of a spar or oar—there were no trees on that part of the island from which we could cut a pole—and suspending our burden midway between us, bore it along somewhat after the fashion adopted, according to old engravings, by the spies bearing clusters of the grapes of Eshcol from the promised land.

In this manner, taking turns as bearers and chief mourner in the procession, we at last conveyed our burden to the buckboard. Here a new difficulty presented itself—how was it to be stowed? Eventually we managed to rest the head upon the back seat, lash the two front flippers securely to either side, and tuck the hind ones under the front seat. We then left to the keeper the task of conveying the seal to the little pier at Scalasaig, where, swathed in cocoa-nut matting, it was delivered on board the steamer, consigned to Rowland Ward, Piccadilly. The keeper also took with him two letters to post, advising the Museum authorities of the consignment. These letters had been prepared and written in anticipation of the event— fortunately not in vain. The seal duly arrived at its destination, "in good order and condition," within thirty-six hours of the time when his siesta on a rock on the borders of the Atlantic had been so rudely disturbed. The artist we lost in 1913, who by his will benefited the Museum which so many of his masterpieces adorn, made the most of his opportunity, and produced a result which contrasts very favourably with the older specimens. The curious may see our seal "in his habit as he lived" in the case of British mammals at the end of the long bird gallery which runs to the left of the Central Hall.

THE HANGMAN'S ROCK, COLONSAY

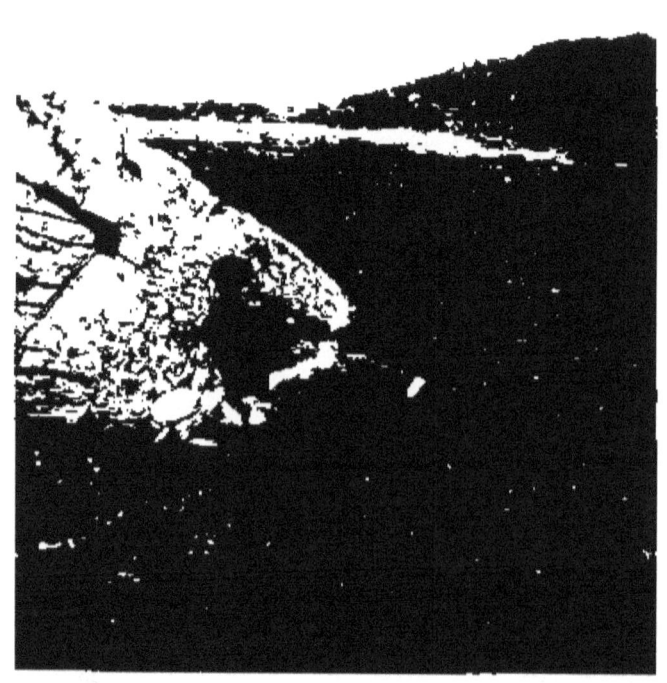

A QUIET PIPE ON THE LINKS

CHAPTER V

GOLF AT COLONSAY

MORE than once during my many visits to Colonsay I caught myself wondering what would be the enhanced value which a proprietor of the island would derive from its golf courses if it could be transported within any reasonable distance of some of the great centres of population. There are certainly five places, if not more, upon the 12,000 acres where a first-class eighteen-hole course could be constructed without any very great expenditure of money and labour. In these days when golf architecture has become a science, and so-called links are constructed on inland parks, suburban commons, and even on the Egyptian desert within hail of the Sphinx and the Pyramids, people have almost forgotten that the game owed its origin to the physical characteristics of those tracts of waste country round most of our seaside resorts which, with their bent-grown hillocks, and short springy turf, are known by the name of links even in the rare instances when they are still unprofaned by driver and niblick.

In such places, far from the madding crowd, the ancestors of our present champions amused themselves by propelling a ball from green to green, a self-selected ball never "standardised" but developed from an unknown quantity to the feather-stuffed, from that to the gutty, and finally, through the misdirected energy of our American cousins, to the rubber core of the present day. No thought had these ancient pioneers, of bunkers constructed to catch a drive, or pots cunningly devised to punish erratic brassy shots. The course had to be taken as it was found, and the players were contented with the bunkers or obstacles nature had provided, in the positions they happened to occupy between the natural plateaus of short grass where it was feasible to putt straight, and where, therefore, the improvised green and hole were necessarily placed. The clubs these ancient heroes wielded were few in number, often home made, and very different in shape and structure from the latest inventions of the ingenious professionals whose beautifully balanced, but perhaps too numerous, implements fill the heavy bag under which the modern caddie staggers round twice daily. There was then a strong natural motive to prevent the undue multiplication of clubs; the player very often had to carry them himself. The game in short was made for the links, and not the links for the game. There was certainly no need to manufacture artificial bunkers. Whins, rushes, and bent grass were left in the profusion provided by bountiful nature, and yawning chasms of sand, unmarked by flags or direction posts, seamed with their gaping mouths the half-explored deserts. If there be still any lover of nature anxious to hark back as far as possible to primitive conditions, he may find them at Machrins on the west coast of Colonsay.

When I was there club and subscription did not exist. The Misses M'Neill, joint tenants of the little inn at Scalasaig, if there were any golfers staying in the island, took care that the greens were mown, and that some mark was put down to indicate the tees. This was really all that was necessary, and there was nothing to prevent a player, if he was of an enterprising turn of mind and liked to try experiments, shifting the position of either greens or teeing grounds, and regulating the length and direction of the holes for himself. Imagination boggles at the notion of any rash individual attempting such a proceeding at North Berwick or St. Andrews. The impious daring of the unfortunate Israelite who laid his hand upon the Ark of the Covenant furnishes the only parallel, and some such penalty as being solemnly stoned with old gutties in front of the club house would alone meet the case, and "make the punishment fit the crime." Perhaps accident might anticipate the execution, as it would be difficult to wander at will over a crowded course in new directions without incurring grave risk of being cut over at every turn.

If you want a match at Colonsay you must take your partner with you or arrange to meet him. I should recommend anyone intending to pay a visit to the hotel for golf to take as companion golf-o-maniac of his own calibre, selecting if possible one who is also a lover of nature and ornithology, content with simple fare and homely surroundings. It may be that caddies will be unattainable. Considering the number of children that flock round the door of every black house or bothy, it is strange how difficult it is to persuade some loose-limbed, barefooted lad to earn a shilling by carrying your clubs. I believe that some indifferent etymologist and translator is responsible for this reluctance. Gaelic is the universal language of the natives, and I am informed that the word caddie is represented in the vernacular by an equivalent which really means something like "rascal," "villain," or "blackguard." Therefore any unfortunate lad who carries clubs is looked down upon, mocked, and derided by his companions, and this "peaceful picketing" has produced something like a strike. I remember the scene once when my boatman tried to persuade his ten-year-old son to undertake the duty, and the urchin fled over the brae pursued by his angry father with a stick.

For myself the difficulty was generally solved by combining my golf with a shooting, boating, or fishing expedition, and my gillies and keepers were quite ready to walk round the links with my clubs, although they could never even affect any enthusiasm for the game.

Sometimes we shot our way to Machrins, spreading in line along the north side of Loch Fada, but more often we sent on the keepers to await us at the first tee, and drove along the road; the buckboard heavily loaded with guns, fishing-rods, golf clubs, cartridges, and a substantial lunch. Gaily we made our way straight for Port Mor, the little boat harbour on the south-west, whence the lobster fishers start on their adventurous voyages through the labyrinth of rocks and breakers which makes the whole of that side of the island unapproachable by yachts or large craft of any description. Among these jagged and tangle-grown islets the big crustaceans still increase and multiply comparatively unmolested, and the daring natives still reap their harvest of the sea without the competition of the innumerable steam-trawlers from distant ports which have well-nigh exterminated the turbot and other flat fish which used to abound on the sandy banks to eastward in the Sounds which divide Colonsay from Jura and Mull. These interlopers have succeeded in ruining the bottom fishing, and you may now toss a long time in your little boat without a bite, where legend tells of great catches of splendid flat fish as an everyday experience. Still abundance of sport may be had with the rod and white fly among the saithe and lythe that cruise round the rocks and haunt the tideways, where it is a joy to paddle along over a translucent ultramarine sea broken by eiders, puffins, guillemots, and cormorants, with here and there the black dog-like head of a seal suddenly emerging close at hand, and turning its large liquid eyes upon you more in curiosity than fear. Sometimes seal have been even known to swallow the fish as it struggles on your hook a few yards astern of the boat.

After reaching Port Mor a sharp turn to the left takes us to Beinn nan Caorach, a bold peak which in spite of its height of only some 412 feet, looks imposing, as it rises straight from the water level. Size after all is a matter of comparison, and on an island where the highest peak only rises to an elevation of some 800 feet or thereabouts, he looks quite a respectable mountain, his grandeur enhanced by the pair of falcons which are nearly always to be seen soaring round his summit in sweeping and majestic circles.

Another hundred yards brings us to the links, where our keepers are reposing at the north-east corner of a broad expanse of lovely springy turf, broken to westward by two bays, Traigh na Tobar Fuar and Port Lotha. Beyond them nothing is visible but the mighty Atlantic, its great waves always restless, although sometimes they rise and fall in billowy undulations as smooth as oil, save where white breakers indicate hidden rocks; or as is more often the case, dash with resistless force against the shore, sometimes on stormy days sending great masses of sea-weed, jellyfish, and barnacles far above ordinary high-water mark. I have known occasions when after a heavy gale the grass has been covered to a depth of two or three inches with a gelatinous and slimy deposit.

To-day, however, there is only a light breeze, the sun is shining, and all is fair. I have for partner my old friend, and connection by marriage, Alan Steward, keen like myself at all outdoor sports, and ready to take a hand to-day with golf clubs, gun, and fishing-rod. We make a good match, as although he has considerably the advantage over me in point of age, I have of recent years enjoyed more opportunities of play, and our handicaps are about equal.

The first tee is just at the edge of a yawning sand bunker, the green being about 250 yards off, the only other hazard being a little burn which meanders through the links to the bay below. The hole is a little tricky, as although any lofted ball is safe to carry the first hazard, a topped one is certain to be severely punished, and the burn is at a distance which a short drive is very likely to find. My partner catches his ball all right, and it finds a rather lucky resting-place just over the burn, but my first drive is a failure, and the new white ball which I have taken in my pride of heart, rolls ignominiously into the yawning gulf below my feet, where the whole party, including the two keepers who are carrying the clubs, are soon engaged in a protracted search. Better would it have been if I had begun with my oldest, blackest, and most battered ball! The sand of the bunker is of a dazzling white, composed of the powdered fragments of shells, and, worse still, it is strewn with water-rounded white pebbles from which a golf ball is almost undistinguishable in shape and size. I tremble to think of the congestion there would be at the starting-place if this bunker was in front of the first tee at North Berwick or Mitcham. At Colonsay there is no hurry, and after a leisurely search my ball is discovered, happily in a place from which I am able to extricate it with a niblick, but I have played two more, and lose the first hole after missing a long putt for a possible half.

The next hole is a short one, and the green can be reached with a full drive if you have the courage to negotiate the angle of two stone dykes which intervene between you and the flag. Next follows a pretty "blind" hole over a high rocky and rushy mound at which you are apt to get into serious trouble if you do not carry the bunker, and to lose your ball in rushes and bracken if you get off the line.

At this point my black spaniel Ben brings me his first rabbit. Like most sporting dogs he has a sovereign contempt for golf as a game, but finds a round on the Machrins links full of incident, as the ground swarms with rabbits, and he seldom fails to pounce on three or four before two rounds are finished. The rabbits are a doubtful blessing on the links, as although they keep the grass so short and fine that a mowing-machine is never needed except upon the putting greens, and might almost be dispensed with there, their burrows go so deep down in the sandy soil, that when a ball disappears down a hole it is often impossible to reach it even with a long driver. I suppose, however, that when a rabbit comes back after a heavy night out and stumbles over a round obstacle in his passage he does not altogether like it, as on subsequent visits I often recovered lost balls at the mouth of the holes, presumably removed there by the occupants.

It would be tedious to describe each successive hole in turn, nor would it be any use even if I was intending to write a guide to the links, for my experience is now many years old, and even during my own visits changes were frequently made. The ninth was just below the site of an ancient prehistoric fort, Dun Gallain, where I used generally to pause and spy with a Zeiss glass, a small single one which I carried loose in my pocket. In Port Lotha, the little bay just below to the south, I could identify most of the birds with the naked eye, and some at least of the seals which frequented its sheltered waters in considerable numbers were generally to be seen swimming about within shot, turning their great liquid eyes upon our moving figures as if they wondered what we were about. Blue rock pigeons darted in and out of the fissures and caves, two ravens winged their heavy flight from a point just below high-water mark where they had evidently been feeding on garbage left by the tide, numbers of eiders and cormorants were fishing in the strong tideway near the mouth, and a flock of a dozen wild ducks feeding close to the bank, not a hundred yards off. It is a favourite spot, where these birds can be successfully stalked from the shore, and if they are not alarmed it will be worth while to come back from our luncheon place where we shall find our guns and cartridges, and try to get a brace. In the distance, where the point of Ardskenish juts out into the sea, the many dots lying on the scattered rocks with which it is fringed when they come into the focus of the glass, resolve themselves into a quantity of basking seals, and a little farther a tiny brown sail shows that Donald the lobster fisher is busy among his pots. A stranger would be ill-advised to risk his life among the cruel-looking jagged points which protrude from that boiling tideway.

After two long holes up and down the narrow peninsula crowned by the fort, we turn northward along the level, leaving a rushy marsh on our left The match finishes, disastrously for me, at a point nearly opposite to the tee from which we started, and then we retrace our steps to Tobar Fuar, the spring from which the adjacent bay takes its name, where a perpetual fountain of the clearest and coldest spring water bubbles up through the sand and discharges quite a considerable stream into the Atlantic. It is by far the strongest and best spring in the island, and the green water-cresses which grow there in profusion give a zest to the meal to which we sit down with hunters' appetites. Half a cold grouse, a roll and butter, some fruit, and slices of cake, are washed down with the clear spring water flavoured to taste from our flasks, and who could ask for a more appetising meal? Then we move to the edge of the bay only a few yards away and smoke our pipes, while we watch another small herd of seals circling below us, diving and gambolling in water so clear that we can see every movement of the long shadowy forms gliding below the surface, and so close that we can count the teeth of one great grey fellow who maintains an almost upright position with his head and shoulders thrown back and his jaws extended in a portentous yawn. A little to the left three choughs are hopping about on the short grass just by the sixteenth green, and on the sand, about fifty yards below the spring, a pair of sheldrakes are feeding among some long green weed in all the glory of their beautiful plumage of white, black, and orange.

There is an interlude before we play our second round. We take our guns, and make off in the direction of Port Lotha, in the hope of getting a shot at the flock of wild duck we noticed from the ninth tee. Keeping about fifty yards apart, we advance cautiously under the shelter of the rock, and, as our heads peer over, the birds rise with loud quacks of alarm, near enough to leave three of their number behind them. At the sound of our shots other flocks of duck and teal rise from various inlets of the bay, and we crouch, in the vain hope that some teal may circle round within shot, as they seldom take a very long flight. We watch them till they settle near the opposite side of the bay, but as they take up too open a position for a stalk we turn back, making a line on our return, through the stretch of rushy marsh we passed on our left during the game. This is always a sure find for a few snipe, and we manage to secure two couple and a half, and a young blackcock, before we return to play a second round.

It is nearly five o'clock when we finish, but the

day's sport is not at an end. We stroll back along the road about a mile, and then walk down across the field to a point near which our boat is waiting for us in an inlet of West Loch Fada. Our rods and tackle are all ready, and we are soon drifting along with the breeze, tempting the trout with a Heckham Peckham and a Zulu. The fish are on the move this evening, and with the assistance of a small phantom minnow trailed in the wake of the boat, as we row up against the wind to take up our position for our second drift, we manage to secure ten beautiful trout of an average weight of about three-quarters of a pound; the largest of which would perhaps turn the scale at a pound and a half. It is getting dark before we leave off, or we might secure a few more snipe and possibly a duck or two by walking home along the edge of the lake, but we have done enough, and we stroll home through the gathering dusk, watching the flighting ducks, and listening to the musical cries of the curlews and plover, well satisfied with our day's amusement.

It is needless to dwell now upon the merits of golf as a game. All must admit that there must be some superlative excellence in a sport which first commended itself to the pawky intellect of Scotland, and then, after planting a few parasitic growths in remote corners of England, at last took permanent root in every part of Great Britain; and in less than a decade invaded and overran two hemispheres, planting its victorious red and white flags in every latitude from the Equator to the Pole. It can be played at all seasons of the year, although extremes of temperature are undesirable; and it is a somewhat doubtful pleasure to hunt a red ball over snow, or to plod over so-called greens parched to a dull khaki colour, with the thermometer at 95 degrees in the shade—where there is any! It can be played at any time of life, although least suited to the torrid energy of youth, or to the tottering winter of extreme old age; still the period of middle life—say between 25 and 80— gives a solid 55 years or thereabouts during which the game may be played with propriety and advantage. A tyro can compete with an expert without spoiling the fun of either player, and under liberal handicap conditions may even win an occasional hole! The scratch man, however unequally matched with an inferior, has his own score to play for, and although he is most unlikely to laboriously note down upon a card the number of strokes he takes at every hole, knows perfectly well how far his round attains to, or falls short of, the standard of perfect golf.

Then the variety of the game is very great. Each stroke is different, and each hole is to a certain extent a new match; elements of chance are provided by changed conditions of wind, sky, ground, and atmosphere, and what are hindrances and obstacles at one time turn to aids and advantages at another. The strong gale which stopped your drive off the first tee, or carried your ball off the course into the rough at the third, becomes your friend at the turn, and helps you to get on to the green in two at the long hole, a feat you have never before succeeded in performing. The hard frost-bound turf which spoils your putting and ruins your iron shots, helps your ball to run a long distance after the carry, or sometimes to skip airily over the wall of some perilous bunker; or the soft and soddened turf which has stopped your drives and ruined your lies, stops an approach shot close to the flag which under ordinary conditions must have gone far beyond holing distance, if indeed it had not trickled into the bunker, or reached the rushes or heather beyond the green. Again, although luck has of course a good deal to say in the game, you cannot, even when fortune favours you most, be said absolutely and incontrovertibly to "fluke" as you do at billiards, when in attempting a cannon you achieve a winning or losing hazard, or when you find your way into a different pocket from the one you aimed at. There is but one pocket at a time at golf, and the player's object is always to get the ball into it in as few strokes as may be. Every drive is intended to propel the ball as far as possible in the right direction, and if, contrary to all probability, a long approach shot finds its way to the bottom of the tin, you have only succeeded beyond expectation, and can still legitimately plume yourself upon a fine shot, if a somewhat fortunate one. Even if a fluke must occasionally be admitted, it only gives you the advantage resulting from the one fortunate accident, and does not, as in billiards, sometimes let you in to make a long break before your adversary has a chance of playing again.

Why then does not everyone play golf? When the merits of the game are so great we cannot wonder at its attracting so many votaries, but must rather begin to look about for some reason to account for the melancholy fact that there are still a few individuals who decline to submit themselves to its fascinations. I think that the deterrent influence is usually self-consciousness. It is a terrible thing for a father of a family—a magistrate, perhaps even an Alderman or a Deputy-Lieutenant—respected in his station of life, and looked up to as a worthy and representative citizen, to stand up before a line of strangers, or still worse, acquaintances, and endeavour to strike a ball off the tee with a strange and unfamiliar weapon, with the moral certainty that his effort will meet with most indifferent success. As he stands waiting his turn, two lithe and active young men, perhaps his clerks, his constituents, or his juniors at the bar, send long drives skimming towards the flag. His own turn comes at last, and waiting to follow him is a hero who, it is darkly hinted, has got into the semi-final in the amateur championship, or stood up at a third with the redoubtable Braid himself. Still the ordeal must be gone through sooner or later; but when the feat that looked so easy has been attempted and the topped ball has trickled into the nearest furze bush, the neophyte feels inclined to apologise, first to his own caddie, and then to all the waiting golfers collected round the tee.

There need be no such discouraging experience if he will only pay a visit to Colonsay. There he may top, foozle, or even miss his tee shot, "far from the madding crowd," with the pleasant consciousness that he is delaying no one, and that his caddie, if he has one, has no standard of criticism by which to measure the degree of his inefficiency. Of course he must take someone to play with who has some notion of the game to initiate him into the elements—a son, a nephew with expectations, or an old friend—for he will find no professional to torture his limbs into constrained attitudes at half a crown a lesson. If he has once spent a fortnight at the little hotel at Scalasaig, and had a dozen rounds on the Machrin Links he will return so convinced of the delights of the game that he will be determined to persevere in spite of crowds and critics, and to submit himself to the local professional with the fixed ambition of one day attaining a fourteen handicap, and perhaps even winning a monthly medal!

CHAPTER VI

SARK: THE GARDEN OF CYMODOCE

It is a "far cry" from Colonsay in the northern Hebrides washed by the rollers of the broad Atlantic, and little Sark, near the coast of France, almost the most southern of the British Isles, but much resemblance may be traced between some of the natural features of these two gems of the sea. On the north coast of Colonsay may be found the same beetling precipices, the same deep caves, and the same natural arches, washed, scooped out, and chiselled by the same rushing and tumultous tideways—

> "Thick-sown with rocks deadlier than steel, and fierce
> With loud cross-countering currents."

Each is a paradise for the naturalist, the botanist, and the artist; and few who have visited either can resist its charm. More than twenty-five years ago I paid my first visit to the Channel Islands and spent a week on Sark. I fell in love with it at once, and afterwards made it a favourite resort for short spring holidays with my wife and children. The poet Swinburne has painted it with all his enthusiasm for beauty and the sea in his melodious rhapsody entitled "The Garden of Cymodoce." It is high praise which he awards it in the apostrophe to the sea, which he calls the "mother of himself and of his song"—

THE GARDEN OF CYMODOCE

> "One birth more divine
> Than all births else of thine,
> That hang like flowers or jewels on thy deep, soft breast,
> Was left for me to shine
> Above thy girdling line
> Of bright and breathing brine,
> To take mine eyes with rapture and my sense with rest."

There is something so unique in the beauty and charm of the little island that lovers of nature and quiet are drawn again and again to its shores, although sport, except sea-fishing, is non-existent, and golf has not yet been introduced, although, as one of the hotel-keepers wrote to me in 1896 (with sublime ignorance of its mysteries), "there are doubtless many places in the hotel grounds where it could be played with advantage"! The gregarious tripper prefers the attractions of Guernsey or Jersey, where he can dash through scenery of great beauty in a four-horse *char-à-banc*, accompanied by congenial souls, and halt at frequent intervals for refreshment where alcoholic stimulants are cheap; or, if he desires to be able to say that he has visited Sark, he crosses by the morning steamer from St. Peter's Port, is conducted as one of a herd to such points of interest as can be visited in a short day with an hour's interval for a heavy midday meal of lobsters and ale; stares into the windows of the Seigneurie, the beautiful gardens and grounds of which are courteously thrown open to the public at stated times, and returns in the evening, after enriching various parts of the island with his autograph, with a hazy impression of cliffs and ocean, and a general conviction that there isn't much to see in Sark, but that at all events he can say that he has been there. To the artist, however, the naturalist or the poet, or to that more numerous class which loves and appreciates nature, beauty and repose, without laying claim to any of those high titles, the little island is replete with interest and charm, and they return again and again where:

> "midmost of the murderous water's web
> All round it stretched and spun,
> Laughs, reckless of rough tide and raging ebb,
> The loveliest thing that shines against the sun."

Sark is a very small island; only about three and a half miles long, and not more than one and a half miles wide in its broadest part, but it is all compact of loveliness; surrounded as it is by cliffs honeycombed with caves hollowed out of its ramparts of gneiss and granite by the action of the sea, in front of which great rocks stand out as sentinels, the home and nesting-place of innumerable sea-birds. Of these the most remarkable are the two great rocks named "Les Autelets."

> "The black bright sheer twin flameless Altarlets,
> That lack no live blood sacrifice they crave
> Of shipwreck and the shrine subservient wave."

On these I have seen cormorants, guillemots and kittiwakes nesting at the same time, each species of bird having appropriated distinct ridges and ledges as its own peculiar property, and none encroaching upon or interfering with that of its neighbour. The guillemots nested highest of all, and their darting flight to the sea in search of food was a revelation of grace and beauty. As I stood below their home at low tide they skimmed over my head at a great height at a pace and angle which would have taxed the skill of a De Grey, although far be it from me to suggest that a great

LES AUTLETS, SARK

shooting expert, or any sportsman one degree removed from barbarism, would molest such harmless and beautiful creatures. I heard of one "'Arry" who fired some shots at them with very indifferent success, but I am glad to say that he was hauled up before the magistrates and heavily fined, as well as having to bear the more disagreeable penalty of exposure.

The wild cliff and rock scenery form a striking contrast to the fertile and flowery interior—the commons blazing with furze blossom, the hedges and banks starred with primroses, the lanes bright with hawthorn bloom. I have nowhere seen primroses grow more luxuriantly. In addition to the ordinary yellow sort, three other varieties—a dark red, a pale pink, and a pure white —are not uncommon, and "sports"—primroses with twelve and even fourteen petals instead of the ordinary five—have been brought under my notice. I am no scientist botanist, but a high authority, Mr. Marquand of the Linnæan Society, in the chapter on "Wild Flowers and Ferns" which he contributed to the *Book of Sark*, says that the indigenous flora is an exceedingly rich one, and that between four and five hundred flowering plants may be found growing wild in the island. Among its floral treasures he enumerates the little bulbous Ixia, and the tiny Capitate rush, which only occur in a single British locality besides the Channel Islands; a miniature Stonecrop of a bright ruby red known as the Mossy Tillaea, a very scarce Blue Pimpernel, and a Yellow Pimpernel, interesting because it is not to be found anywhere else in the Channel Islands. He deplores the danger of the extermination of rare plants by thoughtless collectors, and instances the practical eradication of the Royal

Fern (*Osmunda Regalis*) by the persistent digging up of roots. I need not say how whole-heartedly I sympathise with his views, and applaud his caution in not specifying the particular localities where rare species may be found. The Osmunda has been eradicated in the same way in many places in my beloved Argyllshire, and I made my own protest in a former volume.

The climate of Sark is far more bracing than that of Guernsey, and *a fortiori* of Jersey; indeed the quality of the air of the high tableland surrounded by sea is such that the late Dr. Chepmell—no mean authority—himself a native of the Channel Islands, used to declare that it was the healthiest spot within a thousand miles of London. The marine zoologist finds a rich field for his labours. Crustacea of various kinds abound round the submerged rocks which fringe the coast, the lobster-fishing being particularly good. Many varieties of octopods frequent the bays and pools, and the scene of Victor Hugo's great description of a combat with a devil-fish in the *Travailleurs de la Mer* is laid in the immediate neighbourhood. I never, however, had the good or bad fortune to fall in with a squid sufficiently large and formidable to account for an absconding bankrupt, and retain and preserve his valuables and papers for future production when the exigencies of the situation require such a marine *Deus ex machina*.

Beautiful shells abound on the shore, and that curious univalve, the ormer, known as Venus's ear, may be found adhering to the boulders at low spring tides, and is much sought after for food. I have eaten these molluscs, but did not care much for them, although they are considered a great delicacy by the natives.

THE GARDEN OF CYMODOCE

I found a few shells myself and bought others at first, as welcome gifts for children or bazaars; but further experience taught me where I could always get as many gratis as I cared to take away. It was only necessary to search the dust-heaps at the back of any farm-house or cottage, and numbers of fine specimens could be obtained, far better than the dead shells washed up on the shore, which in addition to their loss of colour usually bear marks of the perforations of their enemies, the cuttlefish and whelks. But it is in anemones, sponges, and zoophytes of a similar character that the island is especially rich. The rocky caverns and hollows covered and disclosed by the great rise and fall of the sea, amounting to as much as twenty-six feet at spring tides, furnish ideal homes for these light-avoiding creatures. One spot especially—the celebrated Gouliot cave—is in itself sufficiently unique to furnish a reason for a visit to the island by any one interested in these beautiful and strange inhabitants. These caves, for there are really two, can only be penetrated at the lowest spring tides, when they must be approached either by a boat, if the sea is sufficiently calm to admit of landing, or by a somewhat precipitous and difficult path from above, not dangerous to any one with a reasonably good head, although Mr. Swinburne, with permissible poetical licence, has given a somewhat exaggerated view of its perils:

"For the path is for passage of sea-mews, and he that hath glided
  and leapt
Over sea-grass and sea-rock, alighting as one from a citadel crept
That his foemen beleaguer, descending by darkness and stealth
  at the last,
Peers under, and all is as hollow to hellward, agape and aghast."

But he cannot exaggerate the beauty of the vision that meets the eye when the seal of the tide

"On the seventh day breaks but a little, that man by its mean
May behold what the sun hath not looked on, the stars of the
    night have not seen.

. . . .

Afloat and afar in the darkness a tremulous colour subsides,
From the crimson high crest of the purple-peaked roofs to the soft-
    coloured sides
That brighten as ever they widen, till downward the level is won
Of the soundless and colourless water that knows not the sense of
    the sun;
From the crown of the culminant arch to the floor of the lakelet
    abloom,
One infinite blossom of blossoms innumerable aflush through the
    gloom."

I have twice had the good fortune to visit these caverns of mystery, once by landing from a boat, once by climbing down the path on the cliff side, and on each occasion managed to penetrate to the extreme depths, although not without a certain amount of wading. Where the two galleries nearly meet a natural shaft pierces upward to the daylight, and it is impossible to exaggerate the loveliness of the jewel-studded arches and walls when the rays of the sun strike down upon them. Most of the anemones are closed, but their brilliant colour remains. Myriads of smaller gorgeous zoophytes and sponges glitter around their big brothers, and the strange *tubularia indivisa* hangs all round, like bunches of white currants, with its flower-like petals closed. It needs no great stretch of imagination for the visitor to fancy that he has forced an entrance into Aladdin's cavern, where, as the old but ever young romance tells us: "The

THE GARDEN OF CYMODOCE

fruit of each tree had a separate colour. Some were white, others sparkling and transparent like crystal; some were red and of different shades; others green, blue or violet, and some of a yellowish hue; in short, there were fruits of almost every colour. The white globes were pearls; the sparkling and transparent fruits were diamonds; the deep red were rubies; the paler a particular sort of ruby called balaz; the green, emeralds; the blue, turquoises; the violet, amethysts; those tinged with yellow, sapphires; and all the other coloured fruits varieties of precious stones."

There are many other caves of great interest, and on a calm day most of them can be visited in a boat. Nothing is more enjoyable than a row completely round the island when the weather is favourable for such an expedition. The deep water comes quite near the shore at high tide, and the passenger is taken close under towering cliffs where he may perhaps see, as I did, a couple of thieving ravens carrying away the eggs from the nesting gulls, pursued and screamed at by the bereaved and outraged parents. Round standing pillars, through natural arches, into deep caves, the boat winds its way, and the colouring of the rocks, and the brilliant blue and translucent clearness of the sea are a revelation of contrasted splendour. Sark is a happy hunting-ground for artists, but I know of no one who has reproduced the actual colouring of the cliffs with such patient fidelity and accuracy as the resident artist, Mr. W. A. Toplis, who has kindly permitted me to make use of an extraordinarily delicate pen-and-ink sketch of "Les Autelets" to illustrate this chapter. He has lived in Sark for thirty years, and during that time many of his faithful portraits of his beloved adopted home have been exhibited on the walls of the Royal Academy, and twenty of his pictures have been reproduced by Messrs. Carl Hentschell & Co. in the *Book of Sark*, published in 1908, with text by Mr. John Oxenham, and chapters on Geology and Botany by Professor Benney and Mr. Marquand. He spares no pains to be accurate in the smallest detail. There are few parts of the beautiful scenery which he has not studied and faithfully delineated either in oil or water-colour.

It seems strange that in an island indented with so many bays and creeks there should be only three places where boats can shelter. In nothing is Sark more unique than in the character of its harbours. Creux Harbour, where steamboats and yachts land passengers at the little pier, is backed by a great wall of cliff apparently impenetrable; and there is a malicious and doubtless untrue story that the Admiralty yacht with the First Lord on board, once came to visit the island in state, but failing to detect the tunnel behind the pier, sailed away, reporting that there was no entrance. Probably the story is by our old friend, Ben Trovato; but there is a peculiar charm in one's first introduction through

> "the dark deep sea-gate that makes way
> Through channelled darkness for the darkling day.
> Hardly to let men's faltering footfall win
> The sunless passage in,
> Where breaks a world aflower against the sun;
> A small sweet world of wave-encompassed wonder."

On the opposite side, near the small island of Brechou, is the little fishing harbour of Havre

THE GARDEN OF CYMODOCE

Gosselin, hardly less peculiar and picturesque than Le Creux; for there the fishermen, to gain access to the boats that float snugly in the little cove, have to climb down the cliff by a precipitous path ending in a perpendicular ladder. The third harbour, "Les Eperqueries," at the northern extremity of the island, is now little used, although before the construction of Le Creux it was the only place where a vessel of any size could land passengers.

I have not yet mentioned the crowning wonder of the island, the well-known natural bridge called the Coupée, where the only road between the two islands—Great Sark and Little Sark—runs for a hundred yards between two precipices 290 feet high without any fence or wall, a track only just wide enough for a small cart to traverse. It is a queer enough place on a windy day, and one across which it would not be pleasant to drive a shying horse; but the natives look on it as all in the day's work, and decline now to fence it with a rail because experience showed that children would swing on it, and that thereby the danger would be increased! It is recorded that when the silver mines were worked in Little Sark (the shafts and buildings are still there, and traces of ore can be found, although the enterprise was a lamentable failure) one of the workmen who was a little convivial, used to try his walking powers on a more protected part of the road a little before reaching the Coupée, and if he found that he swayed too much from one side to the other, used to lie down and sleep off his potations instead of attempting the dangerous transit. For most sober men, however, it has no terrors, and I myself, although

I have a bad head for precipices, never objected to crossing

> "that steep strait of rock whose twin-cliffed height
> Links crag with crag reiterate, land with land,
> By one sheer thread of narrowing precipice
> Bifront, that binds and sunders
> Abyss from hollower imminent abyss,
> And wilder isle with island, blind for bliss
> Of sea that lightens and of wind that thunders."

It was, however, too much for my friend Frank Lockwood, who got a headache after crossing it, and spoke of it afterwards as a "dreadful place."

Dear Frank Lockwood! It was with that brightest and cheeriest of companions and truest of friends that I visited Sark in 1896; and, although the Coupée was too much for him, he thoroughly appreciated the island, with its beauty, its quiet, and its grand scenery. It was the last of those happy Easter holidays when, with his family and friends, he threw off the weight of Parliamentary and legal cares and became a boy once more. Like him, I had my wife and children with me, and I shall never forget that happy gathering, and how devoted all the young people were to the cheery and sympathetic friend who joined so heartily in all their amusements—never patronised or lectured them, but talked to them without pedantry or affectation on a footing of equality. How we all enjoyed the walk we had together when my daughter's little Scotch terrier incontinently fell upon a duck, and nearly slaughtered it in full sight of a cottage, at the door of which the outraged proprietress appeared. How he laughed at the old women holding up their hands at the door,

FANCY

FACT

THE GARDEN OF CYMODOCE

and at the dialogue in dog French which took place between me and a not altogether sober emissary of the duck's owner. "Qui est le propriétaire du méchant chien?" "Moi." "Il faut payer." "C'est juste." And then, when ransom had been duly offered and accepted, at the tough old duck running away apparently none the worse, and the joyful comment, "Il vit encore." I well remember the pencil sketch he drew of the incident, but it has unfortunately disappeared; however I still possess, and value as one of my most treasured possessions, an admirable imaginary portrait of the Seigneur of Sark as he expected to find him, contrasted with the real Seigneur offering him a cup of tea. The mildness in the second sketch is exaggerated in order to heighten the contrast with the bronzed buccaneer with cocked hat, high boots, belted dagger, and bell-mouthed pistol who is truculently consigning his visitor "a la donjon." I framed the two with the visiting card of "The Seigneur of Sark" below them, and I am sure they would heartily amuse their supposed model if he could see them. My son has also preserved two "lightning sketches" made in the course of a game we played one evening after dinner at the hotel. Each of the party was to draw some well-known incident of history or fiction. Frank Lockwood's contributions were Sir Walter Raleigh spreading his cloak at the feet of Queen Elizabeth, and Gilliat's fight with the devil-fish. I think the first of the two was intended to bear some resemblance to a statesman of the present generation.

Frank and I had been thrown much together, having been constant companions and friends from the day when we commenced our careers at the Bar as students. We sat on opposite sides of the House of Commons, but the difference of our political views never interfered with our friendship. Indeed it had its conveniences, for in the Parliament of 1886, when pairs were scarce, we established a "standing pair" from 7.30 to 9.30, which enabled us to get home for dinner. He was my junior by a year, and might have hoped for a long career of usefulness on the Bench, where his high honour and strong common sense would have made him an admirable judge, but his health began to fail early in 1897, and he died in December of that year below the age at which most judges are appointed.

Since that Easter I have never visited Sark again. I have heard that there are more hotels, but I hope they are like those of my time, homely and comfortable quarters, clean and simple with good and wholesome food and personal attention. I should be sorry to hear that a monster palace with gold-laced porters and charges to match sullied the simplicity of the little island, even if it brought golf with it as an additional attraction. There are not too many such oases in the desert of civilisation. As I write, the rich odour of the whins seems once more to delight my nostrils, and the vision of the varied beauties celebrated by the poet rises again before my eyes—

> "O flower of all wind-flowers and sea-flowers,
> Made lovelier by love of the sea
> Than thy golden own field-flowers, or tree-flowers,
> Like foam of the sea-facing tree
> No foot but the sea-mew's there settles
> On the spikes of thine anthers like horns,
> With snow-coloured spray for thy petals,
> Black rocks for thy thorns."

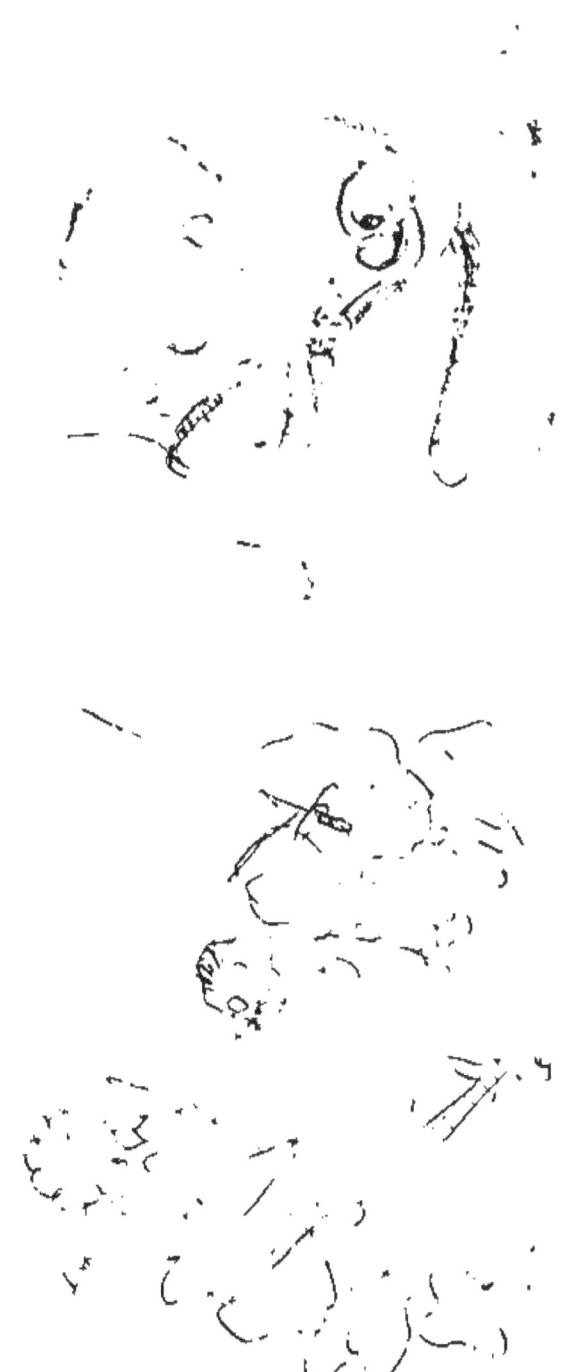

Queen Elizabeth and Sir Walter Raleigh.   The Fight with the Devil-fish.

LIGHTNING SKETCHES BY SIR FRANK LOCKWOOD.

CHAPTER VII

NORWAY IN 1865. MY FIRST SALMON

NEARLY fifty years have passed since my first visit to Norway, where I spent a memorable holiday in 1865; memorable indeed! for then I caught my first salmon. I had always been a fisherman from that first day when, at the age of five or thereabouts, I extracted goldfish with a crooked pin baited with bread from the pond of tepid water which adjoins the Low Moor ironworks. Dace, gudgeon, and perch were my next victims, then small jack, and before I was seven, when on a visit with my parents to the Wrights at Halston, I caught a trout some three inches long in the stream which flows beside the beautiful lake across which the famous Jack Mytton, a later William Tell, had fired and cut the red feather out of his mother's bonnet with a rifle ball. The mark tempted him. "Look out, mother," he cried, and fired, fortunately with a true aim. The incident was told me by my father, who records also among his earliest recollections of Shrewsbury, where he was at school, how he was privileged to behold that hero engaged in the characteristic diversion of making an unfortunate waiter dance by flicking his white cotton calves with a long driving-whip. Now the rest of the acts of Jack Mytton and all that he did, how he dissipated a fine fortune, and ruined an iron constitution, are they not written and illustrated in his biography by Nimrod, of which the first edition has become a rare and valuable classic?

But this singular incident in the history of Halston lake is not half so memorable in my mind as the great event in my piscatorial experiences which I have just recorded. Not only had I caught my first trout, but I was allowed to eat it for my breakfast. From that day I worked my way up from the worm to the spoon, from the spoon to the minnow, from the minnow to the fly, and made up by perseverance for want of skill. I know that in the pond at Blackdown in Sussex I got a trout of two pounds weight on a small spoon attached to my reel line without any gut cast, and landed him without a net, pulling him by main force on to the shore, which was not even sloping; but how it happened I am at a loss in the light of later experience to conjecture. Such miracles of good fortune fall only to the lot of the tyro who is doubtless strong in the faith which enables him to remove mountains of difficulty.

When I left my first school, where I had spent some six very miserable months, my master gave me two books—Spenser's *Faery Queen*, and *Forest Life: a Fisherman's Sketches in Norway and Sweden*, by the Rev. Henry Newland; and after more than fifty years the latter volume is still one of my cherished treasures. My copy is the second edition, published by Routledge in 1855. It gives in the form of fiction the sporting adventures of the author and his companions in Scandinavia, and my mouth waters as I read how those early pioneers wandered without let or hindrance from river to lake, and from forest to fjeld, camping, shooting, and fishing wherever they pleased, and casting their flies on waters then almost virgin, but now let for many hundreds of pounds a season. The book is brightly and amusingly written, and full of anecdotes of the folk-lore, superstitions, manners, and customs, of a country then uncivilised; and as it is now very difficult to obtain, it would well repay reprinting.

As I devoured its picturesque pages the resolve that I would some day visit this Mecca of the fisherman formed itself in my boyish mind. I also was a fisherman! and some day perhaps I might achieve the supreme triumph of landing a salmon. In 1865, just after the birth of his present Majesty King George, I attained this object of my ambition. At that date there was one tackle-maker in London who made a speciality of supplying the needs of the Norwegian angler. This was Macgowan of Bruton Street, who furnished me with an eighteen-foot hickory rod, treble gut casts, and a fly-book and flies, which I believe I have somewhere still, although I cannot at this moment lay my hand upon it. The flies were not the same one uses now—" Jock Scott" and " Durham Ranger" were not. The wings were plainer and the bodies thicker and rougher. To this rule there were exceptions. I remember one special fly for bright weather known as the " Sun Fly," with nearly the whole of the wing made of golden pheasant topping. I have never seen its like in any tackle-maker's shop since, but it caught fish, and I do not doubt that it would do so still if anyone had the temerity to try it.

I was then a Balliol undergraduate, and it was one of my earliest and idlest long vacations. My companion was Alfred Gurney, then a freshman at

Exeter; afterwards for many years the beloved and respected Rector of St. Barnabas, Pimlico. He was not so keen a sportsman as myself, but his acute appreciation of the beautiful, and his well-stocked and poetical mind, made him an ideal companion upon a trip.

I drop a veil over my first experience of the North Sea. The boats were smaller, and the accommodation far rougher than is provided by Wilson's present fleet, and even now a bad sailor does not enjoy the purgatory through which he has to pass on his way to the northern paradise. Some robust and unfeeling fellow-travellers came and scoffed at me in my bunk, and recommended boiled pork. With what joy I beheld them prostrated on the third day when I had recovered my appetite and got my sea legs! At last we reached the sheltered waters of the fjord, and I shall never forget my first experience of the glories of the northern night. The light never left us. Pink sunset streaks ended the long day, and had hardly faded into dusk before the east was again brightening with the first glow of dawn. I was quite sorry when the voyage came to an end, and the boat anchored in the harbour of Christiania.

Our destination was Aak, at the head of the Romsdal valley, then an hotel, but now the site of a villa, the property of the Wills family. We had to make very different preparations for our journey than would have sufficed at the present time. Now there is a railway to Otta, which is shortly to be extended to Dombaas, and from that point I have heard that a service of motor brakes runs through the beautiful Romsdal valley to Vaeblungsnaest during the season.

NORWAY IN 1865

In 1865 practically the whole journey was by carriole.

Our first step on arrival at Christiania was to call upon Bennett, then the "Cook" of Norway, and buy two second-hand carrioles for our use upon the trip. At that time the convenient little stolkjaerres, holding two side by side, which have now nearly supplanted the primitive vehicle, were not in existence. A travelling party had to go in single file along the road, each member occupying a separate conveyance. Portmanteaus and bags were strapped upon the little board behind the seat, and the skydskarl who accompanied you on each stage to take back the horses perched himself or herself upon it. These attendants might be of any age or sex; sometimes a tiny urchin, sometimes a venerable crone, would undertake the duty. One feature they all had in common—a love of, and care for, their four-footed charges. If you hurried the little grass-fed beasts along a stage, frowning faces and muttered exclamations would convey their rebuke; and no liberality in the way of tips, "drinke-penge," would make up for what they not unjustly regarded as cruelty to animals. The patient sure-footed dun beasts are still fortunate in their masters.

Our preparations did not take long, and on the second day we went by rail as far as Eidsvold, then the terminus of the line, and thence on by steamer over the Miosen Lake as far as Lillehammer. Our whole stock of Norwegian consisted in the few phrases contained in Bennett's guide-book, but Norwegian good-nature and English impudence carried us safely through our enterprise. We often had to wait on completing a stage for our two horses to be fetched off the hill or from the plough; in those times the telephone was not, and we were not prepared to face the expense of sending "forbud." But little we recked of delay; all was fresh and new to us as by easy stages we penetrated the enchanted land. Often we had to put up with rough accommodation, and plain if plentiful food; but we consumed our eggs and fish, fladbrod, rye bread, and "gammel ost," a strong-smelling cheese looking like brown windsor soap, with a relish and appreciation the daintiest fare would not provoke in these degenerate days.

Our quarters were by no means as clean as the traveller would now be sure to find everywhere on the most frequented road in Norway; the washing apparatus was primitive, and baths were not. What matter! everywhere in that land of running water there were pools and streams where one could enjoy a refreshing dip, and make an *al fresco* toilet. Once or twice we put our rods together and tried fishing on the way, but only a few small trout rewarded our efforts. Sometimes we came in for very crowded quarters. One occasion still remains very vividly in my memory, when in the half light I awoke in our little double-bedded room startled by a rustling sound, and saw a lad emerge from behind the boughs which masked the open fireplace. He had been slumbering peaceably upon the hearthstone, and was stealing away at dawn to get to his work. At another stopping-place we came in for a wedding festivity, and sat up half the night dancing with the bride and bridegroom and the wedding guests. We did not, like the gentleman whom the ancient mariner buttonholed, "hear the loud bassoon," there was no instrumental music whatever, but the dancers trod their measures to the time—I can hardly call it the tune—of an air hummed by a gawky lad who sat with his legs dangling on a table which had been moved into the corner. When we asked in the morning for our "recnung," we were told there was none. Our hosts were keeping open house in honour of the newly-wedded couple. A small donation towards their housekeeping expenses was however gratefully accepted, with the shake of the hand with which Norwegians still acknowledge any gift however small.

I strain my memory to try to fix upon the points of difference between this, my first journey in Norway, and those of forty years later over the same ground; for twice, in this twentieth century have I driven along the Romsdal valley between Dombaas and Vaeblungsnaest. In the first place, if my recollection serves me right, the road was narrower, steeper, and more winding in 1865. Now a coach or a heavy motor can pass along the broad high-road that runs parallel to the Rauma past the Witches Peaks, towards the foot of the beautiful Romsdal Horn, yet I seem to remember many steep pitches and narrow places on my first visit. I expect also that bears were more common than they are now. In certain places just outside the houses bear skins pegged out to dry were a common object. We met a few English upon the journey, among others two Eton friends, Lord Albert Clinton and Haynes, who were travelling with a "talk," who besides his skill as an interpreter was an accomplished cook, and gave us the benefit of a little variety in our somewhat monotonous bill of fare, and spared us the necessity of signs and references to the phrase book while our parties were together. About four or five days brought us to our destination. During the journey I had passed by many a pool and rapid which made my fingers itch to grasp the rod, and now the day was at hand when I might hope to try for my first salmon.

Of course I was not at liberty to fish wherever my fancy led me, like those fortunate early pioneers whose adventures I had devoured in Newland's fascinating volume. One of his party began harling, and was nearly towed out to sea by a twenty-pounder as soon as the packet had anchored at Christiansand. In 1865 most of the rivers were rented, and the Rauma was in the hands of that prince of sportsmen, Mr. W. Bromley Davenport, who has recorded some of his adventures there in his too short work *Sport*. If there be any among my readers who have not already devoured the fascinating chapter in which he records how, at five in the morning, he caught a forty-three-pounder, and on the same evening lost a salmon so large that the morning fish was, in the graphic words of his fisherman, "only a small piece of this one," let him lose no time in getting hold of the book.

That year he did not occupy at his usual quarters, but had sublet the house and fishing rights to Lord Coventry and Captain Pennant. They had a very long stretch of water at their disposal, and the boatman whom I sent for and engaged on my arrival told me that they very seldom came to the lower pools immediately adjacent to my quarters, and that they might be induced to grant me permission for a short time to wet my maiden line there. With trembling hands I indited a humble petition which I despatched by messenger, and feverishly awaited the reply. It was favourable, and gave me the run of about a mile of water for three days.

The earliest dawn of the following morning of course found me by the stream, accompanied by my fisherman, a wiry old boy of about fifty. I walked by faith and not by sight, put on the fly he selected, cast where he told me, and let out the exact proportion of line which he suggested. After about half an hour of fruitless efforts, during which I only succeeded in catching my fly pretty often in grass or bushes behind me, and knocking off the barb of more than one hook against rocks, fortune favoured my efforts. A sharp stream was running just below me pretty deep near the bank, and as the fly came round in the strong water at the third or fourth cast, I felt the electric shock of a rise and the line began to run merrily through the rings. I was into my first salmon! I cannot recall the incidents of the fight, perhaps because my longing for success was so great, and I was so intent obeying the directions of my mentor, that everything except the glorious consummation has faded from my memory. In about a quarter of an hour I saw my gillie plunge his gaff into the water, and withdraw it with a beautiful silvery fish impaled upon its point. It weighed only nine pounds, but it was a salmon—my first salmon! and if my readers do not know what those words mean to an enthusiastic angler no words of mine can stimulate his torpid imagination. It is always the first triumph that counts—the first century of the cricketer, the first brief of the barrister, the first baby of the happy mother, the first picture of the artist, the first sparrow that falls to the schoolboy's first gun. Who shall draw a comparison between the relative delights of such triumphs as these ?

Before the sun had sunk sufficiently low in the heavens to allow of my sallying forth once more " on high adventure bent," that fish had been cooked and eaten. My palate still recalls its curdy firmness, its incomparable freshness. There was no novelty about the taste of salmon in the abstract; fish, and good ones too, had furnished the staple of nearly every meal of which I had partaken on my journey, and the jaded taste might well have turned from the dainty, as the Israelites did from the quails in the wilderness. My fish, caught with my own rod and line, just fresh from the sea, and boiled before the very next possible meal, was not to be compared to any vulgar salmon of unknown origin with which the guest makes his first acquaintance upon the table. All honour to my fellow-travellers and convives at the midday meal. They played up to my enthusiasm, and shared, or affected to share, my transports with such hearty goodwill that nearly all the dish was consumed.

That same evening I caught two more salmon, weighing respectively twenty-one and fifteen pounds. The three allotted days passed all too quickly, but produced altogether nine fish of the aggregate weight of nearly a hundred and fifty pounds. I at once entered the weight of each fish and the date of its capture upon the first leaf of my fly-book, and although, as I have said, I cannot lay my hand upon the record at this moment, I think my memory, refreshed as it has been many times since by reference to the original document, may be relied upon as substantially accurate. The fish were very kind to me; some, but not many, got away, and I do not think any one of those captured took more than half an hour to kill. Most of them were caught from the boat by harling, a practice which I have since learnt to despise. Certainly the process of rowing a boat across a stream and back again with two or even three rods, and twenty yards of line hanging over the stern from each of them, cannot compare with fishing from the bank, or even with casting from a boat where the likely places to rise a salmon are marked and defined; but in some of the great wide rivers in Norway where a salmon may be lying anywhere, harling is almost a necessity, as even if you were purist enough to insist on going through the form of casting, the stream and the strong arms and local knowledge of the boatman would still be responsible for presenting the lure in the proper position, and the honours of the day up to the moment of hooking the fish would really rest with your attendants.

For a beginner in his early days of sport there is, and ought to be, joy enough in the sudden bending of the rod, the singing of the line through the rings, and the sight of the jumping fish, often first seen in a place you would not in the least have anticipated from the direction towards which the rod is pointed where the line is cutting through the water making a little wake, and scattering showers of spray. At such a moment give good heed to your tackle, and recover your line as quickly as you can. When the fish is travelling up stream, and the line, or what you can see of it, is pointing down, the weight of water on the curve is placing an immense strain upon the stoutest twisted gut and the firmest hold, and you will be lucky if you do not soon feel that heart-sickening "slack" which may mean only that the fish has turned, but generally signifies a definite severance of all connection between the angler and his fish. All such excitements incident to playing the fish fall to the lot of the harler in as full a measure as they do to the more complete angler.

Proud as I was of my success, my average of three fish a day sank into insignificance when compared with the bags of those fortunate fishermen to whom I was indebted for the permission I was enjoying, who had the run of the whole long stretch of water up to the fall beyond which no salmon could ascend. Their keeper came down to see me one day when I was fishing. I am uncertain whether he was an Englishman or a Norwegian, but I remember that he spoke English perfectly, and understood, as do the natives of most countries, the meaning of the verb "to tip." He informed me that the bag of the two rods on the water above on the previous day had amounted to eighteen salmon: the largest thirty-two pounds, and the smallest nine. I never fished the Rauma on my later visits, but from what I heard I should imagine that such a bag would seldom be equalled now. The commercial sale of salmon, and the consequent increase of netting in all the long fjords has gone far to deplete the once prolific waters, and in many places the goose is already dead, and the natives are beginning to miss the golden eggs which it used to produce annually.

My three days were over, but my sport was not altogether at an end. There was still a wide stretch of water at the mouth of the river, I think tidal, where all were free to fish. It was no longer worth while to keep my fisherman, who was dismissed gladdened with an ample guerdon; but Gurney and I used to go daily to this spot, and harl the broad stream, rowing across and across, making up for want of skill by energy and perseverance. What fish we caught were entirely our own, as we were boatmen, fishermen, and gaffers; and we really enjoyed very good sport, especially with sea-trout, which were beginning to run up, and to rise freely. No doubt we should have done even better with them had we not stuck to our big flies in the hope of salmon, of which we got very few; but I remember that on one morning, my best, I got to my own rod six sea-trout of the average weight of six and three-quarter pounds, the largest being rather over nine pounds, and the smallest four. What sport such fellows would have given had I fished for them, as I do in the light of my present knowledge, with small hooks, fine tackle, and an ordinary trout rod and reel, with plenty of stout backing in case your fish wants to run a hundred yards or more at a time. I now look upon it as murder to sacrifice the sport these game fish can and do afford by dragging them out with tackle which gives them little or no chance of resistance.

Indoor amusements were not much wanted. We played a good many games of picquet during the midday hours, and I suppose that in skill or want of skill, at the game we were about equally matched, as only a few shillings changed hands at the close of a month's play. We fished early and late, and did a little climbing and a good deal of walking on the surrounding mountains. Personally I was never any good at mountaineering; I always had a bad head for precipices, and can hardly bear to look down a sheer height even when standing on perfectly safe ground. I remember and confess that on one of these expeditions I left my companion and his guide to finish their scramble above the snow-line without me, and waited their return idly sitting on the slope, and contentedly watching with a glass two diminutive figures fishing the beloved stream below.

All good things must come to an end, so after a sojourn at Aak which passed with lightning rapidity, we had to turn our faces South and traverse once more, in the reverse direction, the valleys of the Romsdal and Gulbrandsdal. We dawdled along the rivers, reluctant to leave them, and had more success with the trout rod than upon our way out. I remember that we caught a good many nice brown trout soon after we had got beyond that fall of the Rauma to which I have alluded, beyond which no salmon or sea-trout could pass, and that we had fair sport at other stages of the journey. We sold our carrioles at Christiania, the difference of price amounting to merely a few dollars, which represented the hire of the vehicles. The whole trip was extraordinarily cheap, posting and the cost of lodging and food being even more moderate than it is now. We spent a night at Christiania, and visited the theatre, where I remember that I was fortunate enough to find the company acting in their own language a familiar English farce, "Little Toddlekins," and was therefore able to follow the dialogue and byplay. On the previous Christmas I had seen the same play acted at Frittenden Rectory, in Kent, by a juvenile amateur company of the children of our neighbours, the Moores and Hoares, the title rôle being taken by one who recently occupied almost the highest position in his Majesty's fleet!

CHAPTER VIII

HVILESTED, 1901

HVILESTED, "place of rest or peace," which was the first spot I visited in Norway when I returned there after long years, stands, or rather stood (for, alas, its very ashes have disappeared), on a plateau overlooking the beautiful Sundal River, some eight miles from Sundalsören. The site of the house was cleared in a wood of Norway pines, many of which shifted their places to its timber walls. It was designed by that most accomplished architect and angler, Mrs. Lort Phillips, and was the first of the many charming residences which owe their origin to the love she and her husband bear to their adopted country. From the verandah can be seen the sharp peaks of the "Seven Sisters," the beautiful ridges that head the valley just where the river turns above Musjerd. Many trees left standing all round the house made it difficult to sketch or photograph. On nearly all of these are bird boxes, where tits of various kinds, flycatchers and woodpeckers, nest and rear their young. Squirrels gambol fearlessly among the boughs, or even on the window-sills, or over the roof; and on the shed below my wife's maid pointed out to her a large bird which she "thought was a duck," but which turned out to be a green woodpecker.

On the south side of the garden a high steep slope

looked down upon the rushing river just above an iron bridge more useful than picturesque. The small rowan bushes on its crest were full of the nests of fieldfares, but by August the young birds had flown. Five salmon pools were visible from the seat overlooking the river; and the stream just below the house could be fished from either side without a boat, and nearly always held both salmon and sea-trout. It was necessary, however, to have a boat at hand and in readiness, for if a fish ran down stream he was sure to get through the bridge and break you, unless you could follow him and shoot the rapids. It was very seldom that after starting down stream they faced the heavy current and ran back again; but on one occasion a very big fish played Mrs. Lort Phillips this trick, going down through one arch, and turning sharp back through the next, with the inevitable result that the cast was cut against the pier, as it was quite impossible to force the boat up again against the rapids.

I never myself caught anything bigger than grilse in this upper bridge pool, but I lost what I imagine to have been a very heavy fish there on the afternoon of the last day of the season on the occasion of my second visit. It was especially disappointing, because I had killed forty-nine fish that year, and was making a great effort to make up the number to fifty. I had flogged every inch of the lower water in vain, and returning crestfallen to the house went down the steps and up to the top of the stream for a last effort. Half-way down the pool something took my Jock Scott deep down in the water, and ran out about ten yards of line with a heavy boring strain. There he stopped in deep water not twenty yards

I

above the bridge, and sulked motionless at the bottom, although I put all the strain upon him that rod and line would bear. Ole ran up and brought the boat down to where I stood upon slippery boulders, in readiness for me to jump on board the moment the fish showed any signs of running down stream. A little gallery—wife, children, and servants—collected above, and still the position continued the same; the salmon only just moved its head from side to side, and bore the strain unmoved. This stale-mate continued for some twenty minutes, then without further incident the fly came away and I was left lamenting. My record for the season was closed at the figure forty-nine! From the way the fish behaved I suspect him of having been an old red kipper who had spent some time in the water.

The great charm of the Sundal River was that nearly every pool could be fished from the bank. Long wading trousers were necessary, as the stream was so rapid that the water very soon got over stockings, when of course the plight of the wearer was much worse than if he had dispensed with any protection for his feet and legs. The bottom was usually shelving, and therefore the wading was not particularly dangerous, although in some places, notably in the lower bridge pool, and in the swift stream known as Carlton, the boulders under water were round and slippery, and a stout iron-shod landing handle was a great support. I used always to carry a landing-net, with the handle passed through a ring attached to my left shoulder by a stout leather thong. When I was using both hands to cast, I let it float in the stream behind me, and when my fly came round I had the support of the staff as I moved two short steps down the stream, as I usually did before making my next cast. In spite of all precautions an occasional stumble was unavoidable, but the worst result I ever experienced was the disagreeable sensation of having my wading trousers filled with water. I carried a gaff in my pocket ready to screw on to the socket, as I preferred when it was possible to land my own fish, whether sea-trout or salmon. My boatman, Ole Grodal, was not a great hand at gaffing, and he had been taught that it was right only to gaff fish in the head, which I have always considered an unnecessary refinement. I remember one occasion when I brought an exhausted salmon up to him under Leding high bank, when with a rapid stroke he severed the gut and let the fish go free. I was angry, and he was sad, but in a few moments I repented of my hot words and said, " Ole, you may have that fish for yourself." He rose to the occasion, thanked me, and asked whether he might have the fly too! As a boatman he was surpassingly good, and knew it.

Our method of fishing the water below the house was to start from the top in a boat, shoot the boiling rapids between the pools, landing at each, and wading from the bank, and after thoroughly exhausting the possibilities of the shore, returning to the boat to fish those parts of the pool which were inaccessible from the bank. It was a breathless experience at first to dash through the white water studded with wicked-looking boulders, but familiarity bred confidence. I soon looked forward to the moments when I reeled up my line and sat looking over the broad stern of the spade-shaped boat, as it danced through the white water guided by the strong and well-timed strokes of Ole's practised arms. The first rapids were just below the iron bridge; then after the lower bridge pool had been fished from the shore came a stretch of broken water, not very deep, down which we floated, Ole holding the boat now and then where it was worth while to make a cast on the chance of a sea-trout, till the next rapid carried us into Loken, a pool over a quarter of a mile in length, fringed on the right side going down stream by a fir wood above a long shelving bank of loose rounded pebbles with deep water running close to the shore. It was not difficult to fish somehow from the bank, but when making long casts it was advisable to look pretty often at the fly, as it was not an uncommon experience to break the barb off against a stone; and I know few things more provoking, when fish are scarce and rises few, than to see or feel a good one for just a second or two, and when the line loosens to discover that your Jock Scott or Silver Doctor was pointless and innocuous through your own fault.

On the opposite side of Loken the stream is shallow and the bottom shelves very gradually, so that one can wade far out and fish without risk of hitting anything harder than water behind; but only sea-trout lie there, and these, though plentiful, are not large. Next the boat shoots down round a bend and over another rapid, and stops at Leding high bank. Here the stream is not nearly so wide, and the deep water is on the left. Fish here carefully, wading cautiously over or between the great boulders, for the green depths are a favourite haunt of great fish, and it will be well to try a large fly to attract their attention. On the opposite shore the water runs more swiftly, and there are more pebbles and fewer rocks, so one can wade in further with safety. When I first knew this place it used to be an almost certain cast both for grilse and sea-trout, and I remember one occasion when I landed four silvery fellows of between five and eight pounds in about forty minutes. A native shepherd sat dangling his legs over the edge of the high moraine from which the pool takes its name, watching the sport with interest. In later years the fish for some reason, probably a change in the bed of the river, quite deserted that side and it became not worth fishing.

The next rapid took the boat down to Leding, where the river swept round in a great horse-shoe, under a wooded bank through which a glacier stream discharged its turbid waters into the lower part of a deep pool. It was not possible to do much here, either wading or from the bank, but the water required and rewarded careful fishing, for it always held big fish. Here it was that I found myself one day with a twenty-pounder running down stream at the end of a hundred yards of line, and the handle of my reel dropped off, rendering it impossible to wind up. For nearly half an hour I played the fish, drawing the slack through the rings as I brought him nearer, and so always keeping the line taut, but expecting at every rush that the line lying in coils at the bottom of the boat would kink and refuse to run through the rings, with the certain result of a break. Fortune favoured me in the end, and I got him, although I would not have given a penny piece for my chance when the accident happened. The days on which such difficulties and dangers are overcome are the red-letter days of sport.

The deep water just below the place where the glacier stream ran in was the scene of more than one curious adventure. Several times I hooked, and occasionally secured, big cannibal brown trout which had seized and attempted to swallow the silvery half-pound sea-trout which had taken my fly. Once on the same day I secured in this way two great ugly big-headed fish weighing between three and four pounds each, and only just failed to land a third, although he took the small fish I had hooked three several times, each time only relinquishing his hold with reluctance just as the landing-net was pushed towards him. Instances of such cannibal ferocity on the part of trout are not very unusual, but I was astonished to find the same thing happening so often, and always in the same place. A little reflection told me the reason. The river was wholly unsuited for brown trout of any size, as it ran over a stony and rocky bed which furnished little food for non-migratory fish. The big brown trout were no doubt bred in some of the lakes or streams on the high fjeld, and washed down by the glacier stream into an environment unsuited for their ravenous appetites, from which they had no means of escape. Half starved and ferocious they clustered round the mouth of the torrent which had wrought their downfall, waiting for the food, worms, small fish, slugs and other delicacies, which came down with the debris, preying upon parr and undersized sea-trout when able to catch them, and looking upon the hooked, and apparently wounded and slow moving fish as a

"Gift the gods provide you."

In order to test the accuracy of my theory I recommended the place to the young footman who had accompanied me from England, who loved to employ his leisure hours in whipping the tributary burns and streams for small trout, which he used proudly to lay out beside the silvery salmon, grilse, and sea-trout we generally brought in and arranged in a row by the steps at the back door, and provided him with a couple of artificial minnows, and gave him permission to use them from the bank at the mouth of the glacier stream. The experiment proved only too successful. He returned minus his cast and minnows, and with the middle joint of his rod broken. The big fish were there all right enough, and as hungry as ever, but they were too much for his skill and tackle, and he was no match for them in the swift broad stream.

I have no doubt that an experienced angler with proper appliances might have secured quite a big basket there by spinning, but it was not worth while to waste time over the experiment, as the ugly brutes were unfit for human food, and the river was full of "metal more attractive." I find among my old photographs snapshots of my wife and myself holding up the cannibal and its meal, but I fear that if I pray them in aid as evidence to the truth of my story, I shall be met by a quotation from Longfellow's poem of "Othere, the old sea captain," and his discovery of the North Cape—

> "And to the King of the Saxons
> In witness of his truth,
> Raising his noble head,
> He stretchèd his brown hand, and said,
> ' Behold this walrus tooth.' "

Strange things do occur in the experience of every

angler and tourist, and often, as in the case of the Abyssinian traveller Bruce, posterity has done tardy justice by accepting the accuracy of records doubted and ridiculed by contemporaries. I do not believe that fishermen as a race are more unreliable than any other class of men when they are recording their own experiences, but I am reminded of one instance which occurred on the upper part of the Hvilested beat where a fisherman gained great distinction as a phenomenal liar by telling a story which he himself absolutely believed, as he had been deceived by a practical joke.

He had come out to Norway as a guest of Lort Phillips, and was experiencing, I will not say enjoying, his initiation into the difficulties of casting at Stor pool, where, *crede experto,* it is by no means easy to get out a decent line without catching the boughs behind you, or breaking the bend of your hook against a rock. He was very hot-tempered, and his misfortunes and difficulties proved too much for his nerves. At last, when Ole had rescued his fly from the bushes for the tenth time or thereabouts, he deliberately broke his rod across his knee, pitched it —reel, line and all—into the deepest part of the pool, and turning upwards to the road walked sullenly homewards, leaving his attendant aghast and dumb with astonishment. The Norwegian race are poor, and count and appreciate every öre and kroner which they earn with such difficulty; and the deliberate sacrifice of so valuable an outfit was unthinkable. Ole repaired to his cottage and there rigged out an impromptu grappling apparatus with which he went back to the pool and recovered the jettisoned treasure. In a few minutes he had spliced together the broken joint, and was playing the fly over the likely parts of the stream, where in a short time he hooked and landed a nice grilse of some eight pounds. Then his sense of humour suggested to him a trick. He knocked the fish on the head, undid his impromptu splice, returned the whole "bag of tricks," including the fish, to the place from which he had fished it out, and sought an interview with his now cooled and repentant master. He was willing to admit that he had acted like a fool, "a d—d fool," and fell in readily with the suggestion that they should return to the scene of their morning adventure and see whether the rod could not be fished out, and the damage repaired. Again the grapnel was brought into use with the same success as before. It soon became apparent that some heavy body was attached to the end of the line, which to the amazement (apparently) of both master and man, materialised in the shape of a silvery fresh-run fish. "The rod," muttered the astonished angler, "does its work better out of my hands than in them." He fully believed that the line and fly had remained in the water and had attracted and captured the fish without human intervention, and often related to a delighted but incredulous audience how the rod and line he had flung into the water caught a fish for itself.

But this digression has detained us too long by Leding pool. However, we have not much further to go. Next we dance over a shallow, then pause at a long stream which in my first year was a certain cast for good-sized sea-trout, but which I found deserted on the occasion of subsequent visits; then a boiling torrent swept the boat round a bend into the last pool of the beat—Hol pool. The last rapid was an exceedingly difficult one to negotiate when the river was low, as boulders projected out of the white water in every direction, and I have known occasions when Ole preferred to leave me on the bank, and guide the boat down without the weight of a passenger in the stern, although he never refused to negotiate it himself. Hol was a deep pool full of large fish, and after all the parts accessible from the shore had been carefully fished, there still remained a deep stretch just above the next line of rapids between the wooded bank and a line of submerged rocks over which Ole used to linger lovingly with the boat, as it was the last and almost the best chance for a big fish. From this point it was about two and a half miles by road and field to the house, and I used either to hire a pony and trap from the farm, or stroll gently home as the spirit moved me. The farmer used as a matter of course to collect the boats early the next morning, and cart them back to their proper places at the tops of the pools. I sometimes passed them in my morning strolls, and have a snapshot of his pretty little children enjoying the opportunity for a ride in the boat.

I generally managed to get back for an eight o'clock dinner. The old stagers, who had spent more than a generation in Norway, used to shake their heads over my incorrigible habit of daylight fishing, and my neglect of the orthodox Scandinavian practice of turning night into day, and only fishing at all when the sun was off all the pools. I was well aware that I could have secured a much greater bag if I had followed their example in this respect, but I got quite sport enough to amuse me my first season, August 2 to September 14, giving a total bag of 50 salmon and grilse, and 480 sea-trout. It was a very dry year, and there was little snow left on the hills to replenish the pools in hot weather, but there was a remarkable run of sea-trout, more than on any subsequent occasion. Day fishing had the advantage, that it was possible to secure capital snapshots of various incidents in our fishing career, but my principal reason was that I could not keep off the water during so long a portion of the days of my delightful holiday. The call of the rushing stream was too alluring, and I had not the many-alternative pursuits, such as gardening, clearing paths, cutting down trees or undergrowth, which made the daylight hours all too short for such energetic habitués as Bertie Lort Phillips, my landlord, best of sportsmen and good fellows. Of course day fishing would have been absurd in the early part of the Norwegian season, June and July, when the sun is at his highest altitude, and his beams hottest; but the lower part of the Sundal River flows through a narrow valley, overshadowed by frowning precipices, and there are many places when in August and September the direct rays never fall on the pools. However, all said and done, I was a heretic and knew it, but preferred a packet of sandwiches by the water-side, a comfortable eight o'clock dinner with a well-earned appetite, and an arm-chair, a book and a chat by the fire, an early bed and a dreamless sleep, to a heavy meal in the afternoon and a night spent at the water-side. I am one of those fortunate people who generally close their eyes as soon as the head is on the pillow, and keep them closed while it remains there, and I found Hvilested during most of my sojourn thoroughly deserving of its name as "a place of rest." Curiously enough my first two or three nights in Norway formed an exception to this rule. Something in the air, or possibly the effects of the very rough voyage, kept me wide-awake in my bed to a quite unprecedented extent, and I only succeeded in breaking the spell of insomnia by taking a delightful trip with my wife to Trondhjem and back by stolkjaerre, a jaunt which occupied the greater part of a week. The scenery all the way was a dream of beauty, especially when the road turned to the north after Gjora, and mounted higher and higher up the hillside till the river threading its way through the deep gorge at the bottom became a mere glistening thread of silver.

We passed few travellers on our way, and only one acquaintance, Mr. Sargent the celebrated artist, who had crossed the North Sea by the same boat, and accompanied us to Sundalsören in the little coasting steamer, the *Ganger Rolf*, which used to ply from Christiansund up the fjord, calling at every hamlet on either bank with mails, goods and passengers. He was driving a carriole along the road above the beat of the river then occupied by Mr. Sandeman, and was doubtless at work upon the picture he afterwards exhibited of a schoolboy (happy lad) recumbent on a boulder with two or three glittering fish beside him. I think this picture figured in the catalogue of the New or Grosvenor Gallery under the title of "His First Salmon." The change of air and scene, and the not unpleasant jolting behind the dear little dun Norwegian ponies quite broke the spell, and during the rest of my time in Norway I was never again troubled by insomnia even in its most modified form. The lost week (from the fishing point of view) should be taken into account as having appreciably diminished the total bag for the season, as my two sons, whom I had left behind me with the whole beat at their disposal, were tempted away on the first of many fruitless expeditions after bears, by the news that a sheep had been killed by Bruin on one of the sheep farms above Grodal. Thus it happened that the water lay idle for six whole days, and those the most likely for salmon of our portion of the season, August and September, when the sea-trout fishing is at its best nearly all the time, but the run of large fish has pretty nearly ceased. As the days shorten the chance of rising a good salmon also diminishes, as those left in the pools grow darker and less eager for the fly. I believe a prawn appeals better to their jaded and depraved appetites, but personally I have always kept to the fly, although I have no doubt that it requires quite as much skill to manage a prawn properly, as to cast and play a Jock Scott.

It was an extraordinarily dry and hot season, and day by day the water became clearer and the pools and streams shallower. Towards the end I found that my daylight fishing could only be carried on successfully with the finest of tackle, and I sometimes tried the fine single gut casts I had been using in May and June on the little Mimram with a dry fly. Needless to say I was frequently broken, but the triumph when I succeeded in landing a really good fish made up for many disappointments.

Hvilested, alas, no longer crowns the eminence

above the bridge of the Sundal. Firstborn of Mrs. Lort Phillips' architectural genius, it was also the first to perish. On one of my latest visits to Norway I was bound for Todal, another of Lort Phillips' fishing quarters, and met on board the *Tasso* that distinguished ornament of the Civil Service, Wilson Fox, who was on his way to join a party of relations at Hvilested. We had reached Stavanger, and had all enjoyed the first few hours of land after a rather stormy passage. Our spirits were damped on our return to the vessel by the news which the Captain had heard from Messrs. Wilson's agent, that one of Lort Phillips' houses had been totally destroyed by fire on the previous day. There was still a chance that neither Wilson Fox nor myself might be personally affected by the calamity, but it was only just over an even chance—to be strictly accurate, five to two—as Lort Phillips has three other fishing quarters, Lilledal, Oxendal, and Alfheim; and if it was one of these we should still find a roof to shelter us when we arrived at our journey's end.

We passed rather a disturbed and anxious time until the arrival of the steamer at Bergen, where we learnt with certainty that it was poor Hvilested which had been totally destroyed by fire. The open hearths, the pride of their designer, had proved its undoing in the end. The tenants or their servants were not sufficiently alive to the danger of fire to which the dry painted and varnished buildings in Norway are liable, and had kept up a fire in the dining-room while absent from the house on a late fishing expedition. Probably a flying ember had ignited the floor; at any rate from some cause or another the whole structure was soon in a blaze, and in a few hours was with most of its contents reduced to a heap of smouldering ashes. The inmates worked hard to save what they could, but a good deal of quaint and curious old Norwegian furniture and carving, and the skins of two fine bears which had been killed in the valley were losses which no insurance could make up for. There is no real necessity to leave fires burning in Norway when you are out of the house. A handful of birch bark, and a few dry logs from the basket by the side of the hearth, will make a roaring blaze in a few minutes.

No one who has had the privilege of being the guest of Lort Phillips at any of his Norway homes will have forgotten the return from a late night on the river. Soup and coffee always stood in readiness on the hearth waiting to be heated up, and in a minute the portly form of the genial host would be seen stooping before the hearth, his jolly face lighted up by the blaze his bellows soon produced. How we relished the smoking soup and boiling coffee, and what Gargantuan meals we managed to consume in the small hours! Such heavy suppers, followed immediately by bed, might have been expected to produce nightmare and indigestion; no such results ever followed in Norway. These open fireplaces were a speciality of our host, and the hearthstone occupied a deep recess in a massive mantelpiece of soft porous stone brought down from the mountains, which had the property of retaining and dispensing heat long after the fire had burnt down. It was certainly a privilege particularly appreciated by Englishmen to get away from the ubiquitous stoves of porcelain or iron which fill the rooms of Scandinavia with a stuffy and smelly heat dear to the natives, and to enjoy the cheerful blaze which so vividly reminds us of home. With proper care and precaution no danger need be incurred, but where houses are constructed of resinous pine logs and planks the risk of fire must always be considerable, as the total destruction of many towns and villages, of which that of Aalsund is the latest example, brings home to every tourist and visitor. It does not, however, take long for a new Phœnix to arise to take the place of the old. Fortunately in the case of Hvilested the fishing party found another unoccupied and commodious house, formerly the summer quarters of a Mr. Cochran, within a hundred yards, and their holiday was scarcely interrupted by their unfortunate experience.

CHAPTER IX

HVILESTED. THE UPPER WATER

WE had all enjoyed our time together at Hvilested too thoroughly to stay long away. In 1903 we became a second time tenants of the well-loved house and fishings, and in the first week in August started from Hull in the old *Salmo*, a merry party. Most of us were not quite so merry soon after we left the shelter of the Humber. The North Sea was in its worst humour, and the attendance at meals, where the fiddles were at once in evidence, was very small indeed. I soon sought my berth, and lay low until we reached Stavanger.

What Messrs. Wilson saved in provisions they must have lost in crockery. Although not in a merry mood, I could not help laughing at a dialogue I heard just outside my cabin door before I dropped off to sleep. A bang, a crash that would have awakened the dead, and then the words, "Oh, stewardess, I hope you have not hurt yourself!" "Hurt myself!" replied the outraged maiden; "of course I have." However we reached Christiansund in good time, started at once by special steamer down the fjord, and found our boatmen, Ole Grodal and Peter Tangen, waiting for us with conveyances for ourselves and our luggage at about four o'clock in the morning.

Their smiling faces indicated that they were as glad to see us as we were to be back in our old quarters. I mentioned Ole and his skill as a boatman in the last chapter, but he deserves a fuller introduction. About fifty years of age, short, slightly hump-backed and thickset, he resembled one of the trolls of the mythology of his native land. He was a personage in the valley, and had, I believe, represented the district for a short time in the Storthing, but had soon tired of town life. He was the proud owner of a delightful little light-coloured dun pony, which used to take us very often to the top of our upper water in the smart stolkjaerre with blue reins which was our temporary property. He did not speak much English, and some of his sayings were quaint enough. In his youth he had been a famous climber, and as we started up the valley from Sundalsören he pointed with pride to a small patch of green on the side of the frowning precipice of Calcan on our right, and related how he had succeeded in reaching it alone out of a large search-party which had attempted the ascent, to rescue a small flock of sheep which had been enticed there by the fresh herbage, but could not make their way back. "How," asked I, "did you get the sheep off when you got there?" He replied, "I let them down by a piece of string."

In spite of his ungainly figure he excelled all his juniors in the Spring dance, and was ready to stay out all night if required, or to turn his hand to any work, from chopping wood to gardening. He took possession of me from the first, and was very jealous if I allowed myself to be accompanied by any other attendant. At first he was inclined to dictate to me where and when I should fish, and to look with ill-veiled contempt at any flies in my box of which he had no previous experience. However, he soon learnt who was master, and I found him a most efficient and zealous boatman and guide, although not a first-rate gaffer. He was possessed of the strange and unaccountable power of water-finding. I have seen the divining-rod twist almost out of his hand as he passed over a subterranean stream. Many, I know, scoff at this phenomenon, and attribute the movements of the twig to imposture, but I myself cannot doubt that there is some strange natural force which compels the motions of the hazel fork in certain hands. Although rather short-sighted, he was extraordinarily clever at seeing fish in the pools.

After a cup of coffee I was glad to turn in for a little, although it was already broad daylight. The journey had been long and tiring, and I had not been able to get much sleep in the cabin of the little steamer which brought our party down the fjord. My son was not so pusillanimous. He was hard at work unstrapping the box of rods, and getting out his reel and tackle long before I had finished my coffee, and was off up stream for Stor pool in a few minutes. His energy was rewarded, for he returned when we were at breakfast, soon after eleven, with a nice silvery fish of about twelve pounds, reporting that the water was in very good order, and that he had risen other two fish. After this encouraging example it was not very long before I too was ready for the fray, ordered the pony to be harnessed while I put my rod together, and soon found myself near the top of the water making my first cast.

The first cast of the year! What fisherman will not understand and sympathise with my feelings? London, its delights and its worries, only four days off in reality, seemed to belong to another age and another world. In front of me was the pool, and just behind me the great rock almost as high as a house beside which I had so often lunched while resting the cast. I gazed hungrily at the eddy where I hooked and lost the last fish of the season two years before. How delightful was the feeling of the first rush of strong water as I stepped into the river from the shelving bed of shingle, let out my line, and cast my fly into the deep strong stream just below white water breaking over a great submerged rock.

I waded down to the bottom of the pool without rising a fish, but what did that matter? The first run of the line through the rings, as one lets it out in successive lengths, the corncrake melody of the reel, the fall of the cast upon the water straight and true, showing that the right hand (not to mention the left) has not forgotten its cunning; after a twelvemonth's fast all these were delights enough without the breathless excitement of the sudden tightening of the line, or the impetuous rush of a hooked salmon. I do not include in this catalogue of delights the sight of the rising fish coming at the fly, as in this river it was the rarest possible thing to see a salmon at all before the sudden check and pull notified that you had hooked one. The rise of a trout was more perceptible and obvious, and was usually followed by a desperate short flurry on the surface before the point of the rod could be raised sufficiently upright to bring you upon terms with him. The sea-trout which escape usually do so either in the first or the last ten seconds of the struggle. The final part of this statement looks like an Irish Bull or a truism, but my meaning, perhaps imperfectly expressed, is that they get off either almost immediately or within ten seconds of the time when, unless the hold gave way, they would be safe in the landing-net. You very seldom lose one while running fairly under water, except from some defect of the cast or hook, unless he manages to get out of the pool and to shoot a rapid.

When Ole joined me with the boat, I determined to get on board and try a different fly over the pool, as the water was high, and some likely places were too far off to be reached by wading. Even the part I had already fished was well worth another try. We had hardly started when my boatman's sharp eye caught sight of something barely covered by the water, just past the edge of the shingle off which we had pushed the boat. He pointed it out to me; it was a large salmon, lying on its side, apparently dead. It seemed to me most remarkable that I had not observed it before, as it was close to the very spot from which I had started to wade, but probably the reason I had missed seeing it was the same which prevented Tilburina in the "Critic" from seeing the British Fleet—it was "not then in sight." We at once pushed back the boat and Ole got out to investigate, but when he took hold of the fish it showed that it was still alive by floundering and endeavouring to escape into the deep water; however, it was too sick to be able to swim away, and a knock on the head with a stone speedily put it out of its misery. It proved to be a fine salmon, and turned the scale at 23 lb. On examining it carefully we found a wound on its head and a mark in the upper jaw, and conjectured that although its end was so inglorious, these honourable wounds must have been received in a desperate battle with some brother angler who had lost it in the moment of victory. The mark in the mouth was without doubt that of a hook; the wound near the eye had almost certainly been made with a gaff.

It was very singular that this dying fish should have been stranded at my feet, but it was even more remarkable that two days later I should have met the man who lost it, and heard from his lips the full details of the fight. I might even have restored him his salmon had I not handed it over as a deodand to the old mistress of the farm. On Wednesday morning Frank Gunnis, a brother-in-law of Lort Phillips, who had been paying him a visit at Hvilested before my arrival, had moved off with him to his mountain home, Alfheim, on the high fjeld. He stopped to lunch with us when on his way down the valley to join the steamer for England. After our first greeting conversation naturally turned on sport, and we began to exchange experiences. "Ah!" he said, with a sigh, "I had a terrible misfortune last Friday. On my way up the valley I met the lessee of the Musjerd beat, who gave me the run of his water for the next day, the last of his tenancy. I hooked a big fish in the top pool, had it on for quite two hours, and after a desperate fight in the strong water at last succeeded in bringing it to the side. My fisherman gaffed it and was lifting it up the bank when it fell off the point and rolled back into the water and escaped. Was there ever such 'a slip between the cup and the lip'?"

The whole story was now complete. The fish made his escape at about three o'clock on Friday afternoon, and from that time until about midday on Monday must have been gradually carried down some ten miles of water, getting weaker and weaker as he was forced through the succession of rapids which bounded the various pools, to be stranded eventually in a dying condition at the very feet of the occupant of the house from which its original captor had so recently departed. To supply a reason for the miracle, we ought to have been in a starving condition, and saved at our last gasp by the opportune arrival of the providential supply; but for those who are satisfied with fish diet such privation is rare in Norway, even when sport is at its worst. Some weary of fish at every meal, but I was always able to relish such fare, giving a preference to the delicate flavoured sea-trout over the richer flesh of salmon. But to appreciate sea-trout thoroughly, they should be eaten in picnic fashion on the bank just after they have been taken out of the water. What meals I recall by Irish loughs and Scotch and Scandinavian rivers! Cook your fish in paper on ashes or a hot stone, toast them on juniper forks, or boil them in a huge pot with plenty of salt, and you will find them delicious.

The scene of this remarkable incident was a very deep pool situated at an angle of the river between two rapid streams, where an immense round cauldron had been scooped out under the opposite bank. The stream below widened into the long pool Fladvad, which generally held salmon, but I fancy that the largest fish usually travelled as far as the sheltered deeps I have just described. Just at the close of my former visit I had a desperate encounter with a salmon which I hooked there on a cast of the finest natural gut such as is generally only used for dry-fly fishing. We had had a long spell of extraordinarily hot and fine weather, and the river had shrunk till the water was so fine and clear that the fish shied hopelessly at salmon or sea-trout casts. Desperate diseases need desperate remedies, and my boldness was not altogether unjustified, although I was often broken. Even the small sea-trout of one to two pounds' weight had a good chance for their lives, and I had to be very careful in regulating the amount of strain to put on a hooked fish, and to avoid striking too hard at a rising one.

On the morning of which I write I had been fairly successful, and was beginning to gain confidence. Something took my fly, an Alexandra, which I had found attractive under the circumstances, although I never found it much good for sea-trout and salmon under normal conditions. The strain, and the way in which the fish hugged the deep water, soon convinced me that I had hooked a salmon, and from the first I had very little hope of landing him. However all went well for more than half an hour; the fish began to show signs of exhaustion, and at last turned on its side, its broad tail breaking the water. I unscrewed my landing-net from the handle, and substituted a gaff, and very cautiously towed the fish towards a still place under the flat rock near the bottom on which I had taken my stand. The fish was almost within striking distance, and I had begun to stretch out my arm with gaff in hand when the gut parted about a foot above the fly, and the spent giant after lying still for a moment rolled slowly back into the depths. The frayed edges of the gut showed that it had been rubbed against a submerged rock, and the cast would not bear the strain of the dead pull. I was beaten! but I think I enjoyed that unsuccessful fight more than many victories.

"Does it never rain in Norway, Ole?" I asked that evening as I got into the cart at Fladvad farm. I think there was just the suspicion of a smile on his wrinkled face as he answered "Sometimes." There came a day in the year of which I am writing when I was to learn what could happen when the floodgates of heaven were opened. On the previous afternoon I had been fishing the long pool at Fladvad full of hope, as I knew that it was full of sea-trout, and it looked in splendid order. I had learnt by experience that it was about the best trout water in the whole of the Sundal. Deep under the south bank on the road side, and sloping gradually from a shingle bank opposite, it had only two faults. The first was that it was somewhat monotonous, as it took quite an hour and a half to fish over, and looked very much the same all the way, although experience proved that fish had their favourite spots. The second drawback was that although it was easy wading and the bottom fairly smooth with a gradual slope, the fisherman got so far out into the stream that it was fatiguing as well as a waste of time to have to wade out and deposit one's fish on the bank every time one was caught, which was often every few minutes. For this reason I invented and adopted what my sons christened my

"Marsupial pouch." This consisted of a stout pocket of net-work buttoned to the front of my wading trousers into which I often deposited as many as half a dozen fish before wading to the shore. Although it was usually well under water, the water ran through the meshes without impeding my progress. However on this occasion the "Marsupial pouch" was not required. Cast after cast was fruitless; in vain I changed the fly over and over again, and tried Greenwells, Blue, Black, and Silver Doctors, Jock Scotts, Dusty Millers, and then smaller patterns such as Green and Drake, and Red and Teal. All was in vain, although the sky looked propitious and the water perfect the fish would not move, and I began to suspect the reason. There is no better barometer than your trout, and it seemed likely that "coming events" had "cast their shadows before," and that we were in for something exceptional in the way of storms.

Heavy clouds were already beginning to gather in the west and to roll up the valley when we started on our homeward journey. The storm broke just after we reached home, and as we smoked our last pipes before turning in, we could still hear heavy rain pattering against the window of the smoking-room.

Before morning I had discovered why Noah, before the art of caulking decks had reached its present perfection, built his ark of such an apparently inconvenient and unseaworthy shape, and with a tiled and slanting roof. I was sleeping very sound after the day's exertions, when in the dead of night—to be accurate it was three in the morning—a hand was laid upon my shoulders and I awoke with a start. It was not burglars or ghosts—it was only my wife—who had been aroused by a stream of water suddenly descending upon her face and pillow. In less than a minute a similar cascade was pouring down on my head, and I shouted for a basin, which was given me, and afforded some temporary protection, but a short reflection convinced me, even in my semi-somnolent condition, that I could not go to sleep holding a basin over my face, and that some other expedient must be devised to secure a dry night's rest. Evidently our pillows were in a position of danger, and our first idea, good as far as it went, was to push the bed a little further into the room and transpose our heads to the position usually occupied by our feet. But when we had moved the bolster, and pushed the heavy piece of furniture nearly into the centre of the room, we found that we had only opened another leak in the roof, and that more streams were pouring down upon us.

At this point, and only just in time, we bethought ourselves of the perilous position of the clothes we had taken off, and took steps to remove them from the drip that had just begun to fall upon them, and to put them away in a place of safety. All this time we could hear perfect torrents of water splashing down upon the roof, and dashing against the windows, while two or three loud peals of thunder indicated that the tempest included an electrical as well as an atmospherical disturbance. I had been dead sleepy, but now began to awake to the position. At first I felt very cross, but fortunately a saving sense of humour came to my rescue, and relieved me of any further irritation at the discomforts of my rude awakening, I began to laugh out loud as the comical side of the situation struck me, and absolute and intense amusement, to the exclusion of any feeling of annoyance, was my condition for the rest of my waking moments.

Baths and basins were placed under the most prominent leaks: some of the deepest pools of water were mopped up with our sponges and towels, and we began to consider what was best to be done for the remainder of the night. Evidently the gutters had been stopped, or were unequal to carrying away such an unusual volume of water; but the suggestion of rousing the servants, and sending them on to the roof was only made to be rejected. Common humanity revolted at such an idea, and while the deluge lasted the effect of any such remedial measures could be only temporary. My wife suggested that we should go downstairs and camp in the drawing-room, but I moved an amendment that we should remove the sheets and sleep in blankets. I had heard the most dreadful accounts of the danger of sleeping in damp sheets, and I believe that my suggestion showed some glimmerings of common sense. As I set to work to carry out my plan, my wife remembered that there was a small camp-bed in my dressing-room; and going on a voyage of discovery found that it was in a dry place, and took refuge there for the remainder of the night, while I rolled myself up in both blankets. For a time I lay awake chuckling, and as I heard the drip, drip of the water into the hip bath which had been placed to catch it, I thought of some old story I had heard of a mediæval form of torture by letting a drop of water fall from a height at intervals on the head of a criminal or suspect. Gradually the sound of many waters mingled with my dreams, then I lost all consciousness and slept soundly, until the housemaid coming in to call us in the morning, was surprised to find me alone and all the furniture in confusion. Fortunately, although the roof leaked in many places, no others of the party had been quite washed out of bed. Although rain had fallen all through the night, the tropical deluge had been only temporary; but I did not hurry to get up. I felt pretty well convinced that for the first time in my Norwegian experiences, fishing would be impracticable even in the shallows and backwaters, so I was content for once to be almost the last at the breakfast-table.

The roof of our house, like that of most of the buildings in Norway, was constructed of birch bark spread over planks, and covered with turf on which long grass grows, giving it a curious and unshaven appearance. The year before, after the long drought, we had been led to expect some leakage, if rain came, from the natural shrinkage of the timber caused by the heat; but there had been sufficient wet this autumn to obviate any exceptional risk of that description. The cause of our ducking was the extraordinary and almost unprecedented volume of water which fell in a short time, which no ordinary gutter could be expected to carry away. I have little doubt that our discomfort was shared by the inmates of many of the farms and dwellings in the district. My first thought was a feeling of thankfulness that the big spate had come on a Saturday, and that there were forty-eight hours for the river to clear and fall before the next "lawful" fishing day. This time at least the Scotch gillie's complaint that the best fishing days were "aye sookit up by the Sabbath" could not reasonably be urged.

Next morning the magnificent river was indeed a sight to gaze upon with admiration and wonder. A swollen torrent dashed against the stone piers of the cast-iron girder bridge with a violence that made us thankful that they were substantial and solid. The stream widened over every backwater and shingle bed, and the top of a solitary bush indicated the spot where under normal conditions a considerable island stands high above a rapid. The water swept over bushes, and half-way up the stems of alders; and the fishing platform between the two rocks at Stran pool, usually many feet above the surface, was completely submerged.

Above more than a mile of the whole river was a foaming mass of white water, while at the bend a little higher up it had completely submerged one rapid, and formed a great lake opposite to Fladvad farm. Down the sides of the mountains, whose tops were white with fresh-fallen snow, hundreds—I might almost say thousands—of miniature cataracts dashed down scarred channels, while the seven or eight permanent cascades fed by glaciers or snowfields, were swollen into large and conspicuous waterfalls. Of course I immediately set to work to put marks by which to ascertain the rise and fall of the water; but although there was little rainfall after the morning, the river continued to wax until past two o'clock when only a few inches of the bough, nearly four feet long, which I had stuck into the grass at high-water mark after breakfast, were visible above the grey water. My fishermen had been out all night looking after the boats, and it was lucky that they had succeeded in dragging them up high and dry; otherwise they would doubtless all have been washed away, as ordinary chains could not have resisted the force of the current.

No wonder the fish would not rise on Saturday!

The farm at Fladvad, a few hundred yards above the long pool, was occupied by a dear old woman who looked after the primitive telephone exchange of the district. We used to leave our cart by the *stabbur* or byre, of this farm, and to turn the pony out in the adjacent fields. Naturally we repaid this hospitality by leaving a goodly supply of fish when we returned with full baskets. This unfortunately aroused the gratitude of the recipient, who adopted a method of showing it which after a time became inconvenient. Every time we fished the upper water she used to come down to the bank about five o'clock, accompanied by a small boy bearing a basket, and signal to us. Generally we were discovered above our waists in water fishing away for dear life, with Ole watching from the shingle. The boat was tied up near the bottom of the pool, and we had to take a weary walk, waste much valuable time, and disturb a lot of the best water by rowing over it, before we could get across. The basket was found to contain hot coffee, always delicious in Norway, with cups and saucers, a clean napkin, and scones, fladbrod, and bread and butter. It was undeniably refreshing, and at first we were duly grateful, and properly appreciated the delicate attention, but when we found that the picnic became an invariable practice we would have given anything to be able to stop it without hurting poor Elie Fladvad's feelings. The "interval for refreshment" occupied about an hour of valuable time at the very best part of the afternoon, and we suspected that the "widow's mite" so generously proffered unnecessarily consumed a good deal of her substance, and put her to considerable trouble. However, we never could hit on any way to stop the unwelcome courtesy without seeming churlish, and I am glad to say we kept up the appearance of surprise and delight, and greeted our "benefactor" with grateful smiles to the end of our stay.

What days and nights we spent, and what numbers of fish we caught in that inexhaustible pool. Two long evenings spent there stand out in my recollection as among the most delightful of my fishing experiences. Before me I have a photograph of the catch we made on the first of these occasions, 24th July 1906, or rather of a portion of the catch, for unless my memory deceives me we left as usual a goodly number at the farm. It portrays Lort Phillips in the centre, Major Darby Griffith on the right, and myself on the left, sitting with rods, gaff, and net behind thirteen fish laid out on a board at our feet. The largest trout, caught by Lort Phillips, weighed nearly twelve pounds; and referring to my diary I find that I got one of nine pounds, one of six and a half, and another of four. It would be tedious to recall all the details, but the masterly way in which Lort Phillips landed his twelve-pounder in the small hours is worth putting upon paper. It was past 2 A.M.; we had done enough for honour and glory, and Darby Griffith and I were already in the boat about to walk to the

A NIGHT'S CATCH

farm and harness the pony, when we saw that our host had hooked something out of the common near the bottom of the pool. He was on the bank running for all he was worth, his reel screaming and his rod bent double. Of course we at once jumped out and followed to see the fun. Once there was a short check and breathing space, but only for a moment, for five minutes later the gallant fish, making light of all the strain put upon him, had actually reached the foaming white water at the bend just above an impracticable rapid. It seemed "all Lombard Street to a China orange" that he would escape, and take the whole "bag of tricks" with him—reel, line, backing, cast, and the "saxpenny flee"—but the gallant sportsman who had hold of him did not abandon hope. He said that there was still just a chance of coaxing him into a small eddy on the right, which might bring him back into the long still backwater which formed the hinder boundary of the bank of shingle on which we stood. Eagerly we watched while a mixture of gentle persuasion and intelligent pressure brought the big fish round, and all breathed again as he sailed about in the perfectly still water. The first time he came within arm's-length Gunder got the net under him, but he was too big for it, and flopped heavily out to have another run for his life. Five minutes more exhausted his strength, and he was towed in and gaffed.

I caught my nine-pounder quite early the same evening more than half a mile higher up in the long rapid stream at the very top of our water where we marched with Stor Fahle, and he certainly gave me an exciting time in the strong water on my little eleven-foot rod. I hooked him on a small double-hooked green fly when I had waded about a third of the way down the pool, and the whole of my thirty yards of line, and a goodly proportion of the backing as well, was off the reel in a moment. I put on all the strain the little red and fine tackle would bear, and followed as quickly as I could, edging towards the bank, which was steep and covered with thick bushes, but the fish soon had put quite 150 yards between us, and continued to dash down stream as if nothing would stop him. It looked as if I should not be able to prevent his getting over the rapids at the bottom, but at last I began to get some control over him and managed to recover fifty yards of backing. By this time it was clear that he was exceptionally heavy, and although I always prefer to land my own fish when possible, I was not ashamed to shout for assistance. Gunder, who was rowing the boat near the top of the pool, brought it to the side, landed, and took my gaff. The fish caught sight of him, and made another violent rush which brought him to the very edge of the foss. It was his last effort. I just succeeded in turning him, and he came to the top of the water and floated almost motionless upon his side. It was quite twenty minutes from the time he was hooked when Gunder got the gaff into him, and deposited him gasping on the stones, a beautiful silvery fellow just fresh from the sea. Although it was not by any means a warm evening, the perspiration was streaming down my face by the time the struggle was over.

One fight with a fish is very like another, at least upon paper, so I will spare further details of that grand night's sport. It became very dark before we left off, and when my fly broke off in my net just after landing my second largest fish, I had great difficulty in selecting and putting on another. Ole stood by me, striking match after match, and I worked by the feeble glow of their light. My knife slipped out of my hand, and I stood perfectly still while a careful search was made round my feet, but it could not be found, and we erected a small pillar of stones on the spot, intending to make another search by daylight. This turned out not to be necessary, as when I took off my heavy waders I discovered the missing article in the right leg just below my knee.

I had a long and weary tramp in waders that night. Having a slight cold, I started to walk homewards along the road before the pony was caught. It so turned out that there was a difficulty in catching him, and I had nearly reached Hvilested before I heard the welcome sound of wheels. The eastern sky was red with the first streaks of dawn before we sat down to a hearty meal of hot soup, coffee, and meats of various kinds by the glow of the blazing wood fire my host speedily kindled. We determined, however, that we would not go fasting so long in future, and three or four nights afterwards, when we had another long and excellent six hours' sport on the same water, we started armed with a huge fish kettle, salt, buttered scones, and biscuits, and picnicked in the small hours on the bank. We boiled three good-sized trout, but there was very little left when we and our attendants had finished our meal. The firm, crisp, flaky flesh would have tempted more fastidious appetites.

The upper water could not be fished, as the lower

was, by shooting the rapids in a boat, and getting out at each pool. Above Stor Pool, a famous cast for large fish, and below Kongen Pool, the way was barred by solidly constructed salmon traps made of pine logs which would have interposed impassable barriers even if the rapids had been practicable for boats, which was not the case. These traps were made on the principle of the lobster pot, with V-shaped entrances through which salmon could ascend but not return. When I was on the Sundal the lawful season for netting or trapping was over, and they were no longer in use, but I was informed that fish which escaped after being hooked in the early part of the season were nearly always caught in the salmon trap next above on the following night, often with the fly still in their jaws. The tenants of the rod fishings used to give a reward of a kroner for every fly returned to them, and were thus able to ascertain the precise weights of many of the fish they lost, which did not always come up to the estimate of their size formed at the moment of parting. The custom of giving a kroner reward for a lost fly was so well known in the valley that it was accounted a huge joke when the coin was offered to a "soeter pige" in the upper valley, who brought us back a Zulu which had been broken off in the hide of an inquisitive black and white heifer when we were fishing one of the lakes.

Norway will never lose its charms for me; I love its mountains, streams, and lakes, and above all I love its people. Three "Ole's"—their name is legion in Scandinavia—have been my friends and comrades on different beats in the Sundal valley. They all differed exceedingly in appearance and temperament, but all

LOW WATER ABOVE STOR POOL: SALMON TRAPS

HVILESTED. THE UPPER WATER

three were the best of sportsmen and the most genial of companions, eager to show sport, and ready for work at any hour of the day or night. My benison upon them, and upon all the simple, industrious, and kindly inhabitants of "Gammel Norge."

CHAPTER X

TODAL AND LILLEDAL. 1903

ANOTHER delightful place which I occupied with my family one autumn, and afterwards visited as the guest of Lort Phillips, was Todal, situated in a most lovely valley upon the upper branch of the long fjord which runs up from Christiansund to the north-west of Hvilested, from which it can be easily reached by pedestrians in a short day by crossing the mountain, a lovely walk over the high fjeld by glaciers and snow-clad peaks. Both places belong to the same owner, and there is telephonic communication between them. When my family occupied Hvilested my sons walked across to pay a visit, taking their guns, and shooting ryper on the way. Engrossed by their sport and novel surroundings, they miscalculated the time necessary for the transit, and darkness had set in while they were still on the high tops. Lort Phillips, who was expecting them, telephoned to us to inquire whether they had started, and seemed somewhat perturbed when he heard that they were benighted on unfamiliar ground. He assured us that they had probably taken refuge for the night in some mountain sœter; but there was anxiety in his tone, and it would have been greater had he known that they were at that moment making a bee-line down the hill towards the guiding lights of his house, a somewhat risky perform-

TODAI.

TODAL AND LILLEDAL

ance, although the slopes on the Todal side are far more gradual than the grim precipice which rises like two walls above the lower part of the Sundal valley. It was nearly midnight before we received a welcome telephonic message announcing their arrival, and we afterwards learnt that they had had to negotiate some nasty ground, and found themselves more than once in rather tight places during their foolhardy descent. On another occasion during my tenancy of Todal, I found a party of five unexpected guests camped in the sitting-rooms when I came down for my breakfast, Lort Phillips and his party having crossed by the regular track, and broken in through the windows in the small hours of the night.

Todal is certainly an ideal place in which to spend an autumn holiday. The house, designed by the same female architect, was an improvement upon Hvilested, with bath-room, and an icehouse outside with a bachelor's room over it. The fishing was certainly not so productive as the lower reaches of the Sundal, but the little river held in good seasons a fair number of salmon and sea-trout, and no boat was required. Many of the pools were artificial, designed by their owner, and made in the winter months by means of barriers formed of boulders, placed upon the ice, and deposited in their proper places when the thaw came in the spring. About two miles above the house a thundering foss of great beauty cleft its way through the rocks, making a barrier which no fish could ascend, and about the same distance below, the river discharges its waters into the beautiful fjords close to a pier, just opposite to a small heathery island where eider-ducks and other waterfowl nest in the spring. The sea-fishing was excellent, and with boating expeditions made a welcome diversion when the river was not in order, or the sun too bright for day fishing. Flounder, whiting, and rock cod abounded, and sometimes the large sea-trout that cruised round the mouth of the river waiting for a spate to carry them up could be prevailed upon to take a spinning bait in the salt water.

The house occupied a commanding position on a plateau overlooking the stream, with a view of the two pools above and below a stone bridge. A garden with many kinds of flowers stretched to the west of the verandah, which extended all round the building. In one of the beds foxgloves, both white and pink, had been sown, and flourished wonderfully, attaining a height of eight or ten feet. The wooded sides of the hills sloped up gradually to the high fjeld, and there were many paths by which pedestrians could reach the numerous lakes which filled the hollows of the upper valleys, and enjoy matchless views over the blue waters of the fjord. The sense of being shut in, which was almost the only drawback to complete bliss on the lower reaches of the Sundal, did not exist here. Although an enthusiastic fisherman has little time to spare for mountain rambles during his short autumn season, it is always a pleasure to feel that it is open to those who wish to do so to scale the heights, and there was something forbidding as well as grand in the frowning ramparts of rock which walled in the valley above Sundalsören. "Truly the light is sweet, and a pleasant thing it is to behold the sun," even if its direct rays falling upon your salmon pools delay your sport for a time.

A LARGE TODAL FOXGLOVE

PART OF A LARGE TODAL FAMILY

Small as the river is, it holds a fair number of large salmon, which run up to a weight of thirty pounds. Mrs. Lort Phillips succeeded in landing one of twenty-six pounds on her little ten-foot Hardy trout-rod, after an Homeric struggle lasting over two hours. On both occasions of my visits to Todal I was, as usual, unfortunate with the monsters. Two at least I hooked, but both escaped; the one through my own carelessness in neglecting to overhaul my tackle before use, the second through the latent defect of the hook upon which my flies had been tied. A giant took my fly at the head of Long Pool, and when he was boring steadily down stream, after a rush which took out more than a hundred yards of line and backing, snapped the rotten hemp as easily as Samson broke his bonds. It was an awful moment! I sat cheerless and forlorn, snapping the remaining backing with so slight a strain as to prove its utter worthlessness; but if my example saves one brother angler from using a reel which has been put away for the winter without thoroughly testing every inch of line, I shall not have suffered in vain. Perhaps the fish was not so enormous as my regretful meditations paint him, but that long steady heavy boring rush down stream was not the effort of a dwarf or weakling. I never saw him, but the twenty-pounder I lost in Lax Stone Pool, the narrow rocky pool just below the point where the river leaves the road above the bridge, showed himself often enough. He was coming to the gaff, beaten and wearied out, when the hold gave way, and the examination—alas! not "post-mortem"—revealed that both the double hooks which had been well imbedded in his upper jaw had yielded to the strain, and completely straightened. They proved to be as ill-tempered as I was after the calamity!

Todal was in the centre of a district more frequented by bears than any other which I have occupied when in Norway. I never myself saw one, although I came upon a fresh track when crossing the hill to Opdal; but frequently sheep were killed by them in the neighbourhood while we were in residence, and my sons were thereby tempted to forsake the river for a time and sleep out by the "kill," always without results. There was a place on the road to the little Norwegian church where the path skirted a rather precipitous wooded bank. At this spot a workman returning to his home one evening rather merry, saw, as he thought, another man leave the road and hide, and heard a rustling in the bushes beneath him. Jumping to the conclusion that this was one of his boon companions intending to play him a trick, he lurched heavily over and rolled down the bank, to find himself almost on the top of a big bear! Fortunately Bruin was as much startled and alarmed as his rash assailant, and made tracks for the mountain in double quick time without resenting the unwarrantable intrusion, while Peder ran home along the road sobered by fright, and determined in future to look before he leaped. When my friend Sir Bargrave Deane was tenant of Todal, a bear killed a sheep near a sœter not three miles distant from the house, and the farmer, knowing his reputation as a rifle shot, sent at once to ask him to come and watch for it. He was much tempted by the offer, but a too wise friend who was his guest for the fishing, and had spent many seasons in Norway, dissuaded him, as I should have

TODAL AND LILLEDAL

done myself, from wasting his time on such a forlorn hope. Although my sons had many times slept out on the fjeld, lured away from the river by similar messages, they had never got a shot at a bear, or even a glimpse at one. However, on this occasion the wise men were wrong, for that night the bear came straight back to the dead sheep within fifty yards of the farmer's son who was watching with his military rifle, and fell an easy victim.

On another occasion a little further up the valley a dark-coloured bull had strayed, and a party went in search of him. They had not got very far when they spied what they imagined to be the truant in an open glade. They surrounded the spot, but when they came to close quarters found themselves face to face with a big brown bear, and having no rifles with them were obliged to let him alone. In the City such a confusion between bulls and bears might have led to more disastrous results. Had they carried glasses, as Scotch mountaineers generally do, they would certainly have got an easy shot, but in Norway even the professional reindeer hunters very seldom use them.

Not far from Sundalsören a narrow ledge some 3000 feet above the sea forms the only passage between two wooded valleys, and here the natives constructed a rough bear-trap by obstructing the passage with a thick fence of bushes, leaving only a small hole, round which they put a rough snare of rope. When my sons visited this spot on one of their wild-goose chases, they found the body of a bear which had been caught in the snare suspended by the rope over the precipice; but it had been there a long time, probably a month or more, the skin was useless, and the only available trophies were the teeth and claws. The natives had not had sufficient faith in their contrivance to take the trouble to pay periodical visits to the spot.

This was the only occasion upon which any of my party encountered a bear in the flesh, dead or alive. Lort Phillips, however, has often described to me an occasion when, accompanied by a friend who has since earned a great reputation as a big game shot, he got quite close to a very fine specimen; but as they were only out to visit the glacier above Leding Pool they were unarmed. He was accompanied by two black spaniels which had just been chasing sheep. He had called them to heel and rated them, when they broke from him again. Following them over the sky-line he came upon a spectacle which he has never forgotten. On the edge of the glacier, set off by the glistening ice and snow, an enormous bear stood erect, the dogs baying him; and he was so occupied with his tormentors that he allowed the two spectators to approach within twenty yards. The wind was right, and bears are very short-sighted, so it was not until Lort Phillips whistled, afraid that his dogs might be injured, that the bear took alarm, and dropping on all-fours proceeded in an easy lolloping gallop up the steep snow-slope on the face of the opposite hill. His companion was so impressed with the sight that he insisted on returning to fetch rifles; but although the party did the ascent and descent in record time, and returned to the glacier utterly exhausted, they saw nothing more of the bear, which had doubtless put ten or fifteen miles between himself and his pursuers during the interval.

TODAL AND LILLEDAL

Todal possessed one distinct advantage over most of my other holiday quarters in Norway; there was excellent brown-trout fishing in the higher reaches of the stream, where it flowed through two fairly flat valleys bounded by meadows and woods. It was a delightful change when the salmon pools were not in order to charter a little stolkjaerre with a particularly quiet pony, and drive up to Kaarvand for a picnic and a day among the trout. These did not run very large, but were free risers and plucky fighters; and there were plenty averaging a little over half a pound, while one got a certain number of pounders. One charm of the sport was that there were many places where it was feasible to fish with a dry fly, though truth compels me to admit that the trout had not been educated up to the standard of their brothers in the Test or Mimram, and were not particular about "drag," or fastidious as to the precise shade of insect offered to them. Indeed, I am not sure that a "chuck and chance it" angler who understood his business would not have been quite as successful as any of my party, but he would have lost the pleasure of the stalking and engaging each particular fish, and the delight of dropping the fly lightly just in the right place, and seeing the trout rise to take it. The water was as clear and translucent as any Hampshire chalk stream, and although there were no weed banks to form a refuge for the hooked trout, there were plenty of other obstacles—sunken snags, branches, roots, and whole trees washed into the water, which furnished many an exciting moment. As I waded through the stream, carefully testing the depth with the stout iron-shod handle of my landing-net, there were endless objects of interest to delight the eye. The banks were carpeted with lovely ferns, berries, and flowers; the lovely oak and beech ferns showing their brilliant green in the interstices of the moss-clad boulders. Wild ducks and mergansers rose from the long pools, lively small birds, tits, mountain finches, and woodpeckers flitted or climbed through and over alders, birches, and pines; and on many shelving banks of sand or alluvial soil—I will not insult it by giving it the name of mud—might be traced the broad impressions of the splay feet of the otter. I never was fortunate enough to catch sight of my four-footed rival, but it is given to few but very early risers to watch his graceful gambols, or to see him emerge from a pool with a captured fish. The sloping heath-clad banks had the reputation of being a favourite haunt of snakes, so much so that my fishermen cautioned the ladies who accompanied us to be careful to look about well before selecting a seat on the ground. I saw and killed one very large adder quite a yard in length which I found basking in the sun on a flat rock. I never saw a specimen of the harmless grass snake either there or in any part of Norway.

The farm of Kaarvand was almost the limit of my wanderings, but I was informed that there was a large lake, just below the two great round hills which bounded the valley on the west, which was at the time of which I write rendered inaccessible to anglers or tourists by the presence on its banks of more than fifty bulls, some of them ferocious. The valley at this point had a very narrow entrance, and as it was easily guarded, the natives used to drive their old and useless bulls up there to graze on the rich pasture before

HEAD OF THE VALLEY ABOVE TODAL

TODAL

killing them and salting the carcases for winter use. A single labourer sufficed to guard the entrance, and feed and look after the herd.

The drive up the valley was very beautiful, but not one to be undertaken with a shying horse. Where it skirted the first foss it was merely a narrow track through the soft sandy surface of a steep slope, and then after a short interval of comparatively flat and easy gradient, where it ran through cultivated land, it once more turned into a wood of pine and birch, where it climbed over rock and boulder above a steep incline, below which the river dashed over great rocks in a succession of rapids and cascades. A false step or a shy would have precipitated the little cart and its occupants into this rocky gorge; but familiarity breeds contempt, and I never found any of my family or guests too nervous to enjoy the lovely drive, where the ferns, mosses, berries, and flowers carpeted the moist slopes in the richest luxuriance. There were many pools among the rapids which must have held big trout, and looked ideal places for the angler to explore with the fly or minnow; but there was so much good trout-water quite easy of access that I seldom troubled to scramble down the brae to stumble over the big boulders at the bottom. The overhanging trees and rocks which hemmed in the stream on both sides would have made it almost impossible to cast a fly properly.

The mile or two above and below Kaarvand farm furnished the most productive water, and if only the fish had been a little larger I could not imagine a more ideal trout river. Clear as crystal, it meandered through fields and woods, presenting an endless succession of beautiful pools and streams. The wading was easy, and I never had any difficulty in filling my basket with good trout, which cut as pink as a salmon, and were excellent eating. On off-days, when I did not care to drive, I found good sport in the reach between the foss and the wood, which could be reached from the house in an hour's walk. The trout here were not quite so large as in the water round Kaarvand, where the river was deeper, and the bed of the stream less rocky. I expect that in the still higher reach, where the water flowed out of the lake, much larger fish could have been obtained, but I never got so far. There were two or three lakes near the house for those who cared to climb the hills, and many delightful excursions could be made to the mountain sœters by tracks along which a pony could convey any ladies or members of the party who did not feel equal to a long stiff climb. There was also excellent anchorage for a yacht at the mouth of the fjord.

Nearly all that I have said about Todal applies also to Lilledal, the beautiful house which stands at the entrance of the lovely little valley which runs up to Torbudal, just opposite to Sundalsören. The second in order of date of the six fishing stations planned and constructed by Mr. and Mrs. Lort Phillips, it is the most attractive for those who are satisfied to dispense with the chance of a salmon. The valley is of unsurpassed beauty, and the little river of some five miles in length is full of magnificent sea-trout, free risers and splendid fighters. It can all be fished with a small rod and without a boat, and waders are not necessary, for most

THE BULL VALLEY ABOVE KAARVAND

of the pools, as the bushes are well cut, have great boulders placed along their sides, from which the angler can cast, passing from one to the other dry-shod in most heights of the water. Fish of fourteen pounds and over have been taken, and five-pounders are quite common. The whole river owes its value, I might almost say its origin, to its present lessor. When he and his associates in the Elverhoi fishings on the Sundal first visited Norway, the Lilledal River was a mere mountain torrent which nobody thought of paying for; though he and other anglers occasionally on an off-day paid a visit to the few pools near the mouth which were accessible and open, to try for the large sea-trout which were known to run up the stream. Seeing its possibilities Lort Phillips acquired the fishing rights, and then set to work to plan and organise the necessary improvements. The torrent was converted into a series of pools by constructing dams across the stream at frequent intervals, and building a great breakwater at the mouth near the sea. This was done in the long Norwegian winter when labour was plentiful and it was easy to move large boulders over the snow on sledges. The river freezes solid in the winter, and the boulders, placed in position then, sink into their proper places when the ice melts in the spring, when a very little additional labour completes the dam.

What I am here writing of Lilledal is true also of Oxendal, another house on the bank of a small river, built by the same skilful amateur architects and engineers; but the Lilledal River owes most to art, and is certainly in my view the most successful and attractive of all the fishing quarters belonging to Lort Phillips. The absence of salmon lengthens the fishing season by ten days, and is therefore to some extent an advantage. In most rivers in August and September, when sea-trout fishing is at its best, the salmon left in the pools are out of condition, and scarcely look at a fly; but the lower reaches of the Sundal are quite close to the house at Lilledal, and a tenant who required salmon fishing might, if he desired it, rent a beat and work it from the house. But the fisherman who could not be satisfied with the splendid sea-trout fishing in the little river would be hard to please.

At the head of the valley, some five miles distant, lies a chain of lakes four in number, full of excellent brown trout. Two great waterfalls dash down into the third lake from the watershed above. On these, alas! industrialism has laid its profane hand, as a scheme has now been authorised by the Storthing for constructing a huge reservoir above, and bringing the water by a tube to the bottom near the fjord, where an immense power-station is to be constructed, with large works for smelting ore, on or near the flat at the bottom by the mouth of the Sundal River. When I last left the valley (29th August 1913) the engineer's red and white flags, planted everywhere, reminded one of a suburban golf course; much of the necessary land had been bought, and it was rumoured that an army of 20,000 workmen would shortly descend upon the spot. Norway is a poor country, and one must not, I suppose, look upon such questions from a selfish point of view, but it is permissible to drop a tear over the threatened peace of the Lilledal and Sundal valleys.

"Sin' I mun doy I mun doy, thaw loife as they say is sweot,
But sin' I mun doy I mun doy, for I couldn abear to seet."

CHAPTER XI

A HOME ON THE HIGH FJELD—ALFHEIM, 1902

THE past week had been fine at Hvilested, and the river had gradually got lower and lower, until fishing had become difficult, and a single grilse or large sea-trout caught after sundown was as welcome as a salmon or half a dozen smaller fish had been a few days earlier. We had been particularly lucky in the time of our arrival, when there had just been a flood to bring up a fresh run of clean fish, and the water had remained for some time at a good height and not abnormally clear. Grand sport had been ours during our first four days, and we were as much surprised as disgusted to find our catch gradually diminishing, and at last to be met by the unwelcome phenomenon of a blank day. Such an experience in our quarters was then rare indeed; usually there were enough hungry sea-trout to save the situation even under the most unfavourable conditions, but for some reason or other these fish were very late that year, and only a few forerunners of the shoals which were still disporting themselves in the salt water at the mouth of the river had made their appearance.

What wonder that my wife and I gratefully accepted a cordial invitation—delivered through the telephone—to visit our friend Lort Phillips in his home on the high fjeld. I love Norway, and can hardly bear

A HOME ON THE HIGH FJELD

to hear it run down, but non-fishing visitors have occasionally been heard to complain that they felt shut in by the massive walls of snow-capped and pine-clad granite which fence on either side the narrow valley through which the Sundal River takes its impetuous course to the fjord, and I must admit that there is some justification for the complaint. This confined character of the valley is not peculiar to our fishing-quarters; most rivers in Norway run through comparatively narrow gorges fringed with a slender margin of pasture-land, wood and tillage. There is therefore some excuse for a desire occasionally to get above the visible mountain-barrier, and breathe the fresher air of the undiscovered country behind.

Visitors seldom prolong their sojourn on the mountain-tops beyond the limits of some brief expedition after reindeer or ptarmigan, and to spend a few hours among the sœters in the upland slopes involves a climb of some 3000 feet, which taken each way cuts "a monstrous cantle" out of the twelve or fourteen hours of daylight. It is seldom that one can enjoy the tonic of the mountain air for any time without elaborate preparations for camping, or taking up one's quarters in some sœter, which, though pleasant enough for the young and hardy, is scarcely suitable for ladies or those who are not prepared to rough it. For this reason my host has for some years occupied a small house on the mountain, to which he has from time to time added fresh rooms and new comforts and conveniences; and there he has been accustomed to spend three or four weeks between his visits to his summer and autumn fishing-quarters.

This delightful mountain home, which he has

named Alfheim, is not many miles as the crow flies from Hvilested, and a moderately expert climber can reach it by a precipitous path above Musjerd in a few hours; but this route requires a good head and sound legs, and certainly would not do for a lady unless she was young and exceptionally active, or a skilled mountaineer.

Our method of progress was necessarily by the longest and easiest route. A good road of about twenty English miles leads to Gjora, at the head of the valley, crossing the river by three bridges at different points. Along this we drove our sturdy little Norwegian pony, which made nothing of our stolkjaerre—loaded though it was with three persons, a side-saddle, and our luggage, which of course we had compressed into the smallest possible compass. The sun was shining when we started at ten o'clock, but we were not so imprudent as to go without our waterproofs, for changes of weather are rapid among the mountains; and although the glass had been rising for twenty-four hours, experience had taught us that this was not inconsistent with the possibility of showers, or even of heavy rain. Some say that in Norway it always rains when the glass rises; and although I would not be a party to such a slight upon the character of the mercury, I do not allow a blind faith to lull me into neglect of ordinary precautions.

Everything was late that year. Very little hay had been saved, and some of it was still uncut; and the barley, rye, and oats—a heavy and promising crop—was only just beginning to colour. Two years ago at this time the fields were cleared and everything was burnt up, but that was an exceptional experience,

SHOOTING THE RAPIDS

OLE AT THE FERRY

A HOME ON THE HIGH FJELD

the result of the hottest and driest season known for more than a decade. The farmers' loss was our gain, for the road was still fringed with innumerable wild flowers, and the mossy banks covered with delicious wild strawberries; a welcome delicacy as we walked up the hills, or strolled ahead while the horse was resting after our first stage. The rushing stream below us dashed over the boulders, now in white rapids, now in clear ultramarine pools. Here and there an angler was trying his luck; one we met strolling down with his attendant bearing rod and gaff, and exchanged experiences, parting with mutual wishes for good luck and "tight lines."

As we approached the bridge above Storfahle we looked with curiosity at the scene of a remarkable fishing incident which had recently been told to us, so remarkable indeed that the narrator, in view of the evil reputation of anglers for veracity, prefers to remain anonymous. Immediately behind a large and very deep salmon pool close below the road the overflow in flood time has hollowed out a large shallow backwater extending parallel to the river for some distance. My friend who was fishing the salmon pool was allowing his fly to trail idly behind him when suddenly he felt a tug at the rod, and before he could turn the line was singing through the rings. Turning, he perceived that he had hooked an otter which had actually taken his fly, probably mistaking it for one of the frogs for which he was hunting in the pool. The line was cut by a low fence at the end of the backwater; and another fisherman of forty years' experience, who had watched the incident from the opposite bank, called out, "It is as well as it is, for you never had a chance of landing him!" In one or two places we expected to see the great fish lying in the pools, but the wind was too strong for us to see any depth even through that translucent water; and a little before two o'clock we left the main river and turned to the right by the banks of a tributary stream which dashed through the gorge at the bottom of the pass through which we were about to make our ascent.

Here we came to a ferry, and sat down to enjoy a sandwich while preparations were being made for our further progress. A saddle-horse for my wife and a cart for the luggage soon appeared on the opposite bank, and everything was shifted and carried across with us in a big ferry-boat. The saddle and saddle-cloth were put on to the big black pony which my wife mounted, and we proceeded on our journey. For a short time I went in the cart with the luggage, but the road soon became too steep and rough for me to drive, and I strolled up the hill in advance of the pony and baggage, resting from time to time to gain breath and to admire the magnificent scenery.

Certainly the view was grand enough to command attention, even from an eye accustomed to the sublimity of valley, coast and fjord. The road wound upward through a beautiful pine-wood; passing among boulders covered with mosses, rock-plants, and masses of oak and beech fern. Great buckler ferns and brackens lifted their heads in the dry places, and long delicate fronds hung down in profusion wherever a streamlet or spring trickled through the stones, which were verdant with mosses of every variety. Canterbury bells, somewhat past their prime, and enormous harebells, flourished in profusion, and campions,

A HOME ON THE HIGH FJELD

willow-herb and buttercups added their various tints; and as we got higher we saw also abundance of beautiful purple monkshood.

The road gradually got further and further from the stream, and higher and higher above it, and dwarf birch-trees, rowans and bird cherry took the place of the fir-wood through which we had started upward. At the head of the gorge, on the left-hand side, a magnificent cataract dashed down into the river, just opposite to our halting-place, Suisdal, the large farm-house at the summit of the pass, where we were refreshed with some excellent coffee and "waffel kok," while the horses were taking a much-needed rest after their severe climb. A stove in the room was lighted to warm us, and although we at once rushed to the windows to let in the fresh air which the natives do not appreciate, we were not sorry to hang up our outer garments to dry, as it had been raining quite hard during our ascent, although we did not notice it sufficiently to put on our mackintoshes. One never seems affected by rain in Norway unless there is an absolute deluge.

After paying the kroner, which is all that was asked for our excellent entertainment, we resumed our progress, and at first I flattered myself that my walk was nearly over, as the early part of the road was quite good for driving, and we seemed to have reached a sort of tableland between two peaks, which I hoped would extend all the way to our destination. But I had reckoned without my host, for the road soon degenerated into a track, strewn with boulders and full of holes, far too rough to drive over, and one that would puzzle a south-country horse, although the sure-footed "best" upon which my wife was mounted made nothing of it; so I left the cart and we continued our journey for another two hours—mostly over a moorland bounded by beautiful snow-tipped peaks, but often passing stretches of undulating pasture-land, with great green glades intersected by coppices and shrubs that might well have formed part of an English park, of which they much reminded me. All over them, among the thick green grass, clustered the leaves of the lilies of the valley, giving some idea of what the prospect must have been when these lovely flowers were blooming in their rich profusion.

At last we reached the margin of a beautiful lake, some four miles in circumference, where we were met by our host and hostess, and rowed home in a two-prowed boat, the ladies being towed behind in a Canadian canoe plentifully provided with cushions. At first I looked in vain for the house, which I had expected to find on the bank, but soon we passed through a narrow channel artificially widened, which my host called the Suez Canal. This miniature channel is like its great original, partly natural and partly artificial. Passing through the reeds we emerged into a second lake, at the far corner of which we perceived the house and boat-house within a few yards of the shore.

The little log-house accommodated quite a large party; everything had been done to economise space, and the rooms were small but very comfortable. The trout caught in the lake were kept alive in a stew just opposite to the drawing-room window, and taken out when wanted for the table, and the supply seldom fell short. I tried for them the next morning, which was

A HOME ON THE HIGH FJELD

bright and sunny, without a cloud to obscure the direct rays of the sun or a breath of wind to ruffle the smooth surface of the lake. When a foot-bath for the accommodation of our fish was put into the boat, I ventured to question whether it was likely to be needed on such an unpromising day, but was assured by my sanguine companion that we were certain to catch something. The boast was unfortunate, as that morning we did not have a single run at our minnows, but in the evening an hour's sport produced seven trout averaging a little more than a pound. I was told that the fish in the lake nearest the house were poor risers, and preferred the minnow to the fly, but that a little further afield there were plenty of places where a good basket could be got with the fly. I had no time on this occasion to test the truth of this, but I proved it most satisfactorily on my next visit.

In the afternoon of the following day we started for a walk over the mountain, and at about five o'clock encamped upon a knoll overlooking the lake, where we lit our fire and had tea. It was curious to note among the wild flowers and heather evidences of the stern climate of winter; the few fir-trees which we passed were gnarled and twisted into grotesque shapes by the weight of snow under which they are overwhelmed in December. Some were dead, but many brave little fellows still contrived to put forth shoots, although their stems were bent back and forced almost to the ground. After tea those of the party who did not care for a steep and long walk left us to return to the house, and we started for the higher ground.

The climb although steep presented no difficulties. At first there were a good many small birch-trees, some of which our host cleared out of the way with the bill-hook he always carries with him on such expeditions. This pioneering work is not done merely to improve the path, but also with a view of making it easy to identify in thick weather; for which reason also we marked our course by raising little cairns of stones upon all the prominent peaks, within sight of each other.

Changes of climate are rapid at these altitudes, and it is no joke to be lost in a mist or storm. Not very long before our visit a farmer, who lived up at Havsaas, was lost on the fjeld for four days, although he was a noted reindeer hunter and practised mountaineer and well acquainted with every inch of the ground. When he had been absent about two days and nights his wife became anxious, and a search-party was organised. His tracks in the snow, which were soon found and followed, meandered about in the most extraordinary manner in loops, curves, and circles, and in one place the party came upon a corniche of snow overlooking a sheer precipice of over a thousand feet through which his staff had pierced into the void. For a short time he had found shelter in an old hut, or he must have succumbed to the effects of exposure, and it was a proof of his dazed condition that he had ventured to leave his place of safety and wandered a second time out into the impenetrable mist. Eventually he was found almost at his last gasp, and quite light-headed; but although he completely recovered, he had so entirely lost his nerve that he could never again be persuaded to tempt the perils of the high fjeld.

The birch-trees on these uplands are in great

SVART SNUTA: THE SUMMIT

SVART SNUTA FROM THE LAKE

request among the natives for the manufacture of sleigh runners, as their method of growth on the sides of the braes gives them naturally the necessary curve.

As we approached the summit level the vegetation altered in character. We had reached the home of the reindeer, and the ground was covered with the various lichens which, although of many different species, all go by the generic name of reindeer-moss, and supply these hardy creatures with food. We also noticed two varieties of ranunculus—a purple and a white—of which the reindeer are so particularly fond that their presence in abundance was considered to be a proof that no herds had been recently frequenting the neighbourhood. A little after seven we reached "Svart Snuta" (Black Beak), a remarkable precipice fifteen hundred feet above our starting-place. The rock literally overhangs the upper valley so directly that a stone dropped over its edge falls to the bottom without touching. Here our host imitated Sisyphus with more success than his prototype, rolling up a huge rock and toppling it over the edge, while we lay peering down from the giddy height to watch its headlong descent and thundering fall when it shivered into a hundred fragments at the foot of the precipice.

To our left stretched a vast extent of corrie, nearly all covered with snow, and we looked without success for the deer which often frequent it. Beyond us was a still higher summit, nicknamed the roof of the world, from which, as we were told, the whole mountain tableland could be seen. A sort of instinct implanted in the human breast makes one always long to get to the top of everything, and we decided to proceed, although it was pointed out that to do so would involve the certainty of a late return. We did not get much of a view when we got to the top, as a sudden change in the weather brought the clouds upon us, and snow began to fall. We stumbled upon several ptarmigan, one of which evidently had a young brood, as she could hardly be induced to fly away from the two black spaniels which accompanied us. We also picked up a gerfalcon's feather—newly shed—and after crossing several snow-slopes, down one of which some of our party glissaded, we got back to the house a little after nine o'clock. The weather below had been much worse than we had experienced above. A perfect deluge of rain had caused a torrent, which had washed away the paths in places where the incline was steep, as the drains were not capable of accommodating so great a quantity of water.

The next day all clouds had disappeared, and every rock and shrub was mirrored in the lake. We spent the morning and part of the afternoon in exploring the immediate neighbourhood, visiting the mountain farm and dairy; greeting the kindly sœter girls, and being initiated into the mysteries of the manufacture of cheese and "waffel-kok,"—a kind of soft cake made by pouring a soft thick paste of barley or rye meal into the front of a pair of flat iron tongs, which are then held over a wood fire for about ten minutes. The logs of which some of these sœters were constructed were nearly three hundred years old, still the timber was perfectly sound, and had only needed planing on the outside to make it indistinguishable from that of the newer log-houses around. The dry keen mountain air has extraordinary preserving

A HOME ON THE HIGH FJELD

qualities, and everything keeps up there wonderfully well. The place where the house stands, and indeed a great part of the valley around it, must once have been a forest of huge fir-trees. In many places their stumps and roots are still visible, although none of the trees are now standing.

It was pleasant enough after two rather hard days' work to lounge on a chair in the verandah, reading the latest English papers—more than a week old—watching the black spaniels Nellie and Bobbie making persevering but unavailing attempts to capture the trout in the stew; or drinking in the magnificent panorama of sky, mountain, and water. An evening row on the lake brought an enjoyable day to a close, and again we had an illustration of the startling rapidity with which atmospherical conditions change. The day had been perfectly still, and the evening so calm that the rings made by rising trout could be perceived halfway across the lake, but before we got to bed—and we did not sit up late—the wind was blowing a full gale, which gradually increased in violence until by the following evening, when we were on our way home, it was difficult to stand upright in exposed places.

We returned by a different route, crossing the watershed in a north-westerly direction and descending a steep pass leading directly to our house. Although the shortest route in distance—only about sixteen miles—no time was saved by adopting it, as it was impracticable for even the roughest cart; but it enabled us to see a new part of the country, and completely to circumnavigate the mountain separating us from our home. We started off about ten o'clock in the morning, having sent our luggage back by the way we came; I and a young lady who was returning to friends in the valley on foot; my wife on a pony which had been sent up for her the night before. The path for the first part of the way was fairly level, but extremely rough, passing through a rugged boulder-strewn moorland between the mountain-tops; but the pony proved equal to the occasion, stepping up and down slippery rocks, and crossing bogs and burns, as only a mountain-bred beast can be trusted to do.

The scenery was comparatively tame until we neared the final stage, when the course of the stream became rapid and the banks rocky and precipitous. Just before the final descent, which although steep is quite easy travelling, the little river broadened into a lake, into which a magnificent cascade poured down from the snow-fields above. The last part of the journey, through a grand gorge down which the stream flows into the Sundal River at Grodal, was very familiar ground, and we reached home about five o'clock, full of the delights of our visit to the high fjeld.

CHAPTER XII

ALFHEIM, 1913

ELEVEN years, to a day, intervened between my two visits to Alfheim. On each occasion I started on the 12th of August, a date which recalled many memories of other hills and moors. The mountains on each side of the road were unchanged on my second journey, but I could not help thinking as I stepped into an automobile at Sundalsören how impossible such a method of transport would have appeared to the simple inhabitants at the time of my former visit. Motors then roused almost as much curiosity, even in London, as an aeroplane does now.

I started from Lilledal after an early breakfast, and old Sivert rowed me over the glassy and unruffled surface of the fjord under a cloudless sky. As we crossed I could see the flounders shooting like miniature kites over the sand as the shadow of our boat disturbed them. There was only one other passenger at the start, a Christiansund banker, who spoke a little English, and sent all sorts of greetings to my host, Lort Phillips, when he heard whither I was bound. But we were not destined to travel light all the way; many other passengers joined the car as we progressed, and we were soon packed as close as herrings in a barrel. However, there was none of the grumbling or ill-humour one sometimes experiences in a crowded railway carriage or omnibus in more civilised regions; everybody seemed to take the inconvenience as part of the fun, and some took children on their knees, while others sat backwards or forwards, compressing their bodies into the smallest possible compass.

One of the first to join the motor was a poor old farmer with a bandage over his left eye, who had been my companion down the valley from Gjora when I arrived on the previous Saturday. The head of a match had flown off as he struck it and burnt his eye, and he had travelled down to consult the doctor. A party of friends escorted him to the ferry, and the driver eagerly questioned him as to the result of his visit. I am sorry to say that no hope was held out to him of ever recovering the sight of the injured eye. He was evidently still in considerable pain, but bore it philosophically and bravely. We soon passed the ruins of poor Hvilested on our left, and next on our right the Grodal pass, down which we had descended on our homeward journey from Alfheim in 1902.

After Gjora the journey became a repetition of the one described in the last chapter. My horse and cart were waiting for me at the post-office at Gjora, in charge of a merry little blue-eyed skydskarl, who persisted in trying to talk to me, regardless of our entire ignorance of each other's tongues. He had never travelled over the route before, and seemed constantly afraid that we were losing our way, although I assured him, in what I imagined to be Norwegian, that there were not many roads on the high fjeld. We crossed the ferry, accompanied by the poor blinded

A LAKE ON THE HIGH FJELD

THE BRIDGE AT VANGEN

man, who was bound for his home at the foot of the Dovre Fjeld, and a young cheery-looking Norwegian with a knapsack, and his companion, a buxom girl of about the same age, either his sister or his bride.

On this occasion the flowers were nearly over. It had been a forward year, and the harvest had been early. Another new feature of the landscape was the scarcity of snow. The fall in the winter had not been a heavy one, and most of the snow had melted early, to the great disgust of the fishermen, who had found their autumn supply of water for the pools lamentably short. A late fall in the beginning of July had temporarily blocked the back door of the mountain home for which I was bound, but of course such unseasonable snow speedily disappears under the hot rays of the summer sun. The steep road to Suisdal, which "wound up hill all the way," seemed to me more difficult to mount than on the former occasion; but perhaps the passage of eleven years had affected not the road but the pedestrian! It speaks volumes for the tonic effect of mountain air, three thousand feet above the sea, that although perilously near threescore-and-ten I was able to manage the four hours' climb without undue fatigue.

I will not repeat my account of the scenery, although perhaps I stopped oftener and longer to look at it than on the former occasion. I saw nothing new until I got within about a mile and a half of Alfheim and passed the imposing new house, Vangen, on an eminence above the east end of the large lake, crossing the river by a fine new stone bridge just below it which seemed to me really a triumph of amateur engineering and construction. It impressed me the more from the contrast it presented to the track over which I had just been passing. Not half a mile back my cart had upset—fortunately I was not in it—and my suit case had been shot over the brae.

It was four o'clock when I reached the house to be welcomed as warmly as usual. I had eaten nothing since an early breakfast, so was glad of a substantial lunch, which was followed almost without a break by five o'clock tea. Time does not exist in Norway, and meals are taken at uncertain intervals. I had a short turn in the boat on the home lake between tea and dinner, catching a few trout for the stew, and drinking in the beauties of the lovely scene, but was glad to turn in early in a funny little room about seven feet square at the back of the dining-room. If there was no room to swing a cat, I did not want to swing one; and there was another room of about the same size next door to it, where my bath was prepared for me in the morning. After spending some ten hours in the open air I slept so soundly that even the untimely notes of a certain white Wyandotte cock, whom the party had christened "Caruso," failed to disturb my repose.

I woke next day quite refreshed but somewhat stiff, and was not sorry to spend a rather lazy morning attending to my correspondence and exchanging home news for the gossip of the valley. A glutton had been trapped at one of the farms above Suisdal at the foot of the Dovre Fjeld. The steel trap had fastened upon his front paw, but he had succeeded in biting it off, and getting away for a time. However, the farmer had contrived to follow the blood trail, and had come up with him and shot him. There was quite a competition for his skin. A bear was going about on the Western slope between the house and the Sundal valley, and had killed a sheep only last week just above Fladvad. Only a day or two ago one of the "soeter pige" herding cattle had come right upon him on the other side of a little birch fence made to protect some mountain hay. "So close," she said, "that she could see his eyes winking at her." In the early part of the year no less than four bears, a male, a female, and two cubs, had been always about near Gjednes, the large farm just over the fjord below Todal. The male broke into the *stabbur* in July, and took two sheep, a most unusual occurrence at that time of the year. Two farm lads got a rifle and went in pursuit; just as one of them had got tired of carrying the weapon, and had put it down against a tree, they came suddenly upon Bruin at close range, and he "hoisted up his fore-paws upon a log and stared at them." They hurried back to the farm, and returning a party of four surrounded the place, and by an exceptional piece of good fortune came upon and secured him. Generally a bear when disturbed covers a long distance before he can be pursued. I told my host that if he wanted to satisfy my greatest wish, he must really contrive to show me a bear; but, alas! he could not manage to gratify my curiosity.

After lunch the whole party started in two boats for Vangen. The sky was bright and clear, and minnows and flies were trailed behind the stern as we progressed over the two lakes. There were four or five fish of a pound and over in the baths before we reached our destination. How they fought! The light rods of the ladies bent almost double as they reeled in line to check the impetuous rush of the game fish; but these were in a taking humour that day, and not many escaped. Soon we landed from deep water just beside a large boat-house built of stone brought from a quarry close at hand, and proceeded up a flight of stone steps to the new building of which its amateur designer may be justly proud. The site is ideal, even more attractive than that of Alfheim, and I can imagine nothing more pleasant than for two parties of friends to spend the summer months as neighbours in such delightful surroundings. The older and less active could find plenty of sport and amusement close at hand, while the young and enterprising could make their summer quarters a centre for long exploring expeditions among snow peaks, glaciers, and lakes. There are any number of sheets of water of all sizes within easy reach, and the river which flows down to Suisdal looked to me, as I gazed at it from the road, as if it had many pools where the votary of the dry fly might enjoy his favourite pastime. The botanist and geologist could ramble over almost virgin ground, and might reasonably hope to make new discoveries.

The new house is very commodious, as I found when taken over it on landing. There are ten bedrooms, a drawing-room, dining-room, smoking-room, and servants' hall, with kitchen and convenient offices. The verandah is not quite finished, but will, when completed, run round the house. It is paved with stone from the same quarry as furnished the materials for the boat-house and bridge, and will be a delightful place in which to sit under cover, and enjoy the grand views of mountain, lake, and river. This verandah is a feature common to all Lort Phillips' houses, and, to judge by my experience, is always a favourite resort. After showing me over, all the party except myself set to work inside and outside the house, my host and one energetic young lady arming themselves with axes and bill-hooks, to clear open spaces and paths round the house by cutting down the thick clusters of birch trees; while the other ladies set to work upon the inside decoration, sewing, hanging curtains, and otherwise making themselves generally useful. I was rather ashamed of myself for not volunteering to help with the work, but I rather suspect that it was thought that I might in my ignorance do more harm than good; anyhow I was excused on the ground of my age and infirmities! and set off to the river with my rod, hoping that at least I might do something for the commissariat department.

I was not as well equipped for the fray as I could have wished. A box containing fishing-tackle, waders, and shooting-boots, which I had sent off a fortnight before starting "to await arrival," so far from awaiting arrival only turned up at Christiansund two days before my departure, and returned with me in the steamer unopened! My reel, line, rod, and casts were all right, but I had no net, and only a few trout flies, wet and dry, which I had borrowed from other members of the party. It was not a good fishing day, as the sun was scorching, and there was no wind, and the river was very low. Nevertheless I attained a sufficient measure of success to whet my appetite for more, and convince me that the river had great possibilities. In rather more than an hour I had caught nine lively little fish without going half a mile from the house, and had lost one of over a pound which I vainly endeavoured to lift on to the rocks with my fine tackle and small fly, of which I could have made certain if I had had a landing net. I brought in quite a respectable basket of plump bright little fish when I returned to tea.

Perhaps everyone may not know a really excellent way of disposing of small burn trout. It is an Alfheim recipe, and, *crede experto*, makes an excellent dish. I adopt the precedent of Izaac Walton, and print it here for the benefit of brother anglers.

"Lay your trout on his side upon a board, and with a very sharp knife cut right down to the bone just below the head. Then pass the blade below the bone and carefully remove it, snip off the fins with a pair of scissors, and put the two fillets at the bottom of a pie dish. When the first layer is complete cover it with butter, bay leaves, a little vinegar, and seasoning to taste, and make more layers until the dish is almost full. Fill up with water, and then bake in an oven. The result comes out in the form of a cake, and makes a delicious cold dish for breakfast or lunch."

To quote *The Complete Angler:* "This dish of meat is too good for any but anglers, or very honest men, and I trust you will prove both, and therefore I have trusted you with this secret."

After a grand tea in the dining-room I tried the river again, but the rise was over. At eight o'clock Gunder, the boatman, took me on board, and I fished with minnow and fly on the two lakes until nine, getting five more good trout on my way home. It was a perfect evening. I never saw anything more lovely than the lights on the hills, and the reflections in and over the water. First the whole range to the

LADIES FISHING AT VANGEN

VANGEN

north was bathed in a warm glow, then the more distant peaks caught fire, and lastly the mountains above the eastern horizon caught the reflection and turned a vivid rose colour. The stars were shining overhead before I landed to enjoy an excellent supper, a primitive rubber of bridge, and then bed.

The two following days were spent nearly in the same way, but with varying success. The next day, when we all had a picnic lunch at Vangen, was a disappointment from a fishing point of view. I started to explore the lower part of the river, full of hope. I had borrowed a landing-net this time to be on even terms with big trout, and confidently offered to bet that I would return with not less than two dozen fish. Fortunately for me there were no takers, for everything went wrong. In the first place I tried the fatal policy of endeavouring to make a short cut, a most foolish thing in an unknown country. As usual my short cut turned out to be an uncommonly long one, and I stumbled up and down hill over boulders and swamps, forcing my way through briars and thick brush, catching my fly in the branches, barking my shins, and getting hotter and crosser every minute. To add to my misfortunes a thick mist came down, and a drizzling rain began, and I had left my mackintosh behind. When at last I reached the river I found before me a long stretch of quite shallow water, and an impassable stream divided me from some big pools which I could see a little lower down. I made my way up to the water in which I had fished the day before, which turned out to be no great distance off, as I had been travelling in a half circle, but had very little success, as the mist had put the fish down.

Soon I was ready for an *al fresco* tea, and my hand mechanically sought my pocket for the sandwich and a small bottle of whisky and milk with which I had furnished myself at starting. The cork had come out, the contents had flooded my pocket, and reduced my sandwich to a pulp!! This was the climax, and I made my way home in a chastened spirit. When I reached the house I had not been delighted as on the previous evening with any beautiful lights and reflections; the whole landscape was obliterated.

> "The white mist, like a face-cloth to the face
> Clung to the dead earth."

I note my little misfortunes only by way of contrast, for I should indeed be churlish and ungrateful if I grumbled at the weather which favoured us during the remainder of my stay. There was some mist from time to time, but only enough to break the outlines of the cliffs, or cling to the little hollows. It was rather bright for fishing, and the breeze generally died away altogether in the evenings, and made it almost impossible to rise the great trout we saw breaking the still water. But I did enough for pleasure, if not for glory. Next day I got thirty-five good trout, and had two hours of exceptionally good sport fishing off the dam which divided the lake from the river. The water was shallow, but the breeze just caught it properly, and nearly every cast produced a rise, although less than a tithe of the fish were hooked, as very naturally they came short in the clear shallow water, taking warning from something they saw before they actually got hold of the fly.

Of course I always kept my eyes open for other

objects as well as fish. Bird life especially interests me, but on the whole I was disappointed at the scarcity of living creatures. In spite of the profusion of berries there were hardly any fruit-eating birds to take advantage of them. The rushy margins of the innumerable lakes promised food and shelter for ducks and water-fowl, and I should have anticipated seeing any quantity of the common wild duck, the most ubiquitous of birds in their range, but I only just "saved my duck" by seeing one flock which rose all round me on my last morning when I was passing in the boat through the Suez Canal on my way to join my cart and luggage at Vangen.

Several times I enjoyed favourable opportunities of watching the great red-throated diver. One day just before our boat emerged from the passage into the big lake, I heard a loud croaking sound difficult to describe. It was certainly not the bark of a raven, although it rather reminded me of it. I should not describe it, as Mr. Frohawk does, as "a mixture between the cackle of a guinea-fowl and the bray of an ass," but it is notoriously difficult to convey a correct idea of sounds by written description. Anyhow the birds whose note I had heard were red-throated divers, five of which we soon spied on our left. We turned the boat towards them, and tried to get as near to them as we could. They were very shy, and after diving once or twice, took wing and flighted round our boat just out of gunshot. They looked as big as geese, and their flight resembled that of an eider. We had no gun with us, or I think my companion would have tried to get a shot at them, as they are very destructive to fish, for which reason the

Norwegian government puts a price on their heads. On subsequent days I often saw a pair of them on the upper lakes, and by remaining absolutely motionless on the bank induced them to come close enough to give me a good view of their brilliant colouring and beautiful laced plumage.

I saw no other water-fowl. One day two magnificent falcons were soaring round a peak, but not near enough for me clearly to determine their species. We picked up during a ramble the wings of a pipit cut clean from the body, which indicated the work of a merlin, but I never caught sight of that beautiful miniature falcon. Kestrels I saw, but not in great numbers. There were a good many hooded crows, but no magpies, although these birds abound in the valley below. We flushed one or two coveys of ryper, and I have no doubt that if I had been accompanied by a dog I should have seen many more. One day my companion actually touched an old cock with the end of his rod before he could induce him to fly. There were plenty of fieldfares, and everywhere along the rocks at the margins of the lakes the white wagtail tripped daintily along, tame and fearless, and performed his work of mercy in reducing the number of flies. My son when hunting reindeer in the neighbourhood shortly after my visit frequently came upon the snowy owl at close quarters.

The only wild quadruped I saw was the blue mountain hare, but I noted tracks of reindeer, fox, and ermine. With luck one might have seen the former, as we were close to their regular haunts, but the scarcity of snow attracted them to higher ground. I believe a cow elk had been seen once or twice in recent years

OLD PINE ON THE HIGH FIELD

ROOT OF SAME

in the neighbourhood, but one must go further north to find these beasts in any numbers. They must have been quite common at one time, as the narrow paths between the lakes and swamps are full of old pitfalls still in excellent preservation dug to capture them. We passed and examined several of these in the course of a delightful walk we all took together one Sunday after tea. Our destination was the lake at the foot of Svart Snuta, the overhanging precipice which we climbed on the occasion of my former visit. Our path started over banks clothed with heather, birch, and different kinds of berries, traversing ground which to a golfer's eye presented great possibilities for the construction of an inland links. At present it would not be easy to get many members for a club, or even to secure a partner for a match, but there is no saying what may happen if the great industrial enterprise at the opening of the valley materialises, and brings a large population. We next passed along a whole chain of lakes, great and small. I counted more than six before we crossed the watershed and reached the large sheet of water opposite to Svart Snuta, where we reclined for a time on the heather and watched a pair of loons fishing under the rocky cliff.

I have alluded before to the great roots and trunks of huge pines which remain, to prove that at one time an immense forest of these trees must have covered the whole valley; but although the time I spent at Alfheim gave me on this occasion an ample opportunity of examining them, I must leave it to wiser heads than mine to account for its total disappearance. I could distinguish many long trunks of trees through the clear water in the shallows at the margin of the lakes; others, moss-covered and fungus-grown, lay prone among the birches, and whenever the soil was disturbed with a spade, more were discovered underground. Some roots clearly showed the marks of an axe, but it is impossible to ascribe the total disappearance of the forest to human agency. There can never have been a large population on these heights, which are now only visited during the short summer season by cattle and the sœter girls who milk and look after them, and by reindeer hunters during two short weeks in September. It would have been impossible to transport the timber into the valley, or to make use of much on the spot, so I can only conjecture that change of climate must have been the cause. The old trees and roots make excellent firewood, and provide an almost inexhaustible supply.

I took photographs of some of these outstanding roots and fallen giants, and tried also, as it was a bright sunny afternoon, to take pictures of some of the most open elk pitfalls; but although my host stood in them with bill-hook in hand, my snapshots unfortunately show nothing but a man looking out of a hole. Even truth, perhaps fortunately, considering her state of deshabille, could defy the photographer when at the bottom of her well! On our return journey we picked up a last year's ryper snare. It was made of a forked stick about a foot and a half high, with a fine wire snare fixed to the bottom of one of its arms. The two ends are planted across a run, and the surrounding ground blocked with brushwood and heather, repeating on a small scale the method adopted with the elk pitfalls and bear snare. Then we botanised, and got some beautiful saxifrages and ferns, and a sprig of white heather for good luck. The ladies also gathered some of the brilliant leaves of the wild geranium for table decoration. Although the autumn tints were not yet at their finest, the hillsides were already a blaze of colour.

The lakes along which we passed in our walk looked very tempting, and I made up my mind to spend most of my remaining time in exploring them. I started the next day for the farthest, the one below Svart Snuta, taking my lunch with me. It was not a first-rate fishing day, there was too much mist hanging in the clefts of the hills, and the trout in the big lake refused to rise. After lunch I tried a small loch quite close to the first, and found it full of trout, which rose to every cast. I got a dozen in less than an hour, all about the same size, something just under half a pound, and then moved on to try the next loch in the hope of finding something bigger. I had excellent sport in this loch, which was bounded on the west by a wall of rock some ten feet high, which went down sheer into deep water, from which feature we christened it "cliff lake." Here the fish I caught averaged about a pound, and I got ten of them in a short time. They were splendid fighters, and when I laboriously clambered down the only place where the edge of the water was accessible, and tried to get them into the net, they nearly always made a second dash for liberty. They were as good for the table as they were sporting, and their flesh cut as red as that of a salmon. Although I sampled all the lakes I could reach, I made that one my favourite haunt, and always hoped to beguile some monster from its depths, as I felt sure that it held far bigger fish than any I caught.

A curious incident marked my second visit to this cliff lake. Somewhat to my surprise I had fished for more than half an hour without a rise, and had nearly reached the limits of my patience when I felt a heavy strain, and really thought that I had at last hooked the patriarch of the lake. Judge of my surprise when on bringing the fish on the top dropper to the surface, I perceived that there was also a fish on each of the other two flies. I carefully climbed down to the water's edge, and more by good luck than good guidance managed to land all three. The two top ones I scooped into the net, and half lifted, half dragged, the bottom one on to a shelving slab of rock. I have often before caught two trout at a time, and occasionally three, but they have generally been small ones. I never before got three at a time averaging a pound each. But the remarkable thing about this particular large draft of fishes was that it was preceded and followed by absolute stagnation; such double or treble events usually come when there is a strong rise, and fish are competing with one another to be the first to secure a fly.

On another occasion I managed at last to get four or five fish out of the big lake below Svart Snuta, but they were poor half-starved creatures with long thin bodies and big heads, good neither for food nor sport. On that morning Lort Phillips and a companion had walked with me as far as the foot of the precipice, and then climbed to the top. While I was lazily reclining on the heather enjoying my sandwich, I heard a signal whistle, and looking up, could just distinguish two moving dots upon the sky-line. I watched while the climbers, as usual, rolled big boulders over the precipice, and was glad to be able to note the effect from below. I wished in vain for my camera to take a snapshot. When the great rock pitched on the cairn at the foot of the cliff a cloud of smoke seemed to rise, and reminded me of the exceedingly free paraphrase by which Pope professed to translate the Sisyphus passage in the *Odyssey* :

"The huge round stone, resulting with a bound,
Thundered impetuous down and smoked along the ground."

There is nothing about either thundering or smoke in the original Greek, but the words give quite a correct impression of the sound and the sight.

My lack of waders or knee-boots restricted me on most of the lakes to a rather limited range. A companion more suitably equipped got a good bag in the shallows near the reedy banks, on an occasion when I did little or nothing from the cliff. It was tantalising to leave many places unfished which I saw dimpled with rises, which could have been reached by a wader without going above the knee. I think I might have been tempted to wade as I was, but for the fact that I was very short of foot-gear of all descriptions. In spite of this I thoroughly enjoyed my sport; boat-fishing is all very well for a change, but I infinitely prefer fishing from the shore, especially in small lakes. I soon get tired of sitting on hard board, and like to wander about, and try to reach rising fish either with wet fly or dry rather than to drift and "chuck and chance it," or row and be rowed trailing a minnow or fly. "Of sitting, as of all carnal pleasures, cometh satiety at the last." So says the monk in Kingsley's *Hypatia*, and I cordially agree with him.

I left Alfheim on the 22nd with many regrets, and with a feeling that if I am ever fortunate enough to visit the dear upland valley again, I may hope to be even more successful with the trout. Perhaps, too, next time I may see the Northern Lights, which did not flash in the heavens on this occasion, as I was told they often do. But I doubt if they could have rivalled in beauty the effect of the August full moon as it rose like a great shield of silver at the head of the valley above Gjora, and reminded me of the lines which Tennyson puts into the mouth of Jephthah's daughter:

> "The balmy moon of blessed Israel
> Floods all the deep blue gloom with beams divine:
> All night the splinter'd crags that wall the dell
> With spires of silver shine."

LILLEDAL AND KALKEN FROM THE FJORD

FARUM ON LILLEDAL RIVER

CHAPTER XIII

LILLEDAL, 1913

My journey to Norway was made this year for the first time overland—by Flushing, Hamburg, Copenhagen and Christiania to Stören, a little south of Trondhjem, and thence by road to Sundalsören. I need not dwell upon the railway portion of it, except to eulogise the extremely comfortable sleeping carriages which run between Hamburg and Christiania, but the last day presented some features of novelty when contrasted with my passage over the same route fifteen years earlier. Now a motor car runs on three days a week between Aune in Opdal and Sundalsören, and our time-tables told us that it was due to start at 3.30 P.M. From Stören, where the train deposited us at 5.30 A.M., to Aune is a distance of over 72 kilometres or about 46 English miles, with six changes of horses. We telephoned on to say we were coming, and received the answer that "the motor would wait for us a little, but we must hurry up." Then commenced a race against time, in which we should have been badly beaten had not the motor waited for us more than two hours.

The road has been vastly improved since I passed over it on my former journeys. Then it was in many places a mere mountain track, now it is wide, well engineered, and with good gradients considering the difficult country over which it passes; while parallel to it a short distance above or below are the cuttings and embankments of the new railway which is to pass through the Dovre Fjeld and join the line to Christiania, which will when completed immensely shorten the railway journey between the ancient and the modern capital. There were not a great number of navvies at work; even primitive Norway has its labour troubles like the rest of the world. All went well till we reached the third posting station; exceptionally good ponies had taken us along the fairly level but rather heavy road at about the orthodox six miles an hour, but at Bjerkager a check came. We had telephoned on, but we found no horse or conveyance awaiting us on our arrival. A bright, cheerful, and buxom Norwegian matron, who talked and understood a little English, condoled with our plight and did all she could to help us; but more than an hour was wasted before a jaded bay pony was brought down from the hayfield and harnessed to the stolkjaerre, to which we had already transferred our light baggage.

The authorities admitted having received our telephone message, but professed to have misunderstood it; as they were getting in their hay, I suspect that the misunderstanding was intentional. How we fretted and fumed at the delay! We could not settle down to anything, as every moment we hoped against hope that our horse would arrive. We were sadly in want of food, as we had had nothing but chocolate and a cup of coffee since 5.30; but were afraid to risk further delays by ordering a meal, so we wandered round the yard sending post-cards from the little branch office, and feeding a small fair-haired baby with much more chocolate than was good for its health. We almost despaired of reaching our destination that night, but when we crawled into Aune after five o'clock, nearly two hours behind time, we found to our delight that the motor was still waiting for us, and that the only passenger, a very nice little Norwegian lady, who had been sitting in the car for nearly two hours, did not seem the least annoyed or out of temper, but took it all in the day's work. All was peace. We telephoned to Lilledal to say when we might be expected in Sundalsören, where a boat was needed to take us across the fjord, and as the driver made no objection to waiting while we fed, we also telephoned to order our "middags mad" at 7 P.M. at the next stage, Gjora.

It was my first experience of motor driving in Norway, and I have no doubt that it was our fellow-passenger's first experience of motor driving anywhere. We were soon under weigh on a really fast and smooth-going car, guided by a good, but dashing driver. Just after starting we met a funeral procession on its way to the little church. More than twenty mourners in carrioles followed the bier. I do not think there was any coffin; it looked, although I could not be quite sure of this, as if the body was wrapped in reeds covered with flowers. Naturally there was great commotion among the ponies, but our careful driver at once stopped and helped to lead them past the alarming object. It was touch and go nevertheless; one pony kicked and plunged and overturned the carriole he was pulling, and his alarm might easily have created a panic among the others which might have led to disastrous results. However, all the vehicles eventually passed us without accident, and we proceeded on our way.

The new road, a really magnificent piece of engineering, takes a lower level than the old rough track along which I had passed on my former journey to and from Trondhjem, but in spite of its numerous windings the gradient down the steep descent to Gjora is a very stiff one, and the track hangs sheer over a beetling precipice far above the Sundal River. Our driver drove very well, but certainly rather fast considering the nature of the country; perhaps he wanted to make up time! Our little Norwegian fellow-traveller was frightened out of her wits, and begged K. to change places with her, as she was on the near side of the vehicle with an uninterrupted view down the precipitous height. There was certainly some excuse for her nervousness, as a skid, or brake failure, might have sent us hurtling down into the gorge. For myself I revelled in the gorgeous scenery, the beloved and well-remembered river winding like a silver thread far below among the pines and rocks, and enjoyed the sensation that we were really progressing, and were certain to reach our journey's end that evening. Norwegian "hests" have not yet become accustomed to mechanical traffic; the drivers of carts or carrioles always got down when we approached and turned their horses' heads well away, leading them into the woods or up the hills. Our driver was certainly no "road hog," as he always stopped the car as soon as any horse-drawn traffic came in sight.

We reached Gjora in good time, and found at

the skyds station an excellent meal of soup, salmon, veal cutlets, compote of fruit, and coffee, which we thoroughly enjoyed after our long fast. There was some further delay at the driver's house, next door to the post-office, where his delightful little son, a baby a little more than a year old, ran about nursing and sometimes hurling about a small kitten, to the delight of a throng of sightseers assembled to see the start. I wish I could have photographed the scene, but it was too late in the evening for an instantaneous exposure. The rest of the journey was pure enjoyment, as well-known scene after well-known scene " swam into my ken." I did not note much change except the bare bank and blasted trees on the height where dear Hvilested formerly stood, and a certain amount of new building, including a bran new Tourist Hotel next to the store at Grodal, where our little Norwegian companion left us with as many smiles and expressions of regret as if we had been her benefactors instead of the unwilling causes of a delay of some hours on her journey. Norwegians really take no count of time, and are never in a hurry. On my return journey from Alfheim along the same route the motor pulled up with a jerk just as we approached Ottem bridge, and while I was speculating whether a tyre had burst or the petrol given out, I saw our chauffeur deliberately cut a stick, and go back some hundred yards to kill a small viper which his quick eye had marked crawling by the side of the road. We reached Sundalsören soon after nine, and found our old friend Ole, Miss Cole's boatman, waiting to row us across the fjord; and in spite of the lateness of the hour our kind hostess was waiting by the boathouse to welcome us. I was soon fast asleep in a comfortable little outside room, as the house was full to its utmost capacity.

I only remained two days, Sunday and Monday, at Lilledal, as I was due at Alfheim for the first part of my stay in Norway, and went on there as soon as my heavy luggage arrived from Christiania. I had neither rods nor fishing things, or even a change of clothes, but Miss Cole lent me a light eleven-foot Farlow rod, and I tried my hand at "Peter Pool," the pool round the first bend above the bridge, on the Monday evening after dinner. Half-way down I hooked a fine fresh-run fish, which gave me great fun in the strong water, for the stream was then pretty high. He really fought like a tiger, and I was afraid that he might get over the dam into the rapids, but in about ten minutes he was safely landed, a beautiful silvery fellow in perfect condition, thick-set and shapely. I hoped he was four pounds, but thought he was about half a pound less, and I found that my eye had not deceived me, as when I weighed him he just turned the scale at $3\frac{1}{2}$ pounds.

Next morning I left for Alfheim, and did not return until Friday, 22nd August, by which time the river had run down so low that there was very little chance of catching big fish. During the time I was away the fishing had been very good, and on the day before I returned my son Geoffrey was lucky enough to beat the record by catching a magnificent fellow of $14\frac{1}{2}$ pounds in the Road Pool. We heard by telephone of his success, and when I drove down the valley next day I found that the fame of the capture was spread abroad! The telephone is a great convenience in Norway, but it

THE RECORD SEA TROUT

LILLEDAL

is as well to refrain from using it to convey any news which it is important to keep secret!

I was taken to see the fish directly after my return. He was a great beauty, quite fresh run and very broad and well-shaped. I was told that he did not take very long to kill, but there was one breathless moment when he nearly went over the foss. Geoffrey wisely adopted the old tactics of slacking the line. Very often the mad rush of a fish towards an impossible place may be checked in that manner; the fish thinks that he is free and turns up stream to seek his old holt. There is of course a risk, but desperate cases need desperate remedies. Many fish of about four pounds had been caught during the week by the other anglers, male and female, who filled the house, but no other monster.

The next day I took my lunch with me, and walked up to Haarstad Bridge to fish my way down. The river was becoming very low and rain was much wanted. There was the threatening of a shower, but it came to nothing. I got one fish of about two pounds, and had two other rises, but did not move anything of any size. I fished every day during the remainder of my stay with the same only moderate success, and no large fish were caught by any other members of the party. The weather continued fine, and the river fell until at last there was hardly any hope of a rise, but there was plenty of other amusement, and it was delightful to spend all day in the open air in such ideal surroundings. On Sunday Miss Cole showed me the remains of a heron's nest in a low birch tree by the side of the path leading down to House Pool, which had been raided by hoodies. I flushed a woodcock not twenty yards from the house on my first morning, and was told that there were plenty of them about, and that they nested close at hand. Green woodpeckers abound. Their laugh may be heard all day, and one actually perched on the flagstaff opposite to the drawing-room window, and to the verandah where I was sitting. The great eagle owl nests in the cliff above Haarstad, and the osprey in the rocks over the fjord, where flocks of eiders congregate and mergansers pilot their numerous progeny.

We spent two afternoons sea-fishing on the fjord, and had a picnic tea at Bügten farm, where a little waterfall now discharges into the sea, just at the spot where it is proposed to make the outlet of the contemplated great power-station. The boats do not cast anchor, but the party fish with hand-lines baited with mussels as they slowly drift. There are plenty of fish—cod, plaice, flounders, saithe, whiting, haddock and ling—but we were not very fortunate on either of the two occasions, although enough were caught for the pot. We saw and pursued a sea-trout of about three-quarters of a pound which was playing on the top of the water, and was apparently unable to get down. After one or two attempts I succeeded in getting him into the landing-net, when we could detect no scar or mark of any injury upon him. The boatmen thought that he was being hunted by some large fish. During our picnic the sky became overcast and there was a slight shower, but as soon as the whole party had enveloped themselves in mackintoshes the sun shone out brightly once more. Changes of weather come very rapidly; that night at three A.M. a heavy gale sprang up, so wild that it blew in the casement and upset the

A RIVAL FISHERMAN: THE OSPREY
(From a Drawing by G. E. LODGE)

looking-glass in the room over my head, and roused most of us from our slumbers, but next morning there was a dead calm and the heat was almost oppressive. But none of these changes brought the rain which was wanted to raise the river.

On 27th August we had a most delightful expedition to the lakes at the head of the valley, which I had never before visited. We breakfasted early, and started soon after ten, a picturesque cavalcade. Four started in two stolkjaerres, and I followed with Ole in a carriole, almost the first time since 1865 that I have occupied that conveyance. We ambled merrily along a road very narrow and steep in some places, especially where it crossed the screed above Peter Pool. The engineers will have their work cut out for them to convey labour and materials for a great reservoir and conduit at the head of the valley over such difficult country, but I was told that they propose to construct a contractor's railway along the lower part, and make a new road higher up. We reached the little farm above Odegaard a little before noon, and were warmly greeted by the handsome athletic farmer and his family. The eldest son, a lad about twelve years old, hurried down from the upland meadow on the other side of the river, where he had been busy getting in the hay, and he and his two blue-eyed fair-haired little sisters were made happy with a present of sweets. We left our horses and conveyances at the farm, and started on foot up a winding path through a natural rock garden rich with ferns, flowers, bright berries, and shrubs. Ole, and Jan Dalen the farmer, followed us, carrying wraps and food baskets. His son, as I was informed, had a very narrow escape for his life when a baby of eighteen months old. He and his cousin Inga had been left in a girl's charge in a light hand-cart just above the rocky slope overlooking Hammeren, and she began playing with the cart, which overpowered her and rolled away down the slope, eventually pitching right over a precipice. The girl Inga jumped or fell out before the most dangerous point had been reached, but the baby was carried down with the cart, and by great good fortune lodged on the right side of a large rock, while the empty cart went right over the brow, and was brought up actually in the river half a mile farther down. The unhappy mother witnessed the awful peril from above, but the child mercifully escaped with only slight injuries.

In about half an hour we reached the boat-house at this end of Stor Vand, a most lovely lake some one and a half miles long, fenced on one side by a great barrier of almost perpendicular granite rock seamed with waterfalls, and on the other by an easier slope of birch-clad hill. We trailed a minnow behind the boat as we rowed along, but the fish were not in a taking humour, and only one bright-spotted trout of about a pound took the lure, and he managed to escape just as he was being brought to the boat side. The level of the lake was so unusually low that we had some difficulty in launching our boat, and getting it out into open water through a narrow channel between great submerged boulders. A squirrel gambolled along the path at the bottom, jumping over the stones and low birch trees, but I saw little or no bird life. At about one o'clock we reached the end of Stor Vand, and landed in a lovely wooded glade with rocks emerging from fringes of birch, bird cherry, and rowan, and turned into a little glen on the right, an ideal place for a picnic. We camped and had our lunch where a little semicircle of level grass formed a natural bower, the rocks at the back being so symmetrically arranged as to look like human handiwork. Here we enjoyed an excellent meal, after which three of the party started on an expedition to Haller Vand, the fourth lake out of which one of the two great cascades visible dashes down from the watershed above, near which the great reservoir which is to supply the proposed power-station below Hammeren is to be constructed.

The path ended by the side of the nearest lake, and the pedestrians were conveyed to the end of Lille Vand in a Berthon boat, which returned for us after depositing its freight. I fished off the rocks until the boat came back, landing two small fish, and afterwards cast from the boat for about an hour without getting a single rise. Ole, who was rowing me, declared that the lake was so low that "all the fish had gone up," and it certainly looked like it. I returned to the landing-place, and scrambled down to the bank of the river which flows for some quarter of a mile through the short peninsula which divides Lille Vand from Stor Vand. I never saw a more beautiful pool than the first to which I came, an ideal place for salmon or sea-trout, if it had been possible for migratory fish to reach it. Deep, clear, and rocky, with great submerged boulders for shelter, its appearance delighted my salmon fisherman's eye. It was full of small trout, and I landed fourteen in a very short time, but nothing of any size, although I was told afterwards that fish of a pound and upwards are often caught there. Shortly after five the pedestrians returned delighted with their long expedition, and after tea at the spot where we had lunched we rowed back along Stor Vand, now unruffled by a single ripple, the great rocks showing so clearly below the smooth translucent surface that it was hard to distinguish reflection from reality, shadow from substance. It reminded me of the Sils Lake in the Engadine when first frozen over, where the skaters on the black ice can then distinguish the piles of the old lake dwellings below their feet. Changing lights—purple, mauve, and golden—glowed on the great peaks. I returned full of gratitude to the kind hostess for having given me so perfect an opportunity of seeing the beauties of the valley while still unprofaned by industrialism! When we got home we heard that workmen had been engaged during the day in cutting down the trees round the little log-house at Hammeren. The next day was my last, and the morning broke sunny, fresh, and clear.

On the following morning I was to join the Aaro at Christiansund for her voyage to Hull, but the special steamer which was to convey me over the fjord was not due till midnight, so I had another day to tempt the trout. It was considered that the Sundal, the big river, presented the best chance, and I was sent there with Ole to fish from the boat. Whether through carelessness or impatience I succeeded, when changing my grouse and red hackle fly for a Greenwell, in driving the hook into my forefinger beyond the barb so firmly that it refused to come out for anything short of a surgical operation, which Ole successfully performed with his knife. I got two nice sea-trout of two and one pound respectively in the morning, but did not succeed in rising anything in the afternoon when I fished House and Bridge Pools in the small river. In spite of my ill success, other anglers proved that it was not altogether hopeless, as one lady caught a fish of three and a half pounds at Haarstad in the morning, and Miss Cole got one of two pounds in the afternoon.

After dinner we played a farewell game of bridge, and shortly after eleven I paid a most grateful farewell to my kind hostess and her party, and started for the boat-house, whither my luggage had preceded me. It was a very dark walk, especially the first part of it, where the path down the slope was overshadowed with trees; but Ole looked after me like a father, and I managed to get on board the boat without a stumble. There was no moon, but the sky above was gemmed with stars as we launched out and made our way over the dark water towards the promontory beyond Hammeren, looking eagerly for the lights of the expected steamer. It was promised before midnight, but it did not actually arrive till 12.40, as it had already made another trip to Christiansund with the party from Todal. The fjord was as calm as glass, and the night warm and still, so the delay did not cause us any inconvenience; but the *Beta* certainly did not hurry herself, as we saw her lights more than half an hour before she reached us. It was a weird experience lying out on the still water in a silence only broken occasionally by the distant cry of some sea-bird or owl, and striking matches from time to time to notify our whereabouts, their flare making the darkness around us seem more intense.

When I at length got on board the *Beta* I bade farewell to Ole and Sivert with many regrets, and turned in the little cabin, laying my head upon the very hardest cushion it has ever been my ill fortune to strike. I could realise Jacob's feelings when he laid his head upon a stone; but I had very little sleep, and no dreams of angelic ladders! At six o'clock the skipper brought me in the bottle of hot coffee which Miss Cole had thoughtfully provided, and it proved a most welcome refreshment. Soon afterwards we dropped anchor at Christiansund, and I got on board the *Aaro*, a fine vessel, and a great improvement on the old *Tasso* and *Salmo* which had conveyed my party on former journeys. I had the very calmest voyage home I ever remember; the North Sea was in its best humour, but we would have welcomed a little wind to dissipate the fog which kept the unfortunate captain and officers on the bridge during the greater part of the last twenty-four hours. The mist only just reached the top of our masts, and we could see blue sky and sun above us, while a sort of rainbow of fog seemed to hang by our starboard bow. It was impossible to see any distance, and the boom of our foghorn, answered by others from time to time, was by no means a pleasant sound as we passed through the fishing fleet on the Dogger Bank. We were some hours late at Hull, and the Custom House examination of our baggage was even more perfunctory than usual. I missed the first train from Paddington, but reached home by six o'clock on 1st September, delighted with my short visit to beloved Norway.

CHAPTER XIV

CHRISTMAS SPORT AT POLTALLOCH

MANY years have passed since I described in *Autumns in Argyllshire* twenty-five years of happy holidays spent in my second home in the Western Highlands. During that time—familiar as the place had become to me—I had never visited it in the winter. I was in the happy position of having two ideal resorts, at each of which my whole family were made welcome at the time when their attractions were greatest, and Christmas used always to be dedicated to Hemsted Park, the Kent residence of my dear father, Lord Cranbrook, where a patriarchal tribe of children and grandchildren, joined towards the end by a fourth generation, gathered round their beloved and venerated head. What memories are awakened by the retrospect: those happy days in the woods where the patriarch long after his eightieth year joined in the sport with a zest exceeding that of the youngest of the party; the hour before dinner when the little ones gathered round their grandfather's knees with their picture-books; the impromptu plays and charades in which Henry Graham and his boys, as they then were, showed their musical and dramatic talents before the most appreciative of audiences; the skating parties on the bay pond, the toboganning down the park slopes on tea-trays, guitar-cases, and other improvised sleighs. " I do not know," said one of his little great-grandchildren when told of his death in 1906, "what dear grandpapa will do without children, he was so fond of them." "Oh," replied the other, "he will find lots of little children to play with in heaven."

I am wandering from my subject; those days are past, and it is my autumn holiday-home which now welcomes myself, my wife, and our grown-up sons to a Christmas gathering almost as numerous and congenial. We join the *Grenadier* on an early morning in December to meet on board a numerous band of nephews, nieces, and grand-nephews bound for the same destination, and to find the deck heaped with luggage labelled " Ardrishaig"—dress-baskets, portmanteaus, gun-cases, perambulators, and mail-carts; just as in the days of yore.

. . . .

Here, for I am nothing if not digressive, my mind goes back to the early days when I first undertook the voyage which is now so familiar. Then there was no Caledonian pier at Gourock, no luxurious sleeping-berths on the night train to Glasgow, no palatial hotel. We used to think ourselves lucky if we could get two sticks on which to put a cushion and stretch our legs to the opposite seat; thrice blest if we could make up a large enough party to secure a family saloon where we could repose at full length. Those who travelled down the day before found their quarters at the old-fashioned " Tontine " at Greenock, and the quarters at that crowded time were not always all that could be desired. I remember one occasion when, finding myself rather hot, I raised the sash to find that the window opened into the kitchen. There was a story of old Gye (of the Opera House, Covent Garden), a keen votary of Highland sport, who found himself shown into a very small room, on a table of which the usual enormous Bible (characteristic of Scotch inns) was displayed. He rang the bell, and asked whether it would be convenient to provide him either with a larger room or a smaller Bible. Then, one recalls the old chestnut about Donald the luggage-man, whose patience, albeit monumental, was on one occasion so entirely exhausted by two tiresome old ladies that he told them to go to hell. The shocked and outraged pair went in hot haste to the Captain and demanded the instant dismissal of the culprit. "Dismiss Donald!" replied the Captain; "what would Hutchinson do without him? You might as well ask me to dismiss Mr. Gladstone, or the Pope of Rome. But he certainly ought not to have spoken to you as he did, and I will make him apologise." Donald was duly summoned and admonished, and returned on his unwelcome errand to make the promised apology. "Are you the leddies whom I told to go to hell?" "Yes," said the eldest, now somewhat mollified, and prepared to accept the *amende honorable*. "Well," replied Donald, "the Captain says you needna go."

On board, the scene is much the same as usual; there are the well-informed trippers explaining to tourists the familiar features of the landscape—Rothesay Bay, the two paint-daubed rocks known as the Maids of Bute, the rugged peaks of Arran, and Ardlamont Point, which has acquired a sinister renown from the tragedy which occurred in the "policies." The gulls still follow the steamer with their easy flight, and scramble for scraps after breakfast and the midday meal. The omniscient purser still greets the familiar faces of residents with a smile of recognition, and the view is still entrancing, although the colour now comes from withered bracken instead of purpling heather. There is the old mixture of smiles and tears—it will be wonderful indeed if you are not driven into the saloon by an occasional shower—but, then, how glorious are the gleams of sunshine on the hills, the flying rainbows, and the cloud-effects in the hollows! All too soon for some the steamer draws up at Ardrishaig, where the beckoning porters compete for the privilege of landing your luggage, and the voyage is at an end.

The hour's drive to Poltalloch passes through familiar ground. The fir-trees at Carnbaan are good-sized timber now; when I killed my first roe there they were hardly up to my knees. At Kilmichael Bridge I cast longing looks at the Add, and note that the height of the water at the "Irishman's Stone" indicates that "she" is in order. But what is the good of this information in December? it will be six months at the earliest before a clean salmon is captured in the Add with rod and line, and if we see the Irishman's Pool at all this Christmas, it will be from the banks of Kirnan when we are after woodcocks and cock pheasants. Next the woods of Ballimore stretch upwards to the right, and there some old blackcocks and quite a number of pheasants are feeding in the field outside on the left. It is close time now for the former, and they are tabooed, although it must be confessed that an occasional "crow" finds its way into the bag sometimes in the winter with a suspiciously lyre-shaped curl about the tail. Human nature is frail, and it is hardly possible to resist a shot at some glorious old polygamist as he sails over your head in all the perfection of his glossy winter plumage. Apart from laws, which, of course, deserve all respect, there is no time of the year when the old blackcocks might not be thinned with advantage. Still, I do not defend any defiance of the Legislature; I am no passive resister, and I cry "Peccavi." Let the motorist who has never exceeded the speed limit cast the first stone.

On we go, past Dunadd, and Crinan Moss, far beyond which across the bay, Scarba, and the low part of Jura, are visible where they almost meet at Corryvreken. Soon the "long walk" brings us to the lodge; and if the steamer has been up to time we shall find an excellent lunch on the table; if not, we shall already have "satisfied our desire of food and drink" with mutton broth and roast beef on board the steamer between Tarbert and Ardrishaig.

I have now reached my destination, and, as the sun sets early at Christmas-time in Argyllshire, there can be no regular shooting to-day; possibly we may try flighting for duck before tea-time, or stroll upon the links to look for a snipe. Still, there is a pause in the proceedings, of which I will take advantage to make another digression, this time upon the subject of winter shooting in Scotland generally. I do not disparage the delights of a grouse drive, or even those of a big day at pheasants in the South, especially if the keeper knows how to show them for sport, and not only for massacre. But as I grow older the mere size of the bag appeals to me less and less, and I become more and more convinced that the best and truest sport is that in which you seek out and get wild game for yourself, with no other companion than some old and tried four-footed friend. If there are any who agree with me in this, and have time and opportunity for a holiday at Christmas, I can recommend Scotland, preferably one of the countless islands, great and small, which constitute the archipelago of the Hebrides. You may answer that the days are short. Well, anticipate Mr. Willett and the Daylight Bill, and make an early breakfast and start, and you will be ready enough for an arm-chair and a pipe by the time the sun sets, if you have worked your hardest through fir plantations and birch scrub, and over rock, heather, and bog. Perhaps it may rain—that I cannot deny—but it will do you no manner of harm if you keep going while you are out, and change into a dry suit and slippers when you get home. If you have any more excuses to urge, I will argue with you no longer. Stick to your covert-side crawling with hand-reared pheasants, your stove-warmed tent for lunch, your three hot courses, and your champagne; but I doubt if your pleasure will equal that of the impecunious sportsman who is spending a brief holiday in some distant and, perhaps, not very commodious inn, round which he has acquired the right of roaming over quite a large tract of country for a sum which does not constitute too heavy a drain upon his scanty means. The bays and inlets will be full of wild ducks, widgeon and pochard; the golden plover will be feeding on the links; you will be pretty sure of getting some snipe and woodcock, and possibly, if you are on an island

and there is hard weather or snow on the mainland, you may happen upon a flight of cock which will give you sport beyond your wildest expectations. If you are a naturalist as well as a sportsman, you will have an unrivalled opportunity of observing and studying the habits of the rarer ducks and the waders and shore birds, and will probably have a chance of fathoming the inner meaning of the proverbial expression "a wild-goose chase." You may also see—but I hope you will not shoot—that magnificent and graceful wild swan, the Hooper. They are regular visitors to Islay, Colonsay, Coll, and Tiree, those paradises of the wildfowler; but I am glad to say they are very rarely interfered with. Although our ancestors liked to have them on their tables, I fancy it was more for show than for food; a young cygnet is fairly palatable, but you will be very unlucky if your day's sport does not furnish something for the pot more palatable and more suitable to the resources of an inn-kitchen than a wild swan.

Now let us hark back to Poltalloch, where, after a game of billiards, the whole party turn in early, rejoicing in the prospect of shooting the home beat the next day. Travelling and sea air make one sleepy, and I can hardly believe that it is time to get up when a knock at the door and the announcement that it is seven o'clock, rouses me from a sound slumber. Breakfast is at eight on shooting days, when we start at ten, as the sun sets soon after three. It is dark enough when I go into my dressing-room, after just forty winks more, but the electric light now deprives early rising of what was formerly its principal drawback. My window looks out over Crinan Bay and the Knapdale Hills, and before very long a faint pink halo begins to tinge the distant horizon, and soon

> "Night's candles are burnt out, and jocund day
> Stands tiptoe on the misty mountain brow."

The morning is all that could be desired; there is just a catch of white frost, and just enough wind to make the pheasants fly. I can see one or two "stops" already in their places on the flat between the window and the sea which divides Calton Mòr wood from Barsloisnach, the high wooded rock above the farm. Devoutly do I hope that they will succeed in keeping a good head of birds in that rather thin covert, for the Barsloisnach pheasant is something of a revelation. I have seen a good many high pheasants in my time: they flew well at Wimpole when Arthur Wood hired it and asked me to his shooting; or, nearer London, they were remarkably tall near the lodge and over the railway at Kingswood Warren, in the reign of Cosmo Bonsor, when even such experts as Mr. Rimington Wilson found their mettle tried. Perhaps the highest birds I have ever seen in England were at Roche Abbey, in Yorkshire, where the guns were placed in a deep valley between two hills, as in the present case, but none equal the height of the Barsloisnach pheasants. We number eight guns, all nearly related by blood or marriage except two—Tom Murray, most genial and trustworthy of Edinburgh writers, and his son. These two are a standing Christmas dish at Poltalloch, as welcome and as necessary as the mince-pies and plum-puddings. One gun goes round to the other side to walk up the road from the lodge, and take any birds that may try to break away to

Mheall; another heads the covert by the old cairn, and the rest form two rows in the park between the woods. There is little choice between the front and back rows; the "gleaning of the grapes of Ephraim" will be as satisfactory as the vintage, and the second row will have more time to see the birds coming, as well as the satisfaction of possibly "wiping the eye" of the first performers. There is no jealousy among the party who stand at attention as the rapping of sticks in the distance tells of the advance of the beaters. The first game to show are three roe, one a fine buck, but, of course, without horns at this time of year. How gracefully and noiselessly the deer glide along, trying first this side, then that, and finally braving the open, and passing close by the whole line of guns; at last, leaping without an effort over the iron fence in the middle, they disappear, unscathed and very little frightened, into Calton Mòr. There is not one of the party who would think of shooting a roe with a shot-gun, or killing one at all with its head bare of its beautiful trophy. True, old Colquhoun, in *The Moor and the Loch*, once a text-book, recommends shooting roe preferably in the winter, because they are then better eating than in the autumn, and also recommends a shot-gun and buckshot as the best method of getting them; but in that respect, like the old Greek, "we boast ourselves to be much better than our fathers," and it is beyond question that we have much better rifles.

The first pheasant is now upon the wing, and it looks as if it meant coming over my head. Diana grant me a good judgment, a straight eye, and a steady hand! I wait until it is nearly over me before I raise the gun to my shoulder; in my opinion there is no surer way of missing a high pheasant than to begin to take aim too soon. It is very high, but I think the choke-bore will reach it, and sure enough, when I swing the barrels well in front of it and pull the trigger, the kind bird collapses and falls, stone dead as I think in the pride of my heart. Not a bit of it! He falls with a thud which one would have thought would break every bone in his body and extinguish the last spark of life if haply any lingered; yet he lifts his head and runs off as if nothing had happened, but, of course, is gathered by the retriever that is waiting behind with the keeper before he has gone any distance. In the *Paradise of Birds*—a book now nearly forgotten, but one which will well repay the perusal of anyone who loves natural history, delicate wit, and true poetry—Courthope puts into the mouth of the nightingale the following verses:

> "Man that is born of a woman
> Man her un-web-footed drake,
> Featherless, beakless, and human,
> Is what he is by mistake.
> For they say that a sleep fell on nature
> In the midst of the making of things,
> And she left him a two-legged creature,
> But wanting in wings.
>
> Therefore ye birds in all ages,
> Man, in his hopes of the sky,
> Caught us and clapped us in cages,
> Seeking instruction to fly.
>   .   .   .   .   .
> But he never can mount as the swallows
> Who dash round his steeples to pair,
> Or hawk the bright flies in the hollows,
> Of delicate air."

We talk of the conquest of the air, and it would seem as if the lesson was at least partly learned; well were it for the hapless aeronauts who almost every day pay the penalty of their daring if they could acquire this second gift of their winged models—that of falling with impunity!

The birds are coming thicker now, and my pride has a fall, as the next two birds pass over my head apparently unscathed. I try to persuade myself that it is not my fault, and that no gun made by human gun-maker would reach them; but my theory is rudely disproved by my youngest son, who, standing immediately behind me, brings down out of the clouds one of the cocks I have just missed. All are now at work, for the pheasants are coming thicker, and great is the jubilation over each successful shot; but although the guns are above the average, many more birds escape than are gathered. As the beaters approach nearer the birds are easier, as they rise from a lower slope and are not flying so fast. I confess I should like to see some of the absolutely first-class guns, such as our present King, Lord Ripon, or Lord Walsingham, try their hands at these high-flyers. I think a fair proportion would still manage to run the gauntlet with success.

The pick-up is not very large when we finish the beat and move across to Calton Môr wood, where we hope to meet not a few of our friends again at somewhat closer quarters, and to gather a few of the high birds that have flown on apparently uninjured to collapse suddenly when out of sight over the brow of the hill. One or two woodcocks have found their way into the bag, but they are not particularly fond of these old coverts; they prefer a young fir plantation, or the natural birch scrub on a hillside. Besides, there has been no hard weather to bring in the flights, which will probably be found in greater abundance on the east coast.

The next beat is not particularly interesting. The wood just round the house is fairly rocky and undulating, but the pheasants, although they fly well, are only fairly good birds. The object of the next two beats is to drive as many as possible into the high wooded hill at the back between the house and the fernery, from which nearly every shot will be at a real rocketer. The only singular incident of the drive is provided by a roe, which charges the high deer-fence that separates the garden from the wood, and gets between the two top strands of wire, about six feet high and less than one foot apart, as gracefully as, nay, far more gracefully than, any coryphee performing in the arena with a paper hoop. It looked, to the eyes of the spectator, as if he had passed through without touching the wire on either side—a truly marvellous feat; but when we examine the place we find a telltale bunch of mouse-coloured hair, which proves that he must have hit the lower wire pretty hard. However, he is certainly not much the worse, for he gallops lightly over the tennis-lawn, takes the stone wall by the gate in his stride, and disappears across the park, heading in the direction of Ach Vean, to the great delight of some of the younger members of the family, who, with their nurses, are watching the sport from the windows.

Then comes the last beat before lunch, that from the high hill at the back already alluded to, and, although there is certainly nothing romantic in the

SPORT AT POLTALLOCH

surroundings, the birds are sure to provide another very enjoyable half-hour's sport. One gun is stationed at the bottom of the rock-garden, the work and gift of William Mitchell, the lifelong friend and, in his latter years, the constant companion of the old Laird, John Malcolm, my father-in-law, and, like him, an ardent collector of drawings and prints by Old Masters, and a generous benefactor to the British Museum. Three years ago, in a green old age, he followed his friend into the silent land, and now, at his expressed wish, he lies in the little burying-ground by St. Columba's Church, hardly a stone's-throw from where we are now standing.

Another gun is placed in the drying-ground, just at the back of the house, and I and the rest of the party are posted at various marks, about thirty yards apart, just below a great bank of rhododendrons, which slopes upwards to the wood we have just left, where, in June, the beautiful plants provide a feast of colour for those eyes which are fortunate enough to behold them. Many of the rare Himalayan and other varieties blossom vigorously here, in the sheltered situation, peaty soil, and damp warm climate which suits them so well. Soon the pheasants begin to come, "first by twos and threes, and then by swarms," and a goodly number take their last flight. The gun in the drying-ground, Alfred Bonham Carter, creates huge delight in the gallery by dropping one bird upon the roof, and another right through the nursery window, where the invaded nurse claims and receives it as a perquisite.

I need not describe the rest of the day. The lunch in the saddle-room, full of beautiful sets of harness now little required in these days of motors, or the afternoon on the rocky slopes of Barrachoan and Barachrome, where we see a sprinkling of black-game, and get a good many more very sporting pheasants, and a fair number of woodcocks. The total bag in the evening is not large according to modern ideas, some two hundred pheasants, and about fifty "various" —woodcock, hares, rabbits, and pigeons. We see, but do not shoot at, a few of the wild turkeys; there are none of the grand but mischievous capercailzie which form such a feature of a Perthshire beat in winter. I believe the Duke of Argyll was one of the first to reintroduce them at Inveraray, but I have never myself seen one on any part of the Poltalloch estate, although I have heard that one or two have been seen on the other side of the Crinan Canal. We have seen a good many more roe, and several fallow deer, both bucks and does; and altogether we are a contented party when we gather in the smoking-room for a pipe and chat before tea. Here the walls are adorned not only with trophies of the chase—moose, red-deer, and kangaroo—but also with the collection of South Sea clubs and other weapons which the great navigator Captain Cook collected in his first and second voyages, and gave to his great friend Dr. Orme, the great-grandfather of the present Laird, just before starting for that fatal third and last journey when he met his death at the hands of those natives to whom he was so true a friend and benefactor.

I will not weary my readers by giving detailed descriptions of all the varied delights of the next fortnight. We have three or four more regular "second times through" before the beaters are dismissed for the season. There is the wild day when we shot the woods on the Moss, Mheall, and Moine-an-Tarbh, when the birds beat the guns so completely at the latter place by twisting back just out of shot—or so I try to believe—and escaping scatheless into the high covert. There are the snipe that rise from the rushy paddocks as we make our way to the castle wood. There are those splendid high birds that rocket over our heads out of Mheall between the keeper's house and the Scoinish burn, some of which splash into the water and float down the swollen stream, which at this time of year is full of spawning salmon and kelts. In the autumn the trout which it contains are mere fingerlings, hardly worth fishing for except on an off-day, although it is visited by an occasional sea-trout and not a few very small flounders. Then there is that delightful day at Barnakil, when we beat the birch-clad slopes which rise out of the moss near Dun-a-Muich, between the bridge over the canal at Bellanoch, and Carn-baan, haunt beloved of the roe, where I have had many a happy hunt in the old autumns. To-day we see plenty of roe, and—*mirabile dictu!*—three red-deer, which, as I learn with great surprise, have taken up their abode in these woods and in the neighbouring plantation of Ballimore. During all my long stay at Poltalloch I had never before seen a red-deer nearer than at Eriden, on Loch Awe side, now no longer a part of the estate; but I was destined to encounter these once again, and at closer quarters. We see also two or more large packs of the old black-cocks which haunt the adjacent Moss. Whether any of them found their way into the bag must remain a mystery. If they did, it was strictly against the

Laird's orders; but we see a really considerable number of woodcocks in spite of the open weather, although the number bagged is not very great. The ground is broken, and it is not possible always to know where the forward and side guns are placed, so there would be some risk of accident if those who walk with the beaters shot at low-flying birds, unless they could see a clear barrier of hill in the foreground. Happily to-day we have a cautious team, who all know and can trust one another not to fire dangerous shots.

Next comes a break for Christmas Day, when, thanks to my rubicund face and silvery locks, I am pressed into the part of Father Christmas, and made to walk round past the window and enter by a circuitous route the drawing-room, where, by the side of a gigantic Christmas-tree, I distribute presents and crackers to a large gathering of delighted children. I appreciate the thoroughness of my disguise when I am condoled with by one of my nephews a little later for having missed the treat. On Sunday afternoon all stroll about, some to Duntroon Castle and to the sea, and others, of whom I am one, to the little plantation on the banks of the Scoinish, where there are tidings of an otter. We do not, of course, see him, but there are abundant indications of his presence. We find no less than three fair-sized salmon with the titbit eaten out of their shoulder and the rest left to the rats and gulls. Ugly red kippers they are, with beaks like reaping-hooks, and no one is disposed to play jackal to the otter's lion, as is often done when the fish are fresh from the sea. We can see the tracks of the marauder well enough, and the broad worn path where he slides down into the water. It would not be difficult to trap him; but the Laird likes to have a few about, in spite of their mischievous habits, and I have a good deal of sympathy with his desire to have all the fauna of Argyllshire fairly represented, even if some of them take toll of the game and fish. If the misguided energy of keepers was transferred from the destruction of peregrine falcons, and even such smaller falconidæ as the hobby and merlin, to the rat and the jackdaw, it would be better both for the game-preserver and the farmer; and the lover of nature would more often be able to watch the magnificent spectacle of the swoop of the peregrine on grouse, curlew, or wild duck, or to see the same performance repeated in miniature by his duodecimo edition, the merlin, in pursuit of pipit, lark, or snipe.

There are only two more days before the beaters are dismissed, on one of which we beat the woods of Largie round Carnasary Castle, while the other is spent in the plantations between Crinan Moss and Duntroon, ending up at Mheall and Moine-an-Tarbh. On neither day does the bag exceed one hundred and fifty head, but quality again makes up for the absence of any considerable quantity. On the whole the weather is kind to us, for although we have "some showers," there is nothing to stop shooting, and we are spared the crowning infliction of heavy snow. This latter is not a very common experience on the West Coast, but I have a vivid recollection of the heavy fall of December 1909, which caught us on the slopes of Kirnan, more than eight miles from home, and rendered the road impracticable for motors on the return journey. It was a long and slippery walk across the hill and through Ballimore before we found our way home, and I felt that I had accomplished something of a feat for a sexagenarian when I changed my heavy boots for slippers in the gun-room. The next day the drifts were so deep that the coach was unable to run between Kilmartin and Ardrishaig, and we had to go without our mail. On the following day some of the party, whose holiday-time was over, only just managed, with two horses in a light dogcart, to struggle over to the pier in time for the boat; but the road a little beyond Kilmichael bridge was still blocked by a huge drift, which had to be circumvented by taking the trap into the meadow to the right, between the road and Dun-a-Muich, driving in at one gate and out at the other.

After the three regular days' shooting were over, there still remained those hardly less delightful days when, with my two nephews, accompanied only by two or three keepers and a couple of spaniels, we devoted our attention to trying to mop up some of the remaining old cock pheasants and any stray woodcocks that happened to have come in. Twenty pheasants was the maximum hoped for, but each bird killed represented a triumph, for it was impossible for the guns to cover the ground, and only a tithe of the birds seen presented themselves within shot. Few birds are more "leary" than a real old wild cock pheasant when he has been beaten for a few times. One day when the keepers were busy and we wanted to walk, we made our way to Ballimore, accompanied by only one gillie, and had a very successful drive from the field on the right-hand, over the road. We saw nearly a dozen old cocks feeding in the roots, and our one beater was able to put them over the guns so

RED DEER IN BALLIMORE WOOD

well that we secured five of their number. As they were making for the top of the wood, which is planted on the side of a steep hill, they were quite satisfactory rocketers as they crossed the road. I must confess that I found it rather hard work walking through the wood in line with the others afterwards, and had to use my hands as well as my feet to help me over the steep hummocks and over the heathery boulders which strew the bottom of the covert, and that most of the few woodcocks that I saw were too quick for me, occupied as I was in looking to my footsteps. I was rewarded, however, for all my toil, when three splendid red-deer, one a royal, if not an imperial, stag, blundered out of the thick fir-wood into an open glade and trotted just in front of me, so near that I might easily have secured the splendid head by planting a charge of number five shot just behind the shoulder. Such things are done in Germany, where the horns are the only part of the stag valued; but I am thankful to say that I know of no forest in Scotland where the coveted royal which has eluded the eager pursuit of the stalker during the season has been slaughtered for his head in the winter by some rifle when in nominal pursuit of the hinds. It is creditable that this should be the case when we reflect how difficult it is in some forests to dispose of all the venison killed, even when a most liberal allowance of haunches has been dumped upon friends and acquaintances.

On off-days the snipe by the Old River, a marsh left by the shifting course of the Add, or on the links by the seashore, or in the rushy fields between them and the Moss, afford an excuse for a ramble, with always the possibility of a duck or widgeon—possibly even a goose, although these latter are not common. Great flocks of wild-fowl are always found between Bellanoch Bridge and Crinan, and again in Port-na-Dewar bay; but the ground is too open to stalk them, and they are "ill to drive." All the more does one feel a sense of jubilation when a successful ambush and a well-arranged drive have enabled us to secure one or two couple. Perhaps one may get a curlew, or put an end to the marauding of a black-backed gull, one of the worst enemies of eggs and young game, and not infrequently also guilty of destroying young lambs and picking out their eyes. The hoarse bark of the raven overhead betrays the identity of the "blot in heaven," which at that distance could not, if silent, be distinguished from rook, crow, or even jackdaw; cormorants wing their flight between Crinan and Loch Fyne, and long-winged herons flap out of the deep drains.

So passes our Christmas at Poltalloch, and the fortnight seems to have flown all too rapidly when we find ourselves once more upon the pier at Ardrishaig waiting for the *Grenadier* to take us South. May we have many more such Christmas visits, and may I be fortunate enough for once to hit upon a season when the guns come in for a real good flight of woodcock! There is a new plantation growing up on Kilchoan banks, between the house and Duntroon, which ought to be an ideal place for these birds in a year or two. Never, I regret to say, have I so far been fortunate enough to hit upon even an average season for cock, and the sportsman always hankers after just the *one* thing he fails to obtain. Why should I be denied the sort of sport my nephew Bonham Carter got at Taynish in January 1910, just after I left Argyllshire, when he and two others bagged nearly two hundred and sixty-six cock in a week—one hundred and eighty-one in three days?

"Little I ask; my wants are few,"

as Oliver Wendell Holmes writes in his well-known lines on contentment. Like him, I only want a little more than I have so far succeeded in obtaining, and if next year only twenty, or at most thirty, woodcocks fall to my gun in a single day's sport, I shall endeavour to be satisfied!

> "If heaven more generous gifts deny,
> I shall not miss them *much* ;
> Too grateful for the blessings lent
> Of simple tastes and mind content!"

CHAPTER XV

HOME AT LAST. DONNINGTON PRIORY

BREAKFAST is over, and it is time to feed the trout which have gathered hungry and expectant just opposite the bow-window of the drawing-room, where the Lambourne flows clear and rapid over a bed of fine gravel shining out brightly between masses of brilliant green starwort, crowfoot, and water-celery. My wife complains, not without some foundation, that visitors who are slow at their meals run the risk of having their plates snatched away and the toast-rack emptied, before they have satisfied their hunger. Certainly there are plenty of hungry mouths outside waiting to be filled. A little concourse of robins, chaffinches, blackbirds, thrushes, and impudent and irrepressible sparrows, have gathered round the bird-table, and Mrs. Wagtail,

"The dainty-stepping duchess of the green,"

has temporarily deserted the numerous and clamorous family in her nest in the *Pyrus japonica* against the wall and, although insectivorous by nature, is as ready for her share of crumbs as any of the party.

Their wants are soon supplied, and it is but a step to the water's edge. There a goodly number of fat trout are waiting for their breakfast, and they fairly jostle one another in their eagerness to swallow the

FEEDING THE TROUT

THE BIG GUNNERA

good things provided. Most of the broken bread and toast is taken almost as soon as it touches the water, and great plops and circles a little lower down betray the presence of an outer ring of pensioners, who take care that not a crumb is wasted. "Of course," says a fair spectator, "you never catch these dear tame fish." "My good lady," I reply, "we do not catch many of them, for they have a very keen appreciation of the difference between floating crumb and the most deftly presented dry fly, and are extraordinarily shy and difficult to please when fished over with a Wickham or an olive quill; tame as they seem, they will hide themselves in the weeds in a moment if the shadow of a rod or line falls on the water. The stream runs sharply, and there is abundance of weed, for I am no believer in leaving fish without food and shelter; and it is no easy thing to put a fly neatly over a rising fish in the narrow channels between the cresses so that it goes over him properly cocked, and without any drag. Still it is occasionally done; but the expert who, from his vantage-ground behind the big Gunnera, has succeeded in beguiling one of these fine fat fellows may justly pride himself upon his lightness of hand, the directness of his cast, and the skill with which he has 'skull-dragged' his prize over the weeds, or guided him down the clear water at the side before he has had time to bury himself in one of those thick patches which generally mean a broken cast and a lost fly. If you should happen to meet that fish upon the breakfast-table you will find that his farinaceous diet has agreed with him, and will be slow to hurl reproaches at his captor."

The next item on the programme is a stroll down

the stream as far as my boundary, but the rod may be left behind for the time being, as my old spaniel Ben expects his morning outing, and hates the sight of a fishing-rod now that his mature years and rheumatism make the pursuit of rats in the backwater and ditches a "fearful joy." To please him I shoulder my gun and pocket half a dozen cartridges, and as soon as he sees the weapon he begins to gambol about like a puppy, in spite of his sixteen years; for no amount of experience has convinced him of the extreme improbability of his having anything to pick up. The jackdaws have learnt caution, the rats will not be about so early, and it is only very occasionally that a casual wood-pigeon passes within range. Off we start together down the stream, I keeping my eyes open to see whether there is any fly on the water; for in the improbable event of an early rise it will only be the work of a few moments to return for my rod which is always in readiness by the terrace-door—a ten-foot split cane, made in one piece, as is best for rods which are not required to be carried off the premises by road or rail. Through the garden we stroll, past the old mulberry-tree; then, leaving the kitchen-garden on the left, we skirt the boathouse where the canoe is kept, and soon come to the meeting of the waters, where the main stream joins the mill-lead just below a little artificial fall, constructed in 1911 to deepen and slacken the stream above. It has been a great success on the whole. At first our domestic engineering was a failure, as the weight of water undermined the sleepers and piles, and the whole structure threatened to give way; but the difficulty was overcome by a mantlet of boards nailed on horizontally,

which directed the rush of water well over the top;
and it has successfully resisted even the exceptional
floods of the winter and early spring, and not merely
serves its purpose as a dam, but also makes a pretty
little fall washing out a big hole, aerating the water,
and keeping the gravel clear and bright in one of the
best spawning-beds in the whole length of water. A
green path between a sort of subsidiary kitchen-
garden and the willow-fringed stream, which here
widens, brings us down to a foot-bridge, the centre
plank of which can be drawn up by a rope to allow
the canoe to pass. This leads to a wooded island,
an acre and a half in extent—a great nesting-place
for all sorts of birds in the spring. In spite of its
proximity to Newbury and the Oxford road, the
island nearly always holds a fox, and occasionally an
otter, and one year a vixen reared a litter of three
cubs under the haystack in the meadow skirting its
farther side. Our path next follows a narrow peninsula between the river and a backwater; the upper
part near the foot-bridge is not very easy to fish, as
an old quince-orchard and numerous graceful willows
are more decorative than useful to the angler. I see
plenty of fish both in the main stream on my right
hand—here broad and somewhat shallow—and in the
backwater on my left, but they are low down in the
water, and take no notice of the very occasional blue-
winged olives, which are the only flies showing yet.
That was the plop of a water-vole into the stream,
but he does not show himself for a shot. I must
admit that I do not look very hard, as I hate to shoot
the pretty creatures, although it is absolutely necessary
to keep their numbers in some check: the repairs and

renovation of the banks rendered necessary by their destructive habits forms no small item of my expenditure. Just below the cattle bridge over the backwater a mallard and his consort circle round, sacred, of course, at this time of year. The duck has, I suspect, a nest or a small family somewhere about in the water-meadows. Last year two nested side by side within a foot of one another under the alder-bush near my boundary-fence, which we are now rapidly approaching, and reared families, of nine and seven respectively, from which I took tithe in August. Here the main stream is separated from Shaw water by a brick-and-iron hatchway, impassable by boat or canoe; but the backwater joins the still wide winding stream below, and a boarded portage across the peninsula sloping into the water on each side makes it easy enough to carry the canoe across when some of the party want to go farther down the stream to enjoy a view of the beautiful Elizabethan house of my hospitable neighbour. There King Charles made his headquarters during the second battle of Newbury, which was fought all round the ground which I and my dog have just been traversing.

Up to now I have seen nothing to shoot, but just opposite to my lowest bridge, over which I shall cross into Horsepools to turn homewards, a mark presents itself. There, in that patch of sedges in the backwater, a dabchick has constructed its absurdly prominent nest, and is now engaged in its maternal but ridiculous habit of working away for dear life covering up the eggs with reeds at the sight of a man, a gun, and a dog. The ostrich, which hides its head in the sand, has become proverbial for its stupidity, but at least its stratagem in no way *increases* the chance of discovery, whereas the industrious dabchick does away with the possibility of your mistaking its nest for a lump of stranded weed or one of the numerous false nests which, like the wren, she is in the habit of making and abandoning before she finally fixes upon that real receptacle for her eggs which she is now advertising with such guileless simplicity. A shot at this range would get rid of

> All the pretty chickens and their dam
> At one fell swoop.

And the shot ought to be fired, for there is, unfortunately, no doubt of the destructiveness of these pretty little fish-eating birds on a trout-stream; but I have not the heart to take advantage of my opportunity, and hasten across the bridge. A kingfisher skims along the little stream, hardly wider than a ditch, which forms the boundary of the island on this side, tracing in its arrowy flight a line of gleaming azure. Knee-deep in the lush meadow-grass, with the green of which their bright fawn-coloured coats form so pretty a contrast, are the three heifer-calves my pedigree Guernseys so kindly provided last year—Sunflower, the eldest; Pease-Blossom, so-called because born on Midsummer night's eve; and Sweet Briar. They are now more than a year old, and well-grown and personable little people, and they receive and seem to appreciate my greeting and caressing hand as they gather round me undeterred by the presence of their old friend Ben. They have been handled and led from babyhood, as no doubt their forbears were in the island of which they are so valuable a product, and their familiarity and engaging little ways well repay the attention. They follow us as far as the line of hurdles, from which at last I catch sight of another possible mark. Three or four young rabbits are sitting out under the haystack; but Ben has seen them too, and by dashing forward in the vain hope of catching one effectually prevents the possibility of getting a shot. So we pass through the gate and home over the "rabbit bridge" just above the fall, so-called because there is a gate and wire-netting to prevent the rabbits crossing into the garden. Then we pass the old sundial and find our way home under the copper-beech and across the lawn-tennis ground, having completed the "trivial round," which takes place nearly every fine morning.

I have seen nothing to tempt me to break my ordinary rule of devoting the morning to work, so it is not until nearly three o'clock that I take down my rod from its hooks, sling my bag over my shoulder, and suspend a light net to a ring attached by a safety-pin to the flap of my left-hand coat-pocket. Ben watches my proceedings with interest, not unmingled with disgust, and displays some curiosity to ascertain in which direction I mean to turn my steps. If I turn to the right and cross the Oxford road to the upper water, above the mill where I make my electric light by the wheel which formerly used to grind flour, he will condescend to accompany me, but if I start in the direction of our morning walk he will not follow me a yard. Well! I may as well humour him, so I turn to the right and cross the road by Donnington Hospital, a picturesque almshouse for old men, the charter of which dates from Richard the

HOME AT LAST

Second, although the existing building is of comparatively modern date. Two or three of the pensioners as usual are leaning over the parapet of the bridge by which the road crosses the mill-stream, watching the trout in the broad shallow reach above. Possibly I might catch one there—it has occasionally happened—but I am not fond of fishing before a gallery; so, passing them and making my way between the almshouse and the mill-stream, I cross the hatch above the mill and find myself in a narrow strip of garden bounded on my right by the deep slow-flowing stretch of water which forms the mill-lead, and upon the left by a small water-meadow. Here I can already see two or three fish quietly rising; but, as I cannot detect any fly coming down the stream, I suspect that they are taking " curses," so decide that the medium-sized Wickham which is attached to the fine point at the end of my cast is as likely to do as any other fly, or, at any rate, that I am too lazy to change it at present. It is by no means an easy place from which to approach a rising fish, as the bank is high, there is a garden below me, and an apple-tree has been planted at the outer edge of the gravel-path upon which I am standing; still I can sometimes manage to switch a long line over a rise without catching the boughs behind me, and this time fortunately, by the help of a favourable up-stream wind, the first cast goes very near the right place without scaring the fish and at the second offer the Wickham floats over him nicely cocked, and he takes it gallantly. A short struggle ensues; but there is no refuge here, except a little riband-weed, which is as useless for shelter as it is for holding food, so in spite of his gallant efforts my fish is soon in the net, a bright shapely trout of about three-quarters of a pound, just over the limit. The Lambourne does not grow such monsters as the neighbouring Kennet, into which it discharges, where there are giants indeed. There fish of five pounds are quite common, and a twelve-pounder was taken under Newbury Bridge in the very middle of the town not a week ago—by what means I had rather not say; but there are compensations, as the fishing in the larger stream is practically confined to a glorious carnival of some three weeks' duration when the May-fly is up, while the little Lambourne gives sport from May until well into September. The *post-mortem* is soon made, and shows that the fish has been taking a few duns, but that the staple of his food has consisted of small round water-snails, swallowed shells and all, and he is deposited with a couple of handfuls of fresh grass in the bottom of the bag.

Let me in passing recommend such of my brother anglers as have not already adopted the practice, always to clean their fish as soon as caught. From a culinary point of view the flesh benefits enormously, and valuable oracles may be read, as of old, from the *spirantia exta*. For south-country anglers I cannot urge the further advantage that it lightens the bag, but there have been days in Norway, and on the Deveron in spring, when I have been glad of a really material diminution of a welcome but heavy burden.

To-day I am not destined to catch anything more before I go through the gate just above the foot-bridge that connects the two portions of the garden at Riverside, and pass out into the open water-meadow. I have put down one rising fish, but the only thing I have caught has been the overhanging bough of a willow behind me, and I deem it fortunate that I have been able to release my fly without a break. Now my task becomes easier, as there are no trees behind me, and it is easy to get out of sight of the fish by keeping down between the main ditch of the water-meadow and the high bank. Fish are almost always rising in this portion of the stream; and in the upper part, where there is a much-frequented shallow, they usually rise so near the opposite bank of a wide stream, that I may stand upright and close to the water on my own side without any risk of their seeing me. But they are very shy risers just here—perhaps because they are a good deal fished for—and the long line required to reach them soon sinks the fly or causes a fatal drag, while the necessary slack makes it very difficult to hook those fish that are persuaded to rise. Two fish in the basket, and three smaller ones returned, is my total when I reach the cart-bridge into the park of Donnington Grove, and the deep hole just above it, into which a weir discharges the waters of an artificial lake, is the limit of my water; but it is a favourite spot, as it always holds some good fish, and they generally rise well and freely. It is surrounded by trees on both sides, but by cutting down the big alder, which now lies horizontally along the shore and forms a solid support for the two or three cartloads of old bricks and rubbish which have been shot here to harden the bank, it has been made possible to reach almost to the broken water of the weir, although it requires care and accuracy to fish it properly.

The weir is, as I have said, the limit of my own fishing, but I have sometimes been privileged by my neighbour's permission to enjoy a day in the water above. There are some fine fish in the lake, although I do not think they are ever as good either for sporting or eating purposes as the real river ones; but I have hardly ever fished there.

I had, however, a funny experience one day from the bridge, now visible about thirty yards above the weir, which carries the road from the lodge over the end of the lake. I was looking over the parapet, and could see quite plainly two or three big fish in the still clear water below. One, a big rather black fellow, was occasionally sucking in the flies that floated over him, and I managed more by good luck than good guidance to float down a black gnat just in the centre of one of his rises, without scaring him. He took it like a lion, and after a brief struggle (for he was in poor condition) was describing circles at the top of the water. But how to land him? The bridge is a parapeted arch quite six feet above the stream, and the road below it is fenced on both sides. To lift the fish must, of course, have resulted in an instant break, and the handle of my landing-net was not nearly long enough to reach the water. At this crisis came the *dea ex machina*, in the shape of one of the maidservants riding home from her shopping in Newbury on a bicycle. I pointed out my difficulty, and entreated her to take my net, go round the corner below and secure my fish, which by this time had not a kick left in him. I could not persuade her to attempt this feat, but with some difficulty prevailed upon her to take my rod and hold it steady while I myself descended and landed the fish, a great ugly brute weighing about two and a half pounds, which ought to have been over three had it been in good condition. I was not going to eat him myself, but I presented him to one of the old men at the almshouse, where quantity is more valued than quality, and received his effusive thanks both before and after the brute had been cooked. Never before, he said, had he eaten such a fish, and I can well believe it!

I once killed an uglier and much larger fish also in a queer way in Mr. Abel Smith's water at Wood Hall in Hertfordshire. There also the river flows through a large artificial lake—the work, I believe, of "Capability Brown"—and falls over a hatch into a large deep pool. I had just reached this spot when a violent thunderstorm came on. I took shelter under an alder-bush, and in the deep hole below me, not three yards off, I spied a giant trout, blear-eyed and black, one of those cannibal brutes which are as great a pest in a stream as a pike. Partly to occupy the time I determined to try to "snatch" him, for there is no need to be particular about the method used to get rid of such vermin. I had no poaching-tackle in my box, but I took off the fine point of my casting-line and attached a big alder to the gut. I sunk it with some difficulty, for I had no weight on, and twice I brought the hook against the side of the fish and struck, but failed to get it in, or, strangely enough, to frighten away the sluggish monster. The third time I was endeavouring to sink the hook the fish turned slowly round and swallowed my alder as if it had been a worm, and in another moment the line was running through the rings as the fish bored heavily into the strong running water below the weir. His weight demanded some caution, but he did not put up much of a fight, and he was soon landed—a very Methusaleh among trout, turning the scale at four pounds twelve ounces, with a head as large as that of a nine-pound grilse. That night I brought him in for inspection, together with two or three beautiful fish fairly caught with the dry fly, and as I handed over my bag I dropped a word of caution against cooking the big one. My caution was in vain. The cook was seduced by his vast if ungainly proportions, and at dinner-time there he was upon the dish. He went down untouched, for I warned my fellow-guests against him, but had I ventured to taste him no doubt he would have recalled the lines on the *volaille perfide* translated in Bulwer Lytton's *Pelham:*

> "Tender no more! behold him on your plate,
> And know while eating you avenge his fate."

But all this time, while I am gossiping about the crimes of my youth, the trout are waiting for me in that top pool of my own water in the Lambourne, to which I must retrace my erratic path. Two fish are rising steadily near the bridge at something that looks like an olive dun, very near the opposite bank under the overhanging bough of a horse-chestnut tree. I change my fly for the required pattern, let out the right length of line, and cast very nearly into the right place, but not quite; for the fly attaches itself to the obstruction above and refuses to yield to my angry jerks, so that I am compelled to go round over the bridge to release it, and of course scare away my rising fish. Still there is another left higher up between the fall and the alder-stump on my own side of the water, and I succeed in rising and hooking him, although the hold gives way just as I am bringing him up to the net. Then I turn back down-stream again; and as I pass cautiously homewards, keeping well away from the water, I see something quietly rising on my own side, and from the appearance of the rise diagnose a grayling. These fish are not yet in good condition, but in the Lambourne we do everything in our power to thin their numbers, even netting them in October, when last year more than five hundred were taken out of my water and the reach below. They were artificially introduced into the stream some thirty years ago, and, like the thistles and rabbits in Australia, have become a perfect plague. For some reason, which I have never been able satisfactorily to explain, they hardly ever rise freely in this river at the time when they are in season, and they cannot be regarded as fairly earning their keep, while they consume a good deal of the food that ought to go to increase the size of the trout, besides destroying a quantity of trout-ova in the breeding season. This one, at any rate, will trouble us no more, for at the fourth offer he rises, and is landed. It is always worth while persisting at a rising grayling until it is frightened away, for, unlike trout, they yield to importunity.

As I pass the house again, on my way down, Ben leaves me, and I wander round with varying success. Many dry-fly fishermen of far greater skill than myself prefer to devote the whole of an afternoon to a third of the extent of water which I usually traverse. I believe that from the point of view of success they are right, but I retain enough of my old North-country habits to like to move about and float a fly over likely spots even when I do not see a rise; but although this plan sometimes succeeds, there can be no doubt that what makes the real charm of dry-fly fishing is the element of "stalking" that comes into it. My eldest son, a very keen rifle-shot and big-game hunter, was never really infected with the microbe of fishing until he came here, although he had had many opportunities of catching both salmon and sea-trout as my companion in Scotland and Norway. In those places the rumour of a bear, or the chance, however remote, of an outlying deer, would draw him away at once, even when the river was in the most perfect order and there was a fresh run of fish.

Here, although the trout are not large and the chances of making anything like a big bag are few and far between, he has become much more eager and persevering, for his skill and cunning are pitted in a premeditated duel with a selected and worthy antagonist. There is no gillie to help or hinder by his well-meant advice, no boatman to do the lion's share of the task of bringing the fly over the habitat of a fish in the right position to attract him, no rough tumbling water to make it a matter of indifference whether the cast touches the surface in the form of an I or of an S, no kindly stream to straighten out the coils and hang the submerged fly at the proper angle. When salmon-fishing, you usually walk by faith and not by sight, and all the conditions tend to equalise the chances of the novice and the expert. But in the clear chalk streams of the South all these conditions are altered, and if you do not give to the challenged the choice of weapons, at least there are certain methods and lures which are tabooed in all well-regulated beats.

A very able, interesting, and suggestive writer on sporting topics, Mr. Earl Hodgson—now, alas! no more—devoted the greater part of a chapter of his book on trout-fishing to proving that even in chalk-streams floating flies were occasionally a mistake, and that bags as good or better could sometimes be secured with the wet fly even on such streams as the Test or Itchen. Really he was forcing an open door. Confining my statement for the moment to this river, the little Lambourne, by which I have taken up my abode, there are many days, when the wind is blowing strongly down stream and the sky overcast, when I could easily fill a basket by resorting to what is technically known as combing the water—*i.e.* by putting on two flies, say a large alder as tail fly and a red spinner for dropper, and casting a long line to the opposite bank and letting the flies sweep round until my rod was pointing down-stream nearly parallel with the near bank. But it is not done, because the trout is too valuable a sporting commodity to be massacred in so simple and uninteresting a way.

Let me distinguish, before appearing to condemn all wet-fly fishing on southern streams. I am no dry-fly purist, and what I advocate is fishing for the fish you see, either rising or in position, in the manner you think most likely to deceive and attract them. There are times when fish are not feeding at the surface, but bulging or taking the submerged nymph, when a wet fly properly floated down is the most skilful, as well as the most expedient, method to adopt. I suppose there is no so-called dry-fly purist so orthodox—or I would rather say so obstinate—as to deny this, and it has been recently advocated and explained at length in the *Minor Tactics of the Chalk Stream* of that very skilful light of the Flyfishers Club, Mr. Skues.

One of the greatest drawbacks of my stretch of the Lambourne is the scarcity of fly. I am told that the May-fly used to abound here, but now, instead of the masses of green drakes which cover the Kennet towards the end of June and the beginning of July, we have but a few occasional stragglers rising here and there, which are generally gobbled up by a cock chaffinch, or some other hungry bird, before they have a chance to settle on the water to propagate their species by depositing their eggs, or to give the fish a chance to make their acquaintance. The trout I have caught with a May-fly during the past two seasons may be reckoned on the fingers of one hand. There are compensations for this. The May-fly carnival, when it really comes off, means a long interval, during which the rod may as well be put by, for the glutted fish take a "cure" of at least three weeks after their surfeit of delicacies, during which apparently their doctor prescribes abstinence from insect food of all descriptions, just as the human race recuperate at Marienbad or Kissingen for a similar period after the excesses of the London season. Then, to my thinking, there is never such charm in taking fish on these large flies with comparatively big hooks as there is in beguiling them with a tiny dun or olive tied on an 00 hook. Where there are a proportion of very big fish, cannibal feeders for the greater part of the year, which only rise at the specially attractive "drakes," and almost always escape if by some extraordinary piece of good fortune you manage to hook them with a tiny dry fly, it is no doubt a great advantage to have a chance of clearing them out of the water by legitimate means, and getting sport in the process. But such giants are so uncommon in the Lambourne that I should be quite willing to dispense with the May-fly altogether if only I might be provided with a few more duns and spinners. I have hardly seen a real good rise this season, and although the cold and gloomy weather may partly be responsible for this, there must be some other cause not yet discovered. I think there is a much better show of fly on the higher reaches of the water, and this leads me to suspect some source of pollution, causing a film through which the insect cannot rise to the surface; but I am unable to trace anything of the kind.

I sometimes doubt whether the elaborate investigation and imitation of the precise shape and colour of the natural fly for the time being on the water, is justified by the results, or whether one would not succeed nearly as well with two or three shades and sizes only; one of these, to my fancy, should be always the Wickham, which is not a precise imitation of any existing insect. But this doubt certainly does not dispose of the question. I have frequently the opportunity of watching one who derives half his pleasure from studying and copying the natural fly, a member of that committee of the Flyfishers Club which is making an exhaustive collection of the different ephemera which frequent our English trout-streams, preserved in formalin and acid in test-tubes, and catalogued and arranged. Like every hobby, it well repays its possessor, and gives an interest to his every moment by the water-side. When the fish are not rising the dredge or the net is used with advantage, and there is always something to watch, and much to interest the mind and occupy the hands and eyes. Grant, if you will, that the fish you beguile with an artistic representation of the precise shade of olive dun which you saw him suck down a few minutes ago might equally have risen to a well-cocked Wickham or "Tup's Indispensable," you would not have had or deserved the same thrill of exultation if that had been the case.

There was a period long before I came to these parts when all the fish in the lower reaches were poisoned by the overflow of some works or mill higher up the stream. From that period, I believe, dates the total disappearance of the crayfish. I have been told by former inhabitants that these crustacea used to swarm in the Lambourne, as they still do in the Embourne and some of the other neighbouring streams. So far as I know, there is not one to be found now in any part of the river, although there have been attempts to reintroduce them. I think I shall make the experiment once more, as I should like to have some in the stream, and I have heard that their immature young provide very good and fattening diet for the trout. As a compensation for their loss we may balance the destruction of the pike, which were totally exterminated at the same time, and have never since returned to torment us. There are none now; but my predecessor here told me that he remembers catching one of twelve pounds weight nearly opposite to the old mulberry-tree, a little below the house. I have often wondered that they have not reappeared from the Kennet, where they are only too plentiful; I believe there is some sort of grating at the point of junction of the two streams, but it takes a lot to exclude such unwelcome visitors. But up to the time of writing (*unberufen*) I have never seen one in this river; and long may their absence continue, for where they once obtain access to a trout-stream they become a nuisance which it is only possible to abate or minimise by constant and relentless warfare.

I have complained of the absence of fly, and expressed some doubt whether accurate imitation of the natural insect on the water is essential to success. There is one exception which I ought to have made— the sedge generally swarms in the evening, when there is almost always a late rise. The bottom of every ditch and backwater is lined with the caddis, from which these insects are hatched, and a silver or cinnamon sedge is unquestionably the proper "medicine" in the evening, and is seldom exhibited in vain. The late comer who labours but for one hour will often prove more successful than one who has borne the burden and heat of the day. So it falls out that a certain industrious barrister, who often takes advantage of his season-ticket and the excellent train service to come down after his day's work and linger by the stream till the darkness becomes too pronounced to distinguish the fly upon the water, usually obtains a better bag than has rewarded his father's desultory efforts extended over a much larger aggregate space of time. Often when dinner is over I have seen a dusky shape take its stand behind the big Gunnera, and have been able to indicate the precise position of some feeding fish near enough to cast over, but invisible to the angler himself. Then comes a moment of supreme interest not only to myself (and the fisherman), but very often also to a feminine gallery. From the seat just outside the dining-room door, or from a window above, one can direct the precise position of the fly and watch every movement of the fish. "Geoff!" I shout, "there is a big fellow lying just parallel to the tuft of reeds at right-angles to the end of the rose-bed. I have not seen him take a fly, but he is pretty high up in the water and seems to be on the look-out. That cast was a little below him; let out about two yards more line. That time you were over him, and he saw and moved at the fly." Once more, *habet;* the line tightens, and the rod bends as the fish makes a dash for the thick bed of water-celery in the centre of the stream. "Hold on to him and guide him down-stream, or he will weed you." The advice is unnecessary, as the angler knows very well what he is about, and has already evaded the most obvious dangers before my well-meant advice could have reached his ears. The struggle is a short and sharp one, watched with breathless interest by the party who have just finished their dessert, and let their coffee cool in the excitement of the scene. Now the net is brought into play, and the trout, a nice fellow of nearly a pound and a half, in perfect condition, is gasping on the grass. I would wager a shilling that another trout, almost the exact counterpart of his deceased brother, will have taken his vacant place to-morrow.

No more fishing to-night. The owl has left her nest in the big elm, and her weird whistle, heard from time to time, directs attention to her shadowy form as she circles round on noiseless wings searching for a supply

DONNINGTON PRIORY

RETURNING FROM CHURCH, DONNINGTON

of field-mice to feed her voracious brood. To-night it is warm for once, and we sit long outside, indolently enjoying the sight, sounds, and scents of a summer night, and guessing at the identity of the dusky shapes that creep or run over the lawn; for this is the hour when the smaller mammals and batrachians resume activity, and my old dog, who has been brought down to share our vigil, often starts forward to inspect some passing toad, but, warned by bitter experience of its acrid taste, lets it severely alone when once he has satisfied himself of its identity.

INDEX

AAK, 116, 126
Aalsund, 144
Add river, 47, 228, 243
Adeane, Captain, 60
Aladdin's cavern, 106-7
Alfheim, 142, 180 *et seq.*, 193 *et seq.*, 216
— the house at, 186
— the pine-forest remains, 191, 205-6
— Vangen, 195-8
Anemones, 105, 106
Angular crab, 50
Ardskenish, 65, 69, 76, 78, 93
Argyll, Duke of, 238
Ashburton, Lady, 14
Asplenium marinum, 35
Autelets, les (Sark), 102, 107

Badminton Magazine, 22
Barsloisnach pheasants, 232
Bears, 119, 141, 170-2, 197
— the bear-trap, 171
Bell, *British Stalk-eyed Crustacea*, cited, 50
Ben, black spaniel, 51, 77, 81, 91, 248, 252, 267
Benney, Professor, 108
Birch-trees for sleigh runners, 188
Bird boxes, 128
Bird life: at Alfheim, 203
— in Colonsay, 38, 43 *et seq.*
Bird memories, 45
Black-backed gull, 51, 244
Black Beak (precipice). *See* Svart Snuta
Blackcock, 38, 94, 228-9, 239
Blackdown pond, 114
Black game, 61, 62, 76, 238
Blinded farmer, the, 194
Boat-fishing *v.* shore-fishing, 209
Bonham Carter, Alfred, 237, 244
Bonsor, Cosmo, 232
Book of Sark, 103, 108
Braemore, 12 *et seq.*
— visitors' book at, 21-2
Bruce, Abyssinian traveller, 136

Bügten farm, 218
Bulwer Lytton's *Pelham* quoted, 258
Buzzard, Common, 59

CADDIE, the, 88
Cailleach, the, 26
Cairns, Lord, 8-12
Campbell, keeper, 76, 81-3
Canterbury bells, 184
Capercailzie, 238
Carnivora, absence of, from Colonsay, 63
Chepmell, Dr., *cited*, 104
Chough, the, 25, 56 *et seq.*, 94
Clinton, Lord Albert, 119
Cole, Miss, 215 *et seq. passim*
Colonsay, 24 *et seq.*, 65
— amusement in, 81
— bird life, 38, 43 *et seq.*
— climate, 32
— coast of, 43
— comparison with Sark, 100
— fauna, 32, 63
— fishing, 29, 31, 65
— game birds in, 29 *et seq.*, 61
— golf at, 85 *et seq.*
— harbour, 28, 32
— lakes on, 31-2
— language, 38
— old beliefs prevalent in, 40-2
— primeval remains in, 28-29
— St. Columba's well, 38
— sanctuary for fauna, as, 63
— seals in, 27, 33-4, 63 *et seq.*, 89, 92, 93
— shooting in, 29-31, 46, 62, 94
— some bags, 30
— Strand, 36, 65
— superstitions prevalent in, 40-2
"Colonsay ducks," 43
Colonsay, Lord, 26
Colquhoun, *The Moor and the Loch*, 233
Columba, St., 29
— well of, 38
Cook, Captain, 238

Cormorants, 54, 92, 102, 244
Coupée, the (Sark), 109
Courthope, *Paradise of Birds*, quoted, 45, 234
Coventry, Lord, 120, 124
Craignish, 20
Cranbrook, Lord, 2, 11-12, 225, 226
Crayfish, 264
Crealock, General, 21
Creux Harbour, 108, 109
Crows, 55 *et seq.*
— hooded, 59, 204, 217
Crustacea, 23, 50, 88, 104, 264
Cuckoo, 60
Curlew, 49, 244

DABCHICK, 54, 250, 251
Dalen, Jan, 219
Dalhousie, Lord, 9
Davenport, W. Bromley, *Sport*, 120
Deane, Sir Bargrave, 8, 170
— Sir James Parker, 8
Deer, 63
— fallow, 238
— red, 63, 239, 243
— roe, 5, 6, 8, 233, 236, 238, 239
— — the high fence, 236
— shooting out of season, on, 243
Deer-stalking, 11-12, 14, 15-18, 22, 80
Diver, Great Northern, 55
— red-throated, 203
Dog-fish, on mutilation of wading-birds by, 49-50
Donald, the luggage-man, 227
Donnington Hospital, 252
— Priory, 246 *et seq.*
— weir at, 255
Dovre Fjeld, 196, 212
Dry-fly fishing, 141, 152, 173, 198, 259 *et seq.*
Duck and dog incident, 110-11
Ducks, 43 *et seq.*, 54, 62, 77, 92, 94, 174, 218, 230-1, 250
Duntroon, yacht journey to, in fog, 18-20

EAGLE, golden, 59
— owl, 218
Eider-down industry, 44-5
Eider ducks, 43-5, 92, 218
Elk cow, 204
— pitfalls, 205, 206
Eperqueries, les (Sark), 109
Erle, Chief Justice, 26
Ermine, 204
Evans, Henry, 59

FADA, Loch, 25, 95
Fairy tales of Oronsay, 39
Falcon and raven, 55
Falcons, 55, 59, 190, 204
— destruction of, 241
Falling birds, 234-5
Family affection among birds and beasts, 45
Farmer, the blinded, 194
— the, lost on the fjeld, 188
Fasque, 6
— snipe bog at, 7
Ferns, 14, 35, 104, 174, 184
Ferreting, failure of, in Colonsay, 63
Fieldfares, 129, 204
Fish attacking birds, on, 49, 50
Fishermen's stories, 136
Fishing, 29, 147 *et seq.*, 160 *et seq.*, 216-7, 221, 253 *et seq.*, *et passim*. (*See also under* Salmon, Sea-fishing, Sea trout, Trout)
— author's early experiences,113-4
— benefits of cleaning fish as soon as caught, 254
— boat *v.* shore, 209
— combing the water, 261
— Hvilested, at: the first season's bag, 139
— picnicking by night, 163
— rewards for lost flies, 164
— Scandinavian practice, 138
— Sundal river, in, 130 *et seq.*, 222
— trailing, 95, 197, 209, 220
Fladvad Farm, 158, 159
— Pool, 151-3
Flies, 52, 95, 115, 132, 141, 152, 154, 162, 222, 253, 261 *et seq.*
— floating flies, 261
— May-fly, 52, 262, 263
— sedge, 265
— Wickham, 253, 263
Flight-shooting, 46
Fly-fishing, 141, 152, 154, 173, 198, 259 *et seq.*
Flyfishers Club, 263
Fowler, Lady, 22
— Sir Arthur, 15, 22
— Sir John, 12, 13, 16, 21
— Montague, 15, 22
Fox, 63, 204, 249
Frohawk, Mr., *cited* 203

GAFFING, 131
Gathorne-Hardy, Alfred Cecil, Notes on the Chough, 58-9
— — Notes on Seals, 68, 69 *et seq.*

INDEX

Gathorne-Hardy, Hon. A. E., *Autumns in Argyllshire*, cited, 225
— — early reminiscences, 1-3, 113
— Geoffrey, 59, 75-8, 79, 216, 217, 260, 265-6
— — catches a 14½-pounder fish, 216
— *See also* Cranbrook, Lord
Gjora, 182, 194, 210
Gladstone, Sir Thomas, 6-8
Glendye, 7
Glutton caught by trap, 196
Godwit, 49
Golf, 76, 77, 78, 85 *et seq.*
— charm and variety of, 95-7
— origin of, 85-6
— self-consciousness a deterring influence in, 97-9
— at Colonsay, 85 *et seq.*
— — rabbits and lost balls, 91-2
— — scarcity of caddies, 87
— in Sark, 101
— possibilities in Norway, 205
Gonoplax angulata, 50
Gouliot cave, the, 105, 106
Graham, Mrs., 3
— Sir Henry, 4, 5, 225
Grayling, 259
Great Northern diver, 55
Green woodpeckers, 128, 218
Greenlander's method of seal hunting, Pennant on, 64
Griffith, Major Darby, 160
Grilse, 129, 133
Grodal pass, 192, 194, 215
Grouse, 7, 8, 9, 31, 61, 62
Guernsey, 101, 104
— heifer-calves, 251
Guillemots, 54, 102
Gulls, 51-4, 61, 77
— destruction of ephemera, by, 52
— eggs of, for food, 53-4
Gunder, 161, 162, 200
Gunnis, Frank, 150
Gurney, Alfred, 115, 125
Gye, 227

HAARSTAD, 218, 223
— Bridge, 217
Haller Vand, 221
Halston, 113, 114
Hangman's Rock, Colonsay, 35-6
Harcourt, Sir William, 21
Hare, blue mountain, 204
Harling, 4, 12 *note*, 120, 123, 124, 197
Harp seal, 72
Havre Gosselin, 109

Haynes, 119, 124
Hemsted Park, 225
Hen harrier, 60
Herons, 217, 244
High fjeld, the, 180 *et seq.*
— the roof of the world, 189
— vegetation on, 189
High pheasants, 232, 234
Hodgson, Mr. Earl, 261
Hol pool, 138
Holmes, Oliver Wendell, 245
Hooded crow, 59, 204, 217
Hooper, wild swan, 231
Hugo's *Les Travailleurs de la Mer*, 104
Hvilested, 128 *et seq.*, 140, 145 *et seq.*, 165, 182
— destroyed by fire, 142, 194, 215
— the upper water at, 145 *et seq.*

INVERMARK, 9, 11, 12

JACKDAWS, 55-9 *passim*
Jelly-fish, 55, 90
Jersey, 101, 104

KAARVAND, 173, 174
— the bulls at, 174-5
Kennet river, 254, 262, 265
Kestrels, 59, 204
Killoran House, 25, 28, 29, 31, 34, 37
— garden of, 34-5
— seal's head and skin at, 74
Kingfisher, 251
Kingsley's *Hypatia*, 209
Kingswood Warren, 232
Kittiwakes, 51, 102
Kongen Pool, 164

LAMBOURNE river, 246, 254 *et seq.*
— crustacea in, 264
— May-fly on, 262, 263
Landseer, Sir Edwin, 21
Laughing gulls, 51, 53
Lax Stone Pool, 169
Leding Pool, 133, 137, 172
Lichens, 189
Lilledal, 142, 176-9, 193, 211 *et seq.*
— expedition to the lakes, 219
— improvements on the river, 177-8
Lille Vand, 221
Lobster-fishing, 30, 50, 88, 104
Lockwood, Frank, 110-12
Loken Pool, 132
Longfellow's *Othere*, 135
Lort Phillips, Mrs., 128, 129, 169, 176

Lort Philips, Mr., 128, 136, 139-43 passim, 150, 166-80 passim, 208
— home of, on the high fjeld, 181-6
— improvements by, on the Lilledal River, 177-8
— twelve-pounder trout, 160-1

MACALLUM, Duncan, 50
Macgowan, tackle-maker, 115
M'Hardy, stalker, 15-17
Machrins links, 65, 76, 91-2
M'Neill, Sir John, 25, 32-4, 59, 73
— portrait of, by Princess Louise, 34
— protection of seals by, 33, 63
M'Neill, Malcolm, 65
M'Neill, the Misses, 37, 86
Magpies, 204
Malcolm, John, 237
Malcolm, Lord, of Poltalloch, 24
Mallard, 250
Marquand, contributions to the *Book of Sark*, cited, 103, 108
"Marsupial pouch," the, 154
May-fly, 52, 262, 263
Mergansers, 47, 54, 218
Merlin, 59, 204, 241
Millais, Sir J. E., 5, 21, 22
— J. G., *British Mammals*, cited, 69
Millden, 8-11
— dogs at, 8-10
— grouse at, 9
Miller, boatman, 4
Mitchell, William, 237
Moncrieff, Sir Thomas, 11
Mount Battock, 7
Mountain air, preservative qualities of, 190
Mountaineering, 126
Murray, Mrs., *Summer in the Hebrides*, 39, 40
— Tom, 232
Murthly Castle, 3-6, 12
— mixed bag at Murthly, 5
Murthly Moss, 5
Musjerd, 128, 182
Mytton, Jack, 113

NATURAL HISTORY MUSEUM, seal in, 84
Newland, Rev. H., *Forest Life*, 114-5, 120
North Esk, 8
Norway in 1865, 113 *et seq.*
— accommodation, 118
— bears in, 119, 141, 170-2, 197
— carrioles, the, 117, 126
— climate, 152, 188, 190, 191, 195, 218

Norway, climate, rain, 153 *et seq.*, 182, 185, 190
— — winter, 187
— cost of trip, 126
— eider-down industry in, 44
— fires, danger of, in, 142-4
— fish food in, 151
— fishing, 120 *et seq.*, 139
— home life in, 143, 159, 185, 196
— house roofs in, 157
— insomnia in, 140, 141
— journey to, 116
— — overland, 211
— motor travelling in, 193-4, 213 *et seq.*
— posting journey in, 117-8, 211-3
— rivers in, a characteristic of, 181
— stolkjaerres, the, 117
— telephone in, 216
— time, native attitude to, 196, 215
— wedding festivity, 118

ODEGAARD, 219
Ole Grodal, 130, 131, 132, 137, 138, 145-7, 149, 215
Orme, Dr., 238
Ormer, the, 104
Oronsay, 35, 36
— fairy tales current in, 39
Osmunda Regalis, 14, 35, 104
Osprey, the, 14, 59
Otter, 68, 174, 240
— taking salmon fly, 183
Owl, snowy, 204
— wood, 60
Oxendal, 142, 177
Oxenham, John, 108
Oyster-catcher, 49, 50, 77

PARTRIDGE, 6, 61
Pearson, Col., 73, 74
Pennant, *Arctic Zoology*, cited, 64
Pennant, Captain, 120, 124
Pennatulidae, 23, 50
Peregrine, 55, 59
Peter Pool, 216, 219
Petrel, fork-tailed, 61
Phalarope, red-breasted, 47-8
Pheasants, 232 *et seq.*, 242
Pigeons, 30, 60, 76, 92
Pike, 264, 265
Pine-forest remains, the, 191, 205-6
Plovers, 49, 66, 77
Poltalloch, Christmas sport at, 225 *et seq.*
— pheasants at, 232
— the bag at, 238, 241

INDEX

Pope's *Odyssey*, quoted, 209
Port Lotha, 90, 92
Port Mor, 88
Prawn as bait, 141
Prawning, 40–1
Primroses, 103
Ptarmigan, 190
Puffins, 54

RABBITS, 61, 63, 77, 252
— on the Machrins golf links, 91–2
Ranunculus, 189
Rats, 63
Rauma river, 120 *et seq.*
Ravens, 55, 92, 107
Razor-bills, 54
Red-breasted phalarope, 47–8
Redshank, 49, 66
Red-throated diver, 203
Reindeer, 189, 204, 206
Reindeer-moss, 189
Rhododendrons, 237
Richardson's skua, 51
Road Pool, 216
Roche Abbey, 232
Rocketing pheasants, 236, 237, 243
Roe, 5, 6, 8, 233, 236, 238, 239
Romsdal valley, 116, 119
Rooks, 56–8
Ross, Edward, 10
Ryper, 166, 204
— snare, 206

SALMON fishing, 4, 8, 12 *note*, 120 *et seq.*, 129, 141, 148–53, 169, 178, 260
— author's first, 113, 115, 120 *et seq.*
— dying salmon, the, 149–51
— traps for, 164
Sandeman, Mr., 140
Sargent, Mr., 140
Sark, 100 *et seq.*
— an artist's hunting-ground, 107
— Autelets, les, 102, 107
— caves, 105–7
— climate, 104
— crustacea, 104
— flora of, 103
— Gouliot cave, 105, 106
— harbours, 108–9
— molluscs, 104
— natural bridge, 109
— octopods, 104
— Seigneur of, the, 111
— silver-mines, 109
— zoophytes, 105, 106
Scalasaig, 27–8, 37

Scotland, winter shooting in, 229
Sea-fishing, 29, 89, 168, 218
Sea pie (oyster-catcher), 49, 50
Sea trout, 125, 129, 132, 141, 149, 152, 168, 176–80 *passim*, 218, 222
— a hunted fish, 218
— cooking, 151
Seals in Colonsay, 27, 33–4, 63 *et seq.*, 89, 92, 93
— breathing of, 72
— colour and appearance, 65, 66, 67, 69, 89
— diving powers, 71–2
— feeding on duck, instance of, 68, 72–3
— food of, 72
— fore-flippers of, 70
— great grey seal (*Halechœrus gryphus*), 63, 68, 69, 73–4
— habits, 67, 69 *et seq.*
— Harp seal, 72
— melanism in, 68
— notes on, 69 *et seq.*
— parasites in, as to, 70
— size of male and female, 74
— stalking, 64, 71, 77–82
— — best time for, 75
— — difficulties of conveying the quarry, 82–3
— stipulations as to, in shooting lease, 63
— weight, 74
— young, 68, 74
Sedge fly, 265
Seigneur of Sark, the, 111
Sgoltaire, Loch, 25
Sheldrakes, 47, 77, 94
Sils Lake, Engadine, 222
Sivert, 193, 224
Skua, Richardson's, 51
Skues' *Minor Tactics of the Chalk Stream*, 262
Smith, Abel, 257
Snakes, 174, 215
Snipe, 7, 62, 94, 239, 243
Snow at Poltalloch, 241
Snow bunting, 61
Snowy owl, 204
Sœter girls, 190, 197, 206
Sœters, 190
Solan geese, 54, 61
Spate in Norway, a, 153–7
Speyside, 8
Spider crab, 23
Sponges, 105, 106
Squids, 104

Stag. *See* Deer
— author's first, 14 *et seq.*
Stag shooting out of season, on, 243
Stalking. *See under* Deer
Steward, Alan, 90
Stewart Wortley, A., 6
Still-hunting, 5
Stor Pool, 136, 147, 164
Storfahle, 183
Stor Vand, 220
Stran Pool, 158
Strathcona, Lord, 33
Suisdal, 185, 195, 196, 198
Sundal River, 128, 130 *et seq.*, 158, 167, 168, 180, 181, 192
— fishing in, 130 *et seq.*, 222
— in flood, 158
Sundal Valley, construction of power station in, 178–9, 205, 218, 219, 221, 222
Sundalsören, 168, 192
"Svart Snuta," 189, 205, 208–9
Swan, Hooper, 231
Swinburne, *Garden of Cymodoce,* quoted, 100 *et seq. passim*

TANGEN, Peter, 145
Tarbert, 27
Taynish, bag at, 244
Teal, 46, 47, 50, 68, 94
Telescope, view of a stalk, 79
— as to signalling, 79–80
Tennyson quoted, 210
Tern, 54
Timber, preservative qualities of mountain air for, 190
Tobar Fuar, 41, 93
Todal, 166 *et seq.*, 197
— fishing at, 167 *et seq.*, 175
Toplis, W. A., 107
Torbudal, 176
Traigh na Tobar Fuar, 41, 66, 90, 93
Tree sparrow, 61
Trondhjem, trip to, 140
Trout, brown, 126, 134, 173, 178, 257–8
— cannibal, 133–5, 257–8

Trout fishing, 95, 148, 152–4, 160 *et seq.*, 173, 175–6, 187, 196–209 *passim*, 220, 221, 247, 253–4, 258 *et seq.*
— chalk streams, in, 261
— three fish at once, 208
— kept alive in a stew, 186, 191
— recipe for cooking, 200
— record of two evenings' sport, 160–2
— sea trout. *See that heading*
Tubularia indivisa, 106
Turkeys, wild, 238

VAN DYCK cited, 57
Vangen, 195–8
— verandah at, 198
Vegetation on the high fjeld, 189
Venus's ear, 104

WADING-BIRDS, 36, 48–9, 66
"Waffel-kok," 185, 190
Wagtail, white, 204
Walton, Izaac, *The Complete Angler,* quoted, 200
Ward, Rowland. 75, 84
Water-finding, 147
Water-rail, the, 54
Water-vole, 249
Westbury, Lord, 26
Wet-fly fishing, 261
Widgeon, 243, 244
Wild swan, 231
— turkey, 238
Williams, Vaughan, 26
Wilson Fox, 142
Wilson, Rimington, 232
Wimpole, 232
Wood, Arthur, 232
Wood Hall, 257
Woodcock, 62, 235 6, 240, 244
— bag at Taynish, 245
Woodpeckers, green, 128, 218

YACHT journey to Duntroon in fog, 18–20
Young, Captain, 11

ZOOPHYTES, 105, 106

Printed by BALLANTYNE, HANSON & Co.
at Paul's Work, Edinburgh

www.ingramcontent.com/pod-product-compliance
Lightning Source LLC
Chambersburg PA
CBHW031250230426
43670CB00005B/112